COOKING THAT COUNTS

COOKING THAT COUNTS

1,200- to 1,500-Calorie Meal Plans to Lose Weight **DELICIOUSLY**

Published by Oxmoor House, an imprint of Time Inc. Books, a division of Meredith Corporation
225 Liberty Street, New York, NY 10281

Senior Editor: Rachel Quinlivan West, R.D.
Editor: Cathy Wesler, M.S., R.D.
Project Editor: Lacie Pinyan
Designers: Amy Bickell, Chris Rhoads
Junior Designer: AnnaMaria Jacob
Photographers: Iain Bagwell, Jen Causey, Greg Dupree, Victor Protasio
Prop Stylists: Kay Clarke, Audrey Davis, Thom Driver, Lindsey Lower, Claire Spollen
Food Stylists: Margaret Dickey, Kellie Kelley
Recipe Developers and Testers: Robin Bashinsky, Jiselle Basile, Adam Hickman, Julia Levy, Callie Nash, Marianne Williams, Deb Wise
Senior Production Manager: Greg A. Amason
Associate Manager for Project Management and Production: Anna Riego
Copy Editors: Jacqueline Giovanelli, Dolores Hydock
Indexer: Mary Ann Laurens
Fellows: Audrey Davis, Kyle Grace Mills, Natalie Schumann

ISBN-13: 978-0-8487-4950-7
Library of Congress Control Number: 2016955288

First Edition 2017

Printed in the United States of America

10 9 8 7 6 5 4

Time Inc. Books products may be purchased for business or promotional use. For information on bulk purchases, please contact Christi Crowley in the Special Sales Department at (845) 895-9858.

We welcome your comments and suggestions about Time Inc. Books.
Please write to us at:
Time Inc. Books
Attention: Book Editors
P.O. Box 62310
Tampa, Florida 33662-2310

CONTENTS

FOR SOMEONE LIKE ME WHO LOVES FOOD

and loves to cook, I have always avoided diets. As a younger person, I didn't need to diet. But then somehow, as I got older, everything changed. Exercise alone wasn't cutting it. My clothes were getting tighter. I was unhappy being tired all the time.

Three months on the Cooking Light Diet changed everything. I lost 14 pounds, went down a belt notch, and felt incredible. I loved getting back into the kitchen and trying new recipes that didn't overwhelm me on a weeknight. Having preplanned meals and shopping lists was a huge time-saver, giving me more time to shop and cook. My family was excited about the new meals and gave them rave reviews—what more could a home cook ask for?!

We've learned what eating well truly means: cooking real food, eating realistic portions, trying new ingredients, and having fun together in the kitchen. Most importantly, my relationship with food has changed for the better. The Cooking Light Diet helped me realize that taking care of my health is the greatest gift I can give myself and my family.

A year later, we are still enjoying the plan. It has brought my family back to the table. For that, I will be forever grateful and a lifelong fan. For us, the Cooking Light Diet isn't just a way to lose weight—it's a way to live a good life.

—Katie Anderson,
Wife, Mom, Blogger, Food Lover
Newnan, GA

INTRODUCTION TO MEAL PLANS

Make Your Meals Count

THINK ABOUT THE TYPICAL APPROACH TO DIETING. It's often framed as can'ts and quick fixes. You can't eat this, you shouldn't eat that, you have to eat this for those results, do this for that amount of time, and so on. Not only are these approaches discouraging and often driven by deprivation, they're also not sustainable. What happens when those X-amount of days are up, or when you've dropped the desired pounds by not eating certain food groups without a thought as to what happens next? You end up right back where you started. If a diet is to truly work, it needs to be a long-term commitment to a healthier lifestyle, one that allows you to enjoy the foods you love, including dessert. It needs to change—and break—all those bad eating habits that have you dieting in the first place. And that change can be extremely difficult, especially since there are so many questions that need answering first: Will I be able to make this work with my schedule? Will I see the results I'm looking for? Is this sustainable?

The goal of *Cooking that Counts* is to help you figure out what this new, healthier lifestyle looks like for you. Each of the meal plans in this book is meant to guide you, introducing you to a delicious way to eat that's filled with wholesome, satisfying foods in proper portions—it's a way to eat for a lifetime rather than just for swimsuit season. We also know that desserts and a celebratory drink are a part of life, so those haven't been omitted from this book. They've just been served up in ways that empower you to work them into your diet when you like. We also realize that many of our readers may have dietary restrictions, so we've identified recipes using the key at left that fit a range of criteria.

RECIPE KEY

- DF **DAIRY FREE**
- GF **GLUTEN FREE**
- LC **LOW CARB**
- V **VEGETARIAN**

This book originated from the Cooking Light Diet, an online, subscription-based service created to help people eat healthier and happier. When building the diet, we harnessed our vast, ever-growing archive of healthy recipes to help families eat better, while also addressing the age-old questions: "What's for dinner? And lunch? And breakfast?" Driven by an emphasis on portion control and three basic principles—PLAN, SHOP, and COOK—we believe we've done just that. Here's a little bit about how the Cooking Light Diet works:

With PLAN, menus are generated based on your preferences: vegetarian, gluten free, SmartCarb, dairy free, tree nut and peanut free, and more. From there, you can designate how often you'd like to cook, whether it's breakfast, lunch, snack, and dinner every day of the week, dinners only, or however much you're able. You make the menus work for your life, not the other way around. If you want to plan for two weeks at a time, you can do that, too.

SHOP then generates a grocery list based on the recipes you've selected. The list can be customized to only include certain meals or meal days, and formatted

BEEF FLATBREAD TACOS WITH CUCUMBER AND YOGURT SAUCE, PAGE 165

to include two weeks' worth of recipes, eliminate ingredients you already have on hand in the kitchen, and add nonfood items to your list. Then you simply email or print when it's store-ready. Our SHOP feature takes all the hassle out of grocery store trips, and eliminates the chances of buying junk food you don't need by arming you with a ready-made list.

Lastly, COOK provides you with beautiful images of the recipes you're cooking along with recipe instructions, nutritional information, cook times, and options to mark favorite recipes for later reference or indicate whether you want more or fewer recipes like the one you're cooking. And all recipes you've ever cooked are archived so you can schedule them into future menus.

Purchasing this book is a great step towards making a commitment to cooking your way towards a healthier lifestyle. We encourage you to use it to expand your recipe wheelhouse, experiment with ingredients, and experience firsthand the joy of cooking. Then take the next step and join the Cooking Light Diet. You can use code CTC50CLDIET to receive 50% off your initial subscription price (expiration: 7/3/2017). Read the success stories in the pages that follow to see how other people have incorporated this plan into their lives. And then take the guesswork out of your meal planning by utilizing the CLDiet in your day-to-day. You won't regret it.

Must-Have Ingredients

AN IMPORTANT STEP TO LOSING WEIGHT and maintaining that weight loss is stocking your kitchen with the ingredients you need to create healthy meals. The following 12 essential kitchen staples are the basis of many recipes in this book. You'll find a mix of ingredients that emphasize flavor without excess calories. Stock your pantry, fridge, and freezer with these items and watch your weekly shopping list grow shorter.

HEART-HEALTHY OIL:
Olive oil and canola oil are Cooking Light Diet essentials for sautéed and roasted dishes, salad dressings, and more. These two staple oils are high in heart-healthy unsaturated fats and low in artery-clogging saturated fats.

CITRUS:
Lemons and limes (juice and rind) add flavor and depth without added salt in sweet and savory dishes. Citrus is similar in effect to vinegar, but is less tangy in flavor. Store whole citrus in the refrigerator for longer life.

EGGS:
Eggs are a near-perfect food. They're inexpensive, low in calories (72 calories each), high in protein (7 grams each), and an easy choice for any meal—scramble eggs for breakfast, boil a few for lunch, or whip up an omelet for dinner.

GARLIC:
Adding fresh, jarred, or minced garlic transforms vegetables, pasta sauces, marinades, soups, and more with no added calories. It adds complexity to ingredients and livens otherwise plain dishes. Store unused minced garlic in the refrigerator.

GOOD-QUALITY CHEESE:
It's worth spending a little extra on cheeses such as fresh Parmigiano-Reggiano and crumbled Greek feta. Both enhance the quality of a dish. Use it to top off pastas, salads, soups, and more. You won't have to add much—a little goes a long way.

GREENS:
Convenient, nutritious, and low-calorie, greens of all varieties are a must. Keep one or two types on hand each week to use for salads and sandwich toppings, or mix into stir fries, frittatas, or whole grains.

NUT BUTTERS:
Although they're higher in fat, nut butters such as peanut or almond butters are great sources of protein, niacin, and heart-healthy fats. Enjoyed in moderation (2 tablespoons per day), nut butters may reduce your risk of heart disease and diabetes.

QUICK-COOKING WHOLE GRAINS:
Ready in as little as 10 minutes, quinoa, old-fashioned oats, instant brown rice, and whole-wheat pastas can quickly become the center or side dish to any meal. Filled with vitamins, minerals, and antioxidants, whole grains can also help you stay full. Serve alone or toss with veggies, beans, rotisserie chicken, toasted nuts, fresh herbs, or dried fruit.

VINEGARS:
Use vinegar to add brightness to salad dressings, marinades, sauces, pastas, and even soups. Vinegars are strong, so add to dishes in small amounts and taste to decide if you need more. Most recipes will use red wine vinegar, balsamic vinegar, rice vinegar, or cider vinegar.

LEAN PROTEINS:
Stock your refrigerator and freezer with lean proteins, especially when they're on sale. Good options to keep frozen are skinless chicken breast cutlets, lean ground beef and turkey, and peeled shrimp. You can defrost them in minutes and make quick tacos, burritos, stir-fries, or pasta dishes.

GREEK YOGURT:
With twice the protein of regular yogurt, Greek yogurt's creamy, rich texture makes it the perfect healthy replacement for sour cream or mayo in recipes. Stir in honey, nuts, or dried fruit for a quick snack, spoon over baked potatoes, or use as a dip or spread.

CANNED BEANS:
Although canned beans are higher in sodium than fresh, you can opt for unsalted varieties and season them yourself, which allows you to control the sodium. Having a few on hand can significantly speed up meal prep. Plus, canned beans are high-quality, inexpensive sources of fiber and protein.

HEALTHY COOKING BASICS

Oil
Canola oil
Extra-virgin olive oil
Toasted sesame oil
Cooking spray

Vinegar
White vinegar
Cider vinegar
Balsamic vinegar
Red wine vinegar
White wine vinegar and/or rice vinegar

Stock/broth
Unsalted chicken, beef, and/or vegetable

Spices & Seasonings
Kosher salt
Table salt
Black pepper/black peppercorns
Crushed red pepper
Ground red pepper/cayenne
Garlic powder
Ground cumin
Curry powder
Chili powder
Ground paprika
Ground cinnamon
Ground nutmeg
Dried oregano
Dried thyme

Baking
All-purpose flour
Whole-wheat flour
Baking powder
Baking soda
Cornstarch
Light brown sugar
Granulated sugar
Vanilla extract
Chocolate: bittersweet and semisweet squares/chips
Unsweetened cocoa powder

Dairy
Eggs
Fat-free Greek yogurt
Fat-free or 1% low-fat milk
Unsalted butter
Parmigiano-Reggiano block
Feta cheese

Condiments
Canola mayonnaise
Pesto
Roasted red peppers
Honey
Ketchup
Mustard: Dijon, whole-grain, yellow
Worcestershire sauce
Lower-sodium soy sauce
Sriracha sauce
Chile paste (sambal oelek)
Hoisin sauce

Fresh Produce
Garlic
Shallots
Onions: yellow, sweet, red
Potatoes: Idaho, red, Yukon, sweet
Carrots
Celery
Lemons
Limes
Greens: baby spinach, romaine, kale

Frozen
Chicken cutlets, breasts, and thighs
Ground sirloin
Ground turkey
Shrimp
Fresh pizza dough
Vegetables: whole-kernel corn, green peas, shelled edamame, whole green beans, broccoli florets

Canned Goods
Unsalted whole, diced, and/or crushed tomatoes
Tomato paste
Unsalted canned beans: chickpeas, black beans, pinto beans, cannellini beans
Marinara sauce
Olives
Tuna

Middle Grocery Aisle Must-Haves
Breadcrumbs/panko
Whole grains: brown rice, quinoa, farro, bulgur
Quick-cooking/rolled oats
Nut butters: peanut, almond
Nuts: unsalted peanuts, sliced/slivered almonds, cashews, pecans, walnuts
Plain and whole-grain pasta: penne, orzo, farfalle, linguine, fettuccine
Dried fruit: cranberries, golden raisins, cherries

1,200-Calorie 30-Day Menu Plan

CALORIE LEVEL	BREAKFAST	LUNCH	DINNER	SNACK
1,200	300	350	400	150
1,300	300	350	450	200
1,400	300	400	500	200
1,500	350	400	500	250

ONCE YOU KNOW your daily calorie level for safe weight loss, follow this menu plan based on your needs. While this one provides 1,200 calories, it's easy to modify; simply turn to the recipes listed in the menus for any additional items to include for 1,300- to 1,500-calorie plans. For 1,600- to 2,000-calorie plans, turn to page 270 for suggestions for increasing the number of servings and calories for each meal.

HELPFUL TIPS TO STAY ON TRACK:

- **You don't have to cook 3 meals every day.** Swap out any menu with leftovers or enjoy a meal out—just be sure to stay within your daily calorie plan.
- **Mark your favorite menus to have more frequently.**
- **Swap out similar foods to keep calories in check.** To maintain a balanced diet, we suggest you choose meals with a mix of vegetables and protein to sustain a healthy balance of nutrients throughout the week.
- **If eating off the plan, consume the same number of calories as your suggested menu to stay on track.** Make sure whatever you're substituting is comparable calorie-wise to what you're replacing.
- **Look for calories on nutritional labels of packaged foods, and keep the portion size in mind.**
- **Check the nutrition information at restaurants before you go**—many post it on their menus or websites—so you stay on track when dining out.

DAY 1

BREAKFAST

Breakfast Quinoa, *page 28*

Coffee with 1 tablespoon half-and-half

1 clementine

LUNCH

Turkey and Swiss Wrap with Carrot Salad, *page 80*

½ cup grapes

DINNER

Lasagna Bowl, *page 214*

1 (1½-ounce) slice Italian bread, rubbed with crushed garlic and toasted

SNACK

½ cup dried apples

1 mini Swiss cheese wedge, such as Laughing Cow Creamy Original Swiss

DAY 2

BREAKFAST

Raspberry-Yogurt Muffin, *page 34*

1 medium apple

½ cup 1% low-fat milk or milk substitute

LUNCH

Grilled Turkey-Plum Sandwich, *page 83*

8 baby carrots

1 tablespoon hummus

DINNER

Thai Shrimp Scampi, *page 155*

1 cup fresh baby salad greens with 1½ tablespoons reduced-fat Asian sesame dressing

SNACK

Peanut Butter-Chocolate Bar, *page 240*

DAY 3 BREAKFAST

3-Ingredient Pancakes, *page 48*

2 tablespoons maple syrup

LUNCH

Roast Beef Sandwich with Watercress Slaw, *page 87*

DINNER

Tilapia with Lemon-Garlic Sauce, *page 151*

½ cup Sautéed Broccolini, *page 202*

1 cup fresh spinach with 1½ tablespoons reduced-fat vinaigrette

SNACK

Chocolate-Pecan Pie Truffles, *page 257*

DAY 4 BREAKFAST

Chocolate Chip-Hazelnut Muffin, *page 37*

1 scrambled egg

¾ cup 1% low-fat milk or milk substitute

LUNCH

Wheat Berry Salad with Goat Cheese, *page 116*

Pita wedges made from ½ (6-inch) pita bread, split and toasted

DINNER

Creamy Tuna Noodle Casserole with Peas and Breadcrumbs, *page 152*

SNACK

Strawberry Cheesecake Pop, *page 261*

DAY 5 BREAKFAST

Grapefruit, Avocado, and Prosciutto Breakfast Salad, *page 60*

Coffee with 1 tablespoon half-and-half

LUNCH

Tart Apple-Hazelnut Chicken Salad, *page 112*

10 multi-seed gluten-free crackers

2 teaspoons peanut butter

DINNER

Beef and Black Bean Enchiladas, *page 160*

¾ cup fresh pineapple chunks

SNACK

2 fun-size Snickers bars

DAY 6 BREAKFAST

Leftover muffin (either Raspberry-Yogurt Muffin or Chocolate Chip-Hazelnut Muffin)

Coffee with 1 tablespoon half-and-half

1 small banana

LUNCH

Chicken and Feta Tabbouleh, *page 122*

1 mini whole-wheat pita bread, cut into wedges and toasted

DINNER

Pork Medallion with Scallions and Magic Green Sauce, *page 170*

1 cup sautéed or roasted zucchini cooked with 1 teaspoon olive oil

SNACK

Leftover Peanut Butter-Chocolate Bar, *page 240*

1,200-Calorie 30-Day Menu Plan *(continued)*

DAY 7 BREAKFAST

Spinach and Feta Quiche with Quinoa Crust, *page 71*

½ cup fresh cantaloupe cubes

LUNCH

Tortellini Salad with Zucchini and Peas, *page 115*

1 fresh tangerine

DINNER

Crispy Fish with Lemon-Dill Sauce, *page 147*

½ cup cooked brown rice

½ cup steamed green beans

SNACK

Chocolate-Pecan Pie Truffles, *page 257*

DAY 8 BREAKFAST

Cinnamon-Banana Crunch Bowl, *page 31*

½ fresh grapefruit

LUNCH

Tarragon Chicken Salad Sandwich, *page 75*

DINNER

Butternut-Eggplant Vegetable Bowl, *page 213*

1 (1-ounce) slice French bread

SNACK

½ cup fruit sorbet made with real fruit

DAY 9 BREAKFAST

Lemon-Blueberry Oatmeal, *page 24*

LUNCH

Chilled Tomato Soup with Avocado Relish, *page 94*

10 mini gluten-free rice cakes

DINNER

Seared Tilapia with Spinach and White Bean Orzo, *page 148*

SNACK

S'mores Chewy Bar, *page 243*

DAY 10 BREAKFAST

Tuscan Lemon Muffin, *page 44*

1 hard-cooked egg

½ cup orange juice

LUNCH

Smoky Ham and Split Pea Soup, *page 98*

1 cup mixed greens with 2 tablespoons reduced-fat balsamic vinaigrette

DINNER

Ground Chicken Wraps with Chili Sauce, *page 198*

SNACK

4 miniature Milky Way Midnight bars

DAY 11

BREAKFAST

Roasted Plum Breakfast Parfait, *page 56*

LUNCH

Greek Tomato and Cucumber Salad with Farro, *page 120*

½ cup fresh watermelon cubes

DINNER

Quick Fried Brown Rice with Shrimp and Snap Peas, *page 156*

SNACK

Valley Dark Chocolate & Nut Chewy Trail Mix Bar

DAY 12

BREAKFAST

Peanut Butter-Berry Smoothie, *page 55*

1 hard-cooked egg

LUNCH

White Cheddar and Chive Potato Soup, *page 100*

1½ cups Orange and Almond Salad, *page 203*

DINNER

Beef Flatbread Tacos with Cucumber and Yogurt Sauce, *page 165*

SNACK

S'mores Chewy Bar, *page 243*

DAY 13

BREAKFAST

Egg and Hash Brown Casserole, *page 64*

LUNCH

Chicken, Edamame, and Couscous Salad, *page 123*

1 small apple

DINNER

Pork Chop with Balsamic Roasted Vegetables, *page 174*

SNACK

Greek Yogurt and Strawberry Snack, *page 245*

6 multigrain crackers, such as Kashi Original 7 Grain

DAY 14

BREAKFAST

Quick Breakfast Taco, *page 68*

1 cup berries

Coffee with 1 tablespoon half-and-half

LUNCH

Smoked Pork Bánh Mì Lettuce Cups, *page 111*

1½ cups Orange and Almond Salad, *page 203*

1 large pear

DINNER

Spiced Sirloin, Butternut, and Tomato Stew, *page 159*

1 (1-ounce) slice French bread

SNACK

Pistachio-Apple Bar with Chia Seeds, *page 241*

¼ cup grapes

1,200-Calorie 30-Day Menu Plan *(continued)*

DAY 15

BREAKFAST

Chai Spice–Pear Oatmeal, *page 24*

LUNCH

Avocado-Egg Salad Sandwich with Pickled Celery, *page 76*

1 kiwifruit

DINNER

Skillet Chicken and Couscous with Pomegranate Sauce, *page 184*

SNACK

Cranberry-Pistachio Bar, *page 237*

DAY 16

BREAKFAST

Banana Breakfast Smoothie, *page 55*

1 hard-cooked egg

LUNCH

Ham, Cranberry, and Gruyère Sandwich, *page 89*

DINNER

Tomato, Basil, and Corn Pizza, *page 218*

1½ cups chopped romaine, 2 tablespoons reduced-fat Caesar dressing, and 2 tablespoons grated Parmesan cheese

SNACK

1 medium pear

1 (1-ounce) part-skim mozzarella cheese stick

DAY 17

BREAKFAST

Fried Egg and Crunchy Breakfast Salad, *page 59*

½ cup orange juice

LUNCH

Quinoa-Brown Rice Pilaf with Goat Cheese and Watercress, *page 131*

DINNER

Fast Chicken Chili, *page 228*

¾ ounce gluten-free corn chips, about 24 chips

SNACK

1 small apple

1 ounce cheddar cheese

DAY 18

BREAKFAST

Cherry-Blueberry Toasted Oat Scone, *page 47*

2 teaspoons jam

LUNCH

Avocado, Sprout, and Cashew Spread Sandwich, *page 79*

DINNER

Roasted Pork Chop with Cabbage and Carrots, *page 173*

½ cup cooked wild rice

SNACK

¾ cup plain fat-free yogurt

¾ cup fresh raspberries

DAY 19 BREAKFAST

Herbed Frittata with Vegetables and Goat Cheese, *page 67*

1 small banana

LUNCH

Orzo Salad with Spicy Buttermilk Dressing, *page 119*

7 whole almonds

DINNER

Baked Chicken Moussaka, *page 183*

1 cup chopped romaine, ¼ cup cherry tomatoes, 1 tablespoon chopped kalamata olives, and 1 tablespoon vinaigrette

SNACK

2 dark chocolate squares, such as Ghirardelli

½ cup 1% low-fat milk or milk substitute

DAY 20 BREAKFAST

Muesli with Cranberries and Flaxseed, *page 33*

½ cup 1% low-fat milk or milk substitute

LUNCH

Vegetarian Niçoise Salad Jar, *page 104*

DINNER

One-Pan Broccoli-Bacon Mac 'n' Cheese, *page 177*

1 cup Orange and Almond Salad, *page 203*

SNACK

Raspberry-Ricotta Waffle, *page 245*

DAY 21 BREAKFAST

Blueberry-Oatmeal Muffin, *page 41*

¾ cup plain fat-free Greek yogurt swirled with 1 teaspoon honey

LUNCH

Arugula, Italian Tuna, and White Bean Salad, *page 127*

1 (¾-ounce) slice French bread

DINNER

Quick Fried Brown Rice with Shrimp and Snap Peas, *page 156*

SNACK

Salty-Sweet Mix, *page 245*

DAY 22 BREAKFAST

Gluten-Free Oatmeal Pancakes, *page 52*

LUNCH

Chicken Taco Salad, *page 125*

1 cup cantaloupe cubes

DINNER

Whole-Grain Mini Meat Loaves, *page 166*

½ cup sautéed Brussels sprouts

SNACK

7 multigrain baked pita chips, such as Stacy's

2 tablespoons hummus

1,200-Calorie 30-Day Menu Plan *(continued)*

DAY 23

BREAKFAST

Whole-Grain Bran Muffin, *page 38*

1 small banana

½ cup 1% low-fat milk or milk substitute

LUNCH

Pork, Bean, and Escarole Soup, *page 99*

10 multigrain crackers, such as Kashi Original 7 Grain

DINNER

Fast Skillet Chicken Cacciatore, *page 187*

Parmesan Polenta Rounds, *page 202*

SNACK

1 cup fresh mango slices

5 multigrain crackers, such as Kashi Original 7 Grain

DAY 24

BREAKFAST

Pancetta, Fried Egg, and Red-Eye Gravy Oatmeal, *page 24*

LUNCH

Apple and Cashew Spread Sandwich, *page 79*

½ cup cantaloupe cubes

DINNER

Mushroom and Bacon Casserole, *page 178*

1 small whole-wheat dinner roll

SNACK

Oatmeal-Raisin Bar, *page 238*

DAY 25

BREAKFAST

Leftover muffin (either Blueberry-Oatmeal Muffin or Whole-Grain Bran Muffin)

1 small orange

¾ cup 1% low-fat milk or milk substitute

LUNCH

Tuna, Olive, and Wheat Berry Salad, *page 126*

DINNER

Classic Lasagna with Meat Sauce, *page 162*

1½ cups chopped romaine lettuce with 2 tablespoons reduced-fat Caesar dressing

SNACK

Homemade Guacamole and Chips, *page 245*

DAY 26

BREAKFAST

Strawberry-Cream Cheese Waffle Sandwich, *page 42*

Coffee with 1 tablespoon half-and-half

LUNCH

Asparagus and Mushroom Quiche, *page 143*

1½ cups fresh spinach with 2 tablespoons reduced-fat vinaigrette and 7 whole almonds

DINNER

Chipotle-Bean Burrito, *page 210*

SNACK

Oatmeal-Raisin Bar, *page 238*

DAY 27

BREAKFAST

Overnight Honey-Almond Oatmeal, *page 27*

2 slices center-cut bacon

LUNCH

Reuben Sandwich, *page 86*

½ cup sliced cucumber

DINNER

Ginger-Soy Chicken Thighs with Scallion Rice, *page 194*

½ cup Cucumber-Peanut Salad, *page 203*

SNACK

Crunch-Crunch-Crunch Mix, *page 245*

DAY 28

BREAKFAST

Green Eggs and Ham, *page 42*

1 cup berries

Coffee with 1 tablespoon half-and-half

LUNCH

Homemade Chicken Noodle Soup, *page 97*

10 multigrain crackers, such as Kashi Original 7 Grain

DINNER

Butternut Squash and Swiss Chard Tart, *page 206*

½ cup fresh strawberries

SNACK

Butterscotch Bar, *page 254*

DAY 29

BREAKFAST

Ginger, Berry, and Oat Smoothie, *page 55*

1 (1-ounce) part-skim mozzarella cheese stick

LUNCH

Black Bean Tostada, *page 139*

¼ cup cubed avocado

DINNER

Chicken Parmesan with Zucchini Noodles, *page 180*

SNACK

Turkey and Cheese Roll, *page 245*

DAY 30

BREAKFAST

Sausage, Gravy, and Egg Breakfast Sandwich, *page 63*

LUNCH

Chilled Soy-Lime Rice Noodles with Tofu, *page 135*

⅔ cup Miso Mixed Vegetable Salad, *page 203*

DINNER

Sweet and Tangy Glazed Pork Tenderloin with Potato Mash, *page 169*

1 serving Sautéed Broccolini, *page 202*

SNACK

3 cups popcorn

1 kiwifruit

BREAKFAST

Out-of-this-World Oatmeals

Oatmeal is a hearty, filling start to the day and is a fantastic base for a range of topping options. Here are a few to get you started, but first, begin here: Bring ¾ cup water to a boil in a medium saucepan. Stir in ½ cup uncooked old-fashioned oats and a dash of salt. Reduce the heat; simmer 5 minutes, stirring occasionally. Remove from the heat, and finish with one of the following variations.

1. Goat Cheese–Cremini Oatmeal V

Heat a medium skillet over medium heat. Add 1 teaspoon olive oil; swirl. Add ½ cup sliced cremini mushrooms; sauté 4 minutes. Stir 1½ tablespoons crumbled goat cheese, 2 tablespoons half-and-half, ⅛ teaspoon salt, and ⅛ teaspoon chopped fresh thyme into 1 serving of warm oatmeal. Top with mushrooms and an additional 1½ teaspoons crumbled goat cheese.

SERVES 1: CALORIES 277; FAT 13.2g (sat 5.2g, mono 5.1g, poly 1.5g); PROTEIN 9g; CARB 30g; FIBER 4g; SUGARS 3g (est. added sugars 0g); CHOL 21mg; IRON 2mg; SODIUM 510mg; CALCIUM 71mg

2. Lemon-Blueberry Oatmeal V

Stir 1 teaspoon sugar and 1 teaspoon prepared lemon curd into 1 serving of warm oatmeal. Top the oatmeal with 3 tablespoons fresh blueberries, 1 teaspoon mascarpone cheese, and 2 teaspoons sliced toasted almonds.

SERVES 1: CALORIES 304; FAT 10.3g (sat 3.5g, mono 2.2g, poly 1.5g); PROTEIN 7g; CARB 47g; FIBER 7g; SUGARS 19g (est. added sugars 9g); CHOL 27mg; IRON 2mg; SODIUM 161mg; CALCIUM 25mg

3. Pancetta, Fried Egg, and Red-Eye Gravy DF

Heat a nonstick skillet over medium-high heat; add ½ ounce sliced pancetta to the pan. Cook for 2 minutes or until crisp. Transfer to a plate; reserve the drippings in the pan. Add 1 teaspoon flour to the pan, stirring with a whisk. Stir in 2 tablespoons black coffee and 2 tablespoons tomato juice. Bring to a simmer; cook until gravy reduces by half. Heat a small nonstick skillet over medium heat; crack 1 large egg into pan. Cook 2 minutes; sprinkle with a dash black pepper. Top 1 serving of warm oatmeal with the gravy, egg, and pancetta.

SERVES 1: CALORIES 315; FAT 15.3g (sat 4.9g, mono 3.6g, poly 2.1g); PROTEIN 15g; CARB 31g; FIBER 4g; SUGARS 2g (est. added sugars 0g); CHOL 201mg; IRON 3mg; SODIUM 511mg; CALCIUM 52mg

4. Chai Spice–Pear Oatmeal V

Heat a medium skillet over medium heat; coat pan with cooking spray. Add ½ pear, thinly sliced, to pan; sauté 3 minutes. Stir in 1 teaspoon honey. Cook 2 minutes. Stir 1 tablespoon 1% low-fat milk, ⅛ teaspoon cinnamon, ⅛ teaspoon cardamom, ⅛ teaspoon ground ginger, ⅛ teaspoon allspice, and ⅛ teaspoon vanilla extract into 1 serving of warm oatmeal. Top with pear slices and 1 tablespoon chopped toasted walnuts.

SERVES 1: CALORIES 289; FAT 8.8g (sat 1.2g, mono 2.2g, poly 4.6g); PROTEIN 7g; CARB 49g; FIBER 8g; SUGARS 15g (est. added sugars 6g); CHOL 1mg; IRON 2mg; SODIUM 154mg; CALCIUM 41mg

5. Pistachio, Fig, and Saffron Yogurt V

Stir 1 tablespoon fresh orange juice and 1 teaspoon honey into 1 serving of warm oatmeal. Whisk together 2 tablespoons plain 2% Greek yogurt and a dash of saffron threads; dollop on oatmeal. Sprinkle with 1 tablespoon chopped unsalted pistachios and 1 tablespoon chopped dried figs. Drizzle with 1 teaspoon honey.

SERVES 1: CALORIES 284; FAT 7.2g (sat 1.3g, mono 2.8g, poly 2g); PROTEIN 9g; CARB 49g; FIBER 6g; SUGARS 20g (est. added sugars 12g); CHOL 2mg; IRON 2mg; SODIUM 159mg; CALCIUM 47mg

1
2
3
4
5

Overnight Honey-Almond Oatmeal DF V

Hands-on: 5 minutes | Total: 4 hours, 12 minutes | Serves 1

Steel-cut oats soak up water overnight so they're ready to go in the morning. Use a big bowl because the grains will expand.

½ cup uncooked steel-cut oats (such as McCann's)
1¼ cups water
⅛ teaspoon salt
¼ teaspoon ground cinnamon
⅛ teaspoon ground nutmeg
1 tablespoon sliced toasted almonds
1 tablespoon honey

1. Combine the oats and 1¼ cups water in a microwave-safe 4-cup bowl. Cover and refrigerate 4 hours or overnight.
2. Uncover the bowl, and stir in the salt. Microwave, uncovered, at HIGH for 6 minutes or until most of the liquid is absorbed, stirring well after 3 minutes. Stir in ¼ teaspoon cinnamon and nutmeg. Top with the almonds and honey.

CALORIES 250; FAT 5.5g (sat 0.8g, mono 2.8g, poly 1.7g); PROTEIN 6g; CARB 46g; FIBER 5g; SUGARS 19g (est. added sugars 17g); CHOL 0mg; IRON 2mg; SODIUM 292mg; CALCIUM 24mg

serve with:

- 2 slices center-cut bacon (50 calories)

1,300-CALORIE PLAN/1,400-CALORIE PLAN: No changes
1,500-CALORIE PLAN: Add an orange (69 calories).

DIY Instant Oatmeal

You can make your own flavored instant oatmeal mix by combining quick-cooking oats with sunflower seeds, dried fruit, cinnamon, or unsweetened flaked dried coconut. Store the mix in an airtight container, and scoop out ½-cup portions on busy mornings. Add water and microwave for a quick breakfast.

294 TOTAL CALORIES

Breakfast Quinoa DF GF V

Hands-on: 10 minutes | Total: 22 minutes | Serves 3

Toast the coconut if you have time to give it a nuttier flavor and added crunch: Spread flaked coconut in a single layer on a baking sheet, and bake at 400°F for 5 minutes or until it's golden brown. Cool slightly.

½ cup uncooked quinoa
¾ cup light coconut milk
2 tablespoons water
1 tablespoon light brown sugar
⅛ teaspoon salt
1 cup sliced strawberries
1 cup sliced banana
¼ cup unsweetened flaked dried coconut

1. Place the quinoa in a fine sieve, and place the sieve in a large bowl. Cover the quinoa with water. Using your hands, rub the grains together for 30 seconds; rinse and drain the quinoa. Repeat the procedure twice. Drain well. Combine the quinoa, coconut milk, 2 tablespoons water, brown sugar, and salt in a medium saucepan, and bring to a boil. Reduce the heat, and simmer 15 minutes or until the liquid is absorbed, stirring occasionally. Stir the mixture constantly during the last 2 minutes of cooking.
2. Place about ⅔ cup of the quinoa mixture in each of 3 bowls. Top each serving with ⅓ cup strawberry slices, ⅓ cup banana slices, and about 1 tablespoon coconut. Serve warm.

CALORIES 237; FAT 7.3g (sat 5.1g, mono 0.5g, poly 1.1g); PROTEIN 6g; CARB 41g; FIBER 5g; SUGARS 16g (est. added sugars 4g); CHOL 0mg; IRON 2mg; SODIUM 119mg; CALCIUM 29mg

serve with:

- Coffee with 1 tablespoon half-and-half (22 calories)
- 1 clementine (35 calories)

1,300-CALORIE PLAN/1,400-CALORIE PLAN: No changes
1,500-CALORIE PLAN: Add an additional clementine (35 calories) or serve with ¾ cup orange juice (84 calories) instead of the coffee and clementines.

Quinoa

Quinoa (KEEN-wah) is a small whole grain, about the size of couscous, that cooks in 10 to 20 minutes. It needs to be rinsed before cooking to remove the bitter-tasting natural coating (called saponin). Consider cooking extra, as it's great to stir into soups and casseroles, to serve as a dinner side, or as a base for a salad.

Massachusetts Woman Chooses Cooking Light Diet, Loses 50 Pounds

A BOSTON-AREA COMMUNITY MEMBER named Lisa Bennett said that not only was she enjoying the Cooking Light Diet, but she was experiencing profound weight-loss results. From January—when she joined—to September, Lisa lost 50 pounds*.

This veterinary clinic employee said she loves the emphasis on portion sizes and whole, natural foods. "I've done other [diets] where they're trying to steer people towards healthy foods," Lisa said. "But *this* is how you do it. And this is what a good portion looks like. And I like that it's mostly whole foods and not processed foods, although there are some convenience options."

"But *this* is how you do it. And this is what a good portion looks like."

Lisa also appreciates trying the menu variety, picking up a few favorite recipes along the way. "The weird grilled turkey and cheese with mango chutney and Granny Smith apples? That's really interesting and delicious, and I never would've put those together on my own," she said. "I can't say that I've had a bad meal. Obviously there are some that you tend towards and prefer, but there hasn't been one that's like, 'Oh my God, I'm never making that again.'"

And, of course, there's more to Lisa's incredible Cooking Light Diet weight-loss journey. "It was a lot of work in the beginning, but just like anything else, you get used to it," Lisa said. "And I started feeling better and losing weight, so it was kind of easy to keep it going after that," she said.

"When I started, I was 193.6 pounds. When I weighed myself this morning, I was 143.6 pounds. ...Yet the Cooking Light Diet doesn't feel restrictive. Like I've said, the food is awesome, I've never felt hungry on it, and taking the time to cook is kind of distracting me from sitting on the couch after work."

**Members following The Cooking Light Diet lose more than half a pound per week, on average.*

Cinnamon-Banana Crunch Bowl (V)

Hands-on: 5 minutes | Total: 5 minutes | Serves 1

Mix up your morning oatmeal routine by using bulgur in this breakfast bowl. If you prepare the bulgur ahead (see directions at right), it's a quick and easy breakfast of champions.

¼ cup plain fat-free Greek yogurt
1 teaspoon honey
Dash of cinnamon
½ cup cooked bulgur
1 tablespoon chopped walnuts, toasted
1 tablespoon brown sugar
⅓ cup banana slices
Additional cinnamon (optional)

Combine the yogurt, honey, and a dash of cinnamon in a small bowl. Toss together the bulgur, walnuts, and brown sugar. Top with the banana slices. Dollop the yogurt mixture over the bulgur mixture. Sprinkle with additional cinnamon, if desired.

CALORIES 255; FAT 5g (sat 0.4g, mono 1.2g, poly 2.9g); PROTEIN 10g; CARB 46g; FIBER 6g; SUGARS 23g (est. added sugars 15g); CHOL 0mg; IRON 1mg; SODIUM 29mg; CALCIUM 65mg

serve with:

- ½ fresh grapefruit (45 calories)

1,300-CALORIE PLAN/1,400-CALORIE PLAN: No changes
1,500-CALORIE PLAN: Add 1 (45-calorie) slice toasted multigrain wheat bread.

Cooking Bulgur

Bulgur is a quick-cooking whole grain and is best prepared pilaf-style using only the amount of water the grains should absorb by the end of cooking. Bring 1 cup of bulgur and 2 cups of water to a boil in a medium saucepan; cover, reduce the heat, and simmer 12 minutes or until done. Cook times can vary, so start testing for doneness early. The bulgur is done when the raw grain taste is gone but the grains are still chewy. You can add more water as the bulgur cooks if you need to, or drain it if it's ready before all the water has been absorbed.

Muesli with Cranberries and Flaxseed DF V

Hands-on: 7 minutes | Total: 7 minutes | Serves 6 (serving size: ⅔ cup)

Muesli is a popular uncooked cereal made of a mix of grains, dried fruit, nuts, and seeds that have been soaked in milk, fruit juice, or yogurt. Store it in the refrigerator to keep the flaxseed and whole grains fresh longer.

2 cups uncooked old-fashioned rolled oats
½ cup sweetened dried cranberries
⅓ cup toasted wheat germ
⅓ cup ground flaxseed
3 tablespoons slivered toasted almonds
3 tablespoons chopped toasted pecans
3 tablespoons toasted pumpkinseed kernels

Combine all the ingredients in a large heavy-duty zip-top plastic bag or airtight container.
Note: Store in the refrigerator for up to 6 months.

CALORIES 251; FAT 11.5g (sat 1.1g, mono 4.3g, poly 4.9g); PROTEIN 8g; CARB 33g; FIBER 7g; SUGARS 8g (est. added sugars 5g); CHOL 0mg; IRON 2mg; SODIUM 3mg; CALCIUM 17mg

serve with:

- ½ cup 1% low-fat milk or milk substitute (51 calories)

1,300-CALORIE PLAN/1,400-CALORIE PLAN: No changes
1,500-CALORIE PLAN: Increase the serving of 1% low-fat milk or milk substitute to 1 cup (102 calories).

Breakfast Cereal V

Combine 4 cups Muesli with Cranberries and Flaxseed, 3 cups 1% low-fat milk, 2 tablespoons maple syrup, and ½ teaspoon vanilla extract in a large bowl. Cover and chill 3 hours or overnight. Spoon the chilled muesli mix into each of 6 bowls. Top each serving with 1 tablespoon plain fat-free yogurt.

SERVES 6 (serving size: ¾ cup muesli mix and 1 tablespoon yogurt): CALORIES 332; FAT 12.7g (sat 2.1g, mono 4.8g, poly 4.8g); PROTEIN 14g; CARB 44g; FIBER 7g; SUGARS 19g (est. added sugars 9g); CHOL 8mg; IRON 3mg; SODIUM 74mg; CALCIUM 204mg

1,300-CALORIE PLAN/1,400-CALORIE PLAN: No changes
1,500-CALORIE PLAN: Increase the yogurt to ¼ cup per serving (19 calories).

Store-Bought Cereal Rules

GO FOR WHOLE GRAIN
Check the ingredient list and make sure the first ingredient includes the word "whole"—whole wheat, whole grain, etc. If it's bran, that's fine too, but bran technically isn't a whole grain.

GO FOR FIBER
Select a cereal that contains at least 3 grams of fiber per serving.

GO SLOW ON SUGAR
Look for a cereal that has no more than 8 grams of sugar per serving. Most of these sugars will be added to the cereal, but natural sugars from dried fruits, such as raisins, are included in this number as well.

Raspberry-Yogurt Muffins GF V

Hands-on: 13 minutes | Total: 45 minutes | Serves 12 (serving size: 1 muffin)

Muffins have always been a breakfast staple, but they can be laden with fat and calories. These delicious gluten-free muffins are not. This blend of flours is a mild mix, allowing the flavor of the raspberries and vanilla to shine through.

Cooking spray
4.6 ounces brown rice flour (about 1 cup)
2.6 ounces white rice flour (about ½ cup)
⅓ cup plus 1 teaspoon sugar
2 tablespoons potato starch
2 tablespoons cornstarch
1 teaspoon baking powder
1 teaspoon baking soda
½ teaspoon xanthan gum
¼ teaspoon salt
1 cup vanilla fat-free yogurt
¼ cup fat-free milk
2 tablespoons canola oil
¼ teaspoon almond extract
1 large egg
1 cup fresh raspberries
1 tablespoon brown rice flour

1. Preheat the oven to 375°F. Place 12 paper muffin cup liners in the muffin cups; coat the liners with cooking spray.
2. Weigh or lightly spoon 4.6 ounces brown rice flour and the white rice flour into dry measuring cups; level with a knife. Combine the flours, ⅓ cup sugar, and the next 6 ingredients (through salt) in a medium bowl; stir with a whisk. Make a well in the center of the mixture. Combine the yogurt and the next 4 ingredients (through egg); stir with a whisk. Add to the flour mixture, stirring just until moist. Toss the raspberries with 1 tablespoon brown rice flour in a small bowl; gently fold into the batter.
3. Spoon the batter into the prepared cups, and sprinkle with the remaining 1 teaspoon sugar. Bake at 375°F for 22 minutes or until lightly browned and the muffins spring back when lightly touched. Cool 10 minutes in the pan on a wire rack; remove from the pan.

CALORIES 145; FAT 3.4g (sat 0.5g, mono 1.9g, poly 0.9g); PROTEIN 3g; CARB 26g; FIBER 2g; SUGARS 10g (est. added sugars 6g); CHOL 16mg; IRON 0mg; SODIUM 212mg; CALCIUM 70mg

serve with:

- 1 medium apple (95 calories)
- ½ cup 1% low-fat milk or milk substitute (51 calories)

1,300-CALORIE PLAN/1,400-CALORIE PLAN: No changes
1,500-CALORIE PLAN: Increase the serving of 1% low-fat milk or milk substitute to 1 cup (102 calories).

Chocolate Chip–Hazelnut Muffins DF GF V

305 TOTAL CALORIES

Hands-on: 14 minutes | Total: 49 minutes | Serves 15 (serving size: 1 muffin)

Hazelnuts and chocolate are a perfect pair. This muffin uses nondairy buttery spread and coconut milk to create a dairy-free muffin layered with flavors.

Cooking spray
3.6 ounces certified gluten-free oat flour (about 1 cup)
2.6 ounces white rice flour (about ½ cup)
1.05 ounces tapioca flour (about ¼ cup)
½ cup packed brown sugar
1 teaspoon baking powder
1 teaspoon baking soda
½ teaspoon xanthan gum
¼ teaspoon salt
1 cup unsweetened coconut milk
¼ cup nondairy buttery spread (such as Earth Balance), melted
1 teaspoon vanilla extract
2 large eggs
¼ cup semisweet chocolate minichips
¼ cup finely chopped hazelnuts

1. Preheat the oven to 375°F. Place 15 paper muffin cup liners in the muffin cups; coat the liners with cooking spray.
2. Weigh or lightly spoon the flours into dry measuring cups; level with a knife. Combine the flours, brown sugar, and the next 4 ingredients (through salt) in a medium bowl; stir with a whisk. Make a well in the center of the mixture. Combine the coconut milk and the next 3 ingredients (through eggs); stir with a whisk. Add to the flour mixture, stirring just until moist. Fold in the chocolate minichips and hazelnuts.
3. Spoon the batter into the prepared cups. Bake at 375°F for 25 minutes or until lightly browned and the muffins spring back when lightly touched. Cool 10 minutes in the pan on a wire rack; remove from the pan.

CALORIES 156; FAT 6.9g (sat 2.2g, mono 2.8g, poly 1.3g); PROTEIN 3g; CARB 21g; FIBER 1g; SUGARS 9g (est. added sugars 8g); CHOL 25mg; IRON 1mg; SODIUM 195mg; CALCIUM 40mg

serve with:

- 1 scrambled egg (72 calories)
- ¾ cup 1% low-fat milk or milk substitute (77 calories)

1,300-CALORIE PLAN/1,400-CALORIE PLAN: No changes
1,500-CALORIE PLAN: Instead of the serving suggestion above, pair this with scrambled eggs made with 1 egg and 2 egg whites (120 calories) and ¾ cup 1% low-fat milk or milk substitute (77 calories).

DIY Oat Flour

If you can't find oat flour, make your own. Place oats in a food processor, and process until they're a powdery consistency. It adds a robust taste and hearty texture to baked goods. Store it in an airtight container in a cool, dry place up to 3 months or in the refrigerator or freezer for up to 6 months.

Whole-Grain Bran Muffins

Hands-on: 25 minutes | Total: 1 hour, 25 minutes
Serves 12 (serving size: 1 muffin)

This classic recipe uses naturally sweet dates and ripe bananas to give these muffins a health boost. You can freeze these muffins for up to 2 months.

Cooking spray
1¾ cups wheat bran (about 4.5 ounces)
1 cup whole pitted dates (about 6 ounces)
¾ cup fresh orange juice
1 cup nonfat buttermilk
½ cup mashed ripe banana
2 tablespoons butter, melted
2 tablespoons canola oil
1 teaspoon vanilla extract
4.5 ounces whole-grain pastry flour (about 1 cup)
1½ teaspoons baking powder
½ teaspoon baking soda
½ teaspoon ground cinnamon
¼ teaspoon salt
2 large eggs, lightly beaten

1. Preheat the oven to 350°F. Place 12 paper muffin cup liners in the muffin cups; coat the liners with cooking spray.
2. Spread the bran on a baking sheet. Bake at 350°F for 8 to 10 minutes or until lightly browned, stirring once.
3. Combine dates and juice in a saucepan over medium heat; bring to a boil. Cover, reduce heat, and simmer 20 minutes. Remove from heat; uncover and let stand 5 minutes. Place date mixture in a food processor; process until smooth. Add buttermilk and next 4 ingredients; process until smooth.
4. Weigh or lightly spoon the flour into a dry measuring cup; level with a knife. Combine the flour, bran, baking powder, and the next 3 ingredients (through salt) in a medium bowl, stirring with a whisk. Add the date mixture to the bran mixture, stirring just until moist. Add the eggs, stirring just until combined. Spoon the batter into the prepared cups. Bake at 350°F for 28 minutes or until a wooden pick inserted in the center of the muffins comes out clean. Remove the muffins from the pan; cool on a wire rack.

CALORIES 168; FAT 5.4g (sat 1.7g, mono 2.3g, poly 0.9g); PROTEIN 4g; CARB 29g; FIBER 7g; SUGARS 12g (est. added sugars 0g); CHOL 36mg; IRON 2mg; SODIUM 183mg; CALCIUM 89mg

serve with:

- 1 small banana (90 calories)
- ½ cup 1% low-fat milk or milk substitute (51 calories)

1,300-CALORIE PLAN/1,400-CALORIE PLAN: No changes
1,500-CALORIE PLAN: Add ½ tablespoon peanut butter (45 calories) to spread on the banana.

Blueberry-Oatmeal Muffins V

Hands-on: 10 minutes | Total: 30 minutes | Serves 16 (serving size: 1 muffin)

294 TOTAL CALORIES

Tossing frozen blueberries with flour keeps them from sinking and from turning the batter purple while they bake. If you use fresh blueberries, skip that step.

Cooking spray
1⅔ cups uncooked quick-cooking oats
3 ounces all-purpose flour (about ⅔ cup)
2.33 ounces whole-wheat flour (about ½ cup)
¾ cup packed light brown sugar
2 teaspoons ground cinnamon
1 teaspoon baking powder
1 teaspoon baking soda
¾ teaspoon salt
1½ cups low-fat buttermilk
¼ cup canola oil
2 teaspoons grated lemon rind
2 large eggs, lightly beaten
2 cups frozen blueberries
2 tablespoons all-purpose flour
2 tablespoons granulated sugar

1. Preheat the oven to 400°F. Line 16 muffin cups with paper liners; coat with cooking spray.
2. Place the oats in a food processor; pulse 5 to 6 times, or until the oats resemble coarse meal. Place in a large bowl.
3. Weigh or lightly spoon the flours into dry measuring cups; level with a knife. Add the flours and the next 5 ingredients (through salt) to the oats; stir well. Make a well in the center of the mixture.
4. Combine the buttermilk and the next 3 ingredients (through eggs). Add to the flour mixture; stir just until moist.
5. Toss the berries with 2 tablespoons flour, and gently fold into the batter. Spoon the batter into the prepared muffin cups; sprinkle 2 tablespoons granulated sugar over the batter. Bake at 400°F for 20 minutes or until the muffins spring back when touched lightly in the center. Remove from the pans immediately; place on a wire rack.

CALORIES 173; FAT 5g (sat 0.5g, mono 2.5g, poly 1.1g); PROTEIN 4g; CARB 28g; FIBER 2g; SUGARS 14g (est. added sugars 13g); CHOL 23mg; IRON 1mg; SODIUM 245mg; CALCIUM 72mg

serve with:

- ¾ cup plain fat-free Greek yogurt (100 calories) swirled with 1 teaspoon honey (21 calories)

1,300-CALORIE PLAN/1,400-CALORIE PLAN: No changes
1,500-CALORIE PLAN: Instead of the serving suggestion above, serve with 1 cup plain fat-free Greek yogurt (120 calories) swirled with 2 teaspoons honey (42 calories) and coffee with 1 tablespoon half-and-half (22 calories).

Keep It Simple

Mornings can be harried. These easy breakfasts are quick to put together and require only a handful of ingredients.

Breakfast Sandwiches & Toasts

Strawberry–Cream Cheese Waffle Sandwiches (V)

Place 4 ounces ⅓-less-fat cream cheese (about ½ cup), 4 teaspoons brown sugar, and ¼ teaspoon ground cinnamon in a medium bowl; beat with a mixer at medium speed until well blended. Gently fold in ¾ cup sliced strawberries. Toast 8 frozen multigrain waffles (such as Kashi). Spread about 3 tablespoons cream cheese mixture over each of 4 waffles; top the sandwiches with the remaining 4 waffles.

SERVES 4 (serving size: 1 sandwich): CALORIES 269; FAT 9.2g (sat 4.1g, mono 3g, poly 1.3g); PROTEIN 10g; CARB 42g; FIBER 7g; SUGARS 11g (est. added sugars 4g); CHOL 20mg; IRON 2mg; SODIUM 443mg; CALCIUM 91mg

Green Eggs and Ham

Spread 1 teaspoon pesto on 1 slice of toasted ciabatta. Top with 1 (¾-ounce) slice Canadian bacon and 1 scrambled or soft-boiled egg. Sprinkle with thinly sliced fresh basil.

SERVES 1: CALORIES 203; FAT 9.4g (sat 2.5g, mono 3.3g, poly 1.2g); PROTEIN 13g; CARB 17g; FIBER 1g; SUGARS 1g (est. added sugars 0g); CHOL 198mg; IRON 2mg; SODIUM 526mg; CALCIUM 46mg

Cheddar 'n' Apple Cinnamon-Raisin Toast (V)

Melt ¾ ounce shredded sharp cheddar cheese over 1 (1-ounce) slice toasted cinnamon-raisin bread. Top with 1 thinly sliced small Granny Smith apple.

SERVES 1: CALORIES 258; FAT 8.6g (sat 4.5g, mono 1.8g, poly 0.3g); PROTEIN 8g; CARB 36g; FIBER 5g; SUGARS 16g (est. added sugars 2g); CHOL 22mg; IRON 1mg; SODIUM 221mg; CALCIUM 159mg

Ricotta-Pistachio Toast 

Spread 2 tablespoons light ricotta cheese on 1 slice of toasted crusty whole-grain bread. Drizzle 1 teaspoon olive oil over the ricotta. Sprinkle with 1 tablespoon crushed dry-roasted salted pistachios.

SERVES 1: CALORIES 176; FAT 10.9g (sat 2.6g, mono 5.8g, poly 1.6g); PROTEIN 7g; CARB 15g; FIBER 5g; SUGARS 2g (est. added sugars 0g); CHOL 10mg; IRON 1mg; SODIUM 138mg; CALCIUM 176mg

Parfaits

Blueberry-Yogurt Breakfast Parfait (V)

Combine 1 cup plain fat-free Greek yogurt, ¼ teaspoon grated lemon rind, and 2 teaspoons honey in a small bowl. Spoon ¼ cup of the yogurt mixture into a parfait glass. Top with ¼ cup fresh blueberries. Repeat with the remaining yogurt mixture and ¼ cup blueberries. Top with 2 tablespoons multigrain cluster cereal.

SERVES 1: CALORIES 230; FAT 0.6g (sat 0g, mono 0.2g, poly 0.2g); PROTEIN 22g; CARB 36g; FIBER 2g; SUGARS 23g (est. added sugars 12g); CHOL 0mg; IRON 0mg; SODIUM 112mg; CALCIUM 162mg

Raspberry-Yogurt Breakfast Parfait (V)

Combine 1 cup plain fat-free Greek yogurt, ¼ teaspoon grated lemon rind, and 2 teaspoons honey in a small bowl. Spoon ¼ cup yogurt mixture into a parfait glass. Top with ¼ cup fresh raspberries. Repeat with the remaining yogurt and ¼ cup raspberries. Top with 2 tablespoons multigrain cluster cereal.

SERVES 1: CALORIES 225; FAT 0.6g (sat 0g, mono 0.2g, poly 0.2g); PROTEIN 22g; CARB 35g; FIBER 1g; SUGARS 21g (est. added sugars 13g); CHOL 0mg; IRON 0mg; SODIUM 112mg; CALCIUM 162mg

Breakfast Parfaits (V)

Place ⅓ cup apricot preserves in a microwave-safe bowl, and microwave at HIGH for 10 seconds or until the preserves are melted. Add 3 cups sliced strawberries, and toss gently to coat. Spoon ¼ cup vanilla low-fat yogurt into each of 4 parfait glasses; top each serving with ⅓ cup strawberry mixture. Repeat the layers. Sprinkle each serving with 2 tablespoons low-fat granola without raisins (such as Kellogg's) and 2 teaspoons slivered toasted almonds.

SERVES 4 (serving size: 1 parfait): CALORIES 246; FAT 5.1g (sat 1.4g, mono 2g, poly 1g); PROTEIN 8g; CARB 44g; FIBER 4g; SUGARS 28g (est. added sugars 15g); CHOL 8mg; IRON 1mg; SODIUM 123mg; CALCIUM 215mg

Egg Scrambles

START HERE: Beat two eggs (144 calories), add in any of the fillings below, and pour into a nonstick skillet. Cook over medium heat, stirring occasionally to produce larger curds, or more often if you prefer smaller curds.

THE FILLINGS:

- 1 tablespoon chopped sundried tomatoes, 1 tablespoon grated Parmesan cheese, 2 teaspoons chopped fresh basil, and 1 teaspoon pesto (56 calories)
- 2 tablespoons feta cheese and 1 teaspoon chopped fresh dill (50 calories)
- 2 tablespoons goat cheese and 1 teaspoon chopped fresh chives (40 calories)
- 3 tablespoons shredded part-skim mozzarella cheese and 1 cup chopped fresh spinach (70 calories)

Tuscan Lemon Muffins (V)

Hands-on: 13 minutes | Total: 34 minutes | Serves 12 (serving size: 1 muffin)

Using ricotta cheese ensures a light and fluffy texture while also yielding a moist and delicious muffin. Enjoy these lemony treats for breakfast or a sweet snack.

Cooking spray
7.9 ounces all-purpose flour (about 1¾ cups)
¾ cup granulated sugar
2½ teaspoons baking powder
¼ teaspoon salt
6 ounces part-skim ricotta cheese (about ¾ cup)
½ cup water
¼ cup olive oil
1 tablespoon grated lemon rind
2 tablespoons fresh lemon juice
1 large egg, lightly beaten
2 tablespoons turbinado sugar

1. Preheat the oven to 375°F. Place 12 paper cup liners in the muffin cups; coat with cooking spray.

2. Weigh or lightly spoon the flour into dry measuring cups; level with a knife. Combine the flour and the next 3 ingredients (through salt). Make a well in the center of the mixture. Combine the ricotta and the next 5 ingredients (through egg). Add the ricotta mixture to the flour mixture, stirring just until moist.

3. Divide the batter among the prepared muffin cups. Sprinkle the turbinado sugar over the batter. Bake at 375°F for 16 minutes or until a wooden pick inserted in the center of the muffins comes out clean. Cool 5 minutes in the pan on a wire rack.

CALORIES 186; FAT 6.2g (sat 1.5g, mono 3.4g, poly 0.6g); PROTEIN 4g; CARB 30g; FIBER 1g; SUGARS 15g (est. added sugars 14g); CHOL 21mg; IRON 1mg; SODIUM 160mg; CALCIUM 81mg

serve with:

- 1 hard-cooked egg (72 calories)
- ½ cup orange juice (52 calories)

1,300-CALORIE PLAN/1,400-CALORIE PLAN: No changes
1,500-CALORIE PLAN: Increase the serving of orange juice to ¾ cup (76 calories).

Cherry-Blueberry Toasted Oat Scones (V)

Hands-on: 34 minutes | Total: 60 minutes | Serves 8 (serving size: 1 scone)

If you have trouble finding dried blueberries, swap in additional dried cherries or another tender dried fruit.

1 cup uncooked old-fashioned rolled oats
4.5 ounces all-purpose flour (about 1 cup)
⅓ cup granulated sugar
2 teaspoons baking powder
½ teaspoon baking soda
½ teaspoon salt
¼ cup cold unsalted butter, cut into ¼-inch cubes
¼ cup white chocolate chips
¼ cup dried cherries
¼ cup dried blueberries
½ cup low-fat buttermilk
1 large egg white, lightly beaten
1 teaspoon water
2 teaspoons turbinado sugar

1. Preheat the oven to 375°F.
2. Spread the oats on a baking sheet. Bake at 375°F for 10 minutes. Cool.
3. Weigh or lightly spoon the flour into a dry measuring cup; level with a knife. Combine the oats, flour, and the next 4 ingredients (through salt) in a medium bowl; cut the cold butter into the flour mixture with a pastry blender or 2 knives until the mixture resembles coarse meal. Add the chocolate chips, cherries, and blueberries, tossing to combine. Add the buttermilk, stirring just until moist (dough will be sticky).
4. Turn the dough out onto a lightly floured surface; knead lightly 4 to 5 times with floured hands. Line the baking sheet with parchment paper. Pat the dough into a 7-inch circle on prepared baking sheet. Cut the dough into 8 wedges, cutting into but not through the dough.
5. Combine the egg white and 1 teaspoon water in a bowl, stirring with a whisk. Lightly brush the egg white mixture over the dough; sprinkle with the turbinado sugar. Bake at 375°F for 25 to 28 minutes or until golden.

CALORIES 254; FAT 8.6g (sat 4.9g, mono 2.3g, poly 0.6g); PROTEIN 4g; CARB 39g; FIBER 3g; SUGARS 18g (est. added sugars 11g); CHOL 18mg; IRON 1mg; SODIUM 377mg; CALCIUM 106mg

serve with:

• 2 teaspoons jam (50 calories)

1,300-CALORIE PLAN/1,400-CALORIE PLAN: No changes
1,500-CALORIE PLAN: Add 1 cup 1% low-fat milk or milk substitute (102 calories).

Coffee

If coffee is part of your daily routine, pay attention to the add-ins. An 8-ounce cup of coffee has only about 5 calories, but hefty additions can bulk it up to 300 calories or more. If you're a coffee shop addict, consider downsizing your usual order or limiting how often you go. Or keep your order simple with half-and-half (1 tablespoon has 22 calories) and a little sugar (1 packet has 11 calories).

3-Ingredient Pancakes DF V

Hands-on: 10 minutes | Total: 10 minutes
Serves 1 (serving size: 3 pancakes)

These single-serving pancakes are a bit more like the custardy center bite of French toast: fluffy, eggy, and golden delicious.

1 medium-sized ripe banana
2 tablespoons whole-wheat flour
1 large egg, lightly beaten

1. Mash the banana with a fork until smooth. Add the flour and egg; stir well with a whisk.
2. Heat a large nonstick skillet or griddle over medium-high heat. Spoon the batter onto the skillet, using one-third of the batter for each pancake. Cook 2 minutes or until the tops are covered with bubbles and the edges look cooked. Carefully turn the pancakes over; cook 1 to 2 minutes or until the bottoms are lightly browned.

CALORIES 228; FAT 5.5g (sat 1.8g, mono 1.9g, poly 1.2g); PROTEIN 10g; CARB 38g; FIBER 5g; SUGARS 15g (est. added sugars 0g); CHOL 186mg; IRON 2mg; SODIUM 72mg; CALCIUM 39mg

serve with:

• 2 tablespoons maple syrup (104 calories)

1,300-CALORIE PLAN/1,400-CALORIE PLAN: No changes
1,500-CALORIE PLAN: Add 2 slices center-cut bacon (50 calories).

Pancake and Waffle Toppings

Maple syrup is the classic pancake and waffle pairing, but there are plenty of other options. Here are just a handful:

- 1 tablespoon powdered sugar (30 calories)
- ½ cup fresh sliced strawberries or blueberries mixed with 1 tablespoon granulated sugar (75 calories)
- 1 tablespoon chopped toasted walnuts or pecans and 2 teaspoons honey (90 calories)
- ¼ cup plain fat-free Greek yogurt mixed with 2 teaspoons honey (73 calories)

Buttermilk Pancakes (V)

Hands-on: 15 minutes | Total: 20 minutes
Serves 6 (serving size: 2 pancakes)

This easy-to-make mix comes together so fast you'll wonder why you ever bought the premade stuff. With this mix on hand, it's possible to prepare homemade pancakes and waffles on weekdays.

1⅔ cups Pancake and Waffle Mix (recipe follows)
1½ cups low-fat buttermilk
1 large egg
1 large egg white

Lightly spoon Pancake and Waffle Mix into dry measuring cups; level with a knife. Place the mix in a large bowl. Combine the buttermilk, egg, and egg white, stirring well with a whisk. Add the buttermilk mixture to the mix, stirring until smooth. Let the batter stand 5 minutes. Heat a large nonstick skillet or griddle over medium-high heat. Pour about ¼ cup batter per pancake onto the skillet. Cook 2 to 3 minutes or until the tops are covered with bubbles and the edges look cooked. Carefully turn the pancakes over; cook 1 minute or until the bottoms are lightly browned.

CALORIES 174; FAT 1.7g (sat 0.7g, mono 0.5g, poly 0.3g); PROTEIN 7g; CARB 32g; FIBER 1g; SUGARS 7g (est. added sugars 4g); CHOL 33mg; IRON 2mg; SODIUM 472mg; CALCIUM 163mg

serve with:

- 2 tablespoons maple syrup (104 calories)

1,300-CALORIE PLAN/1,400-CALORIE PLAN: No changes
1,500-CALORIE PLAN: Add ⅓ cup peach slices (51 calories).

278 TOTAL CALORIES

Buttermilk in Pancakes

Fresh buttermilk, the low-fat liquid left after churning butter, helps create light, fluffy pancakes because it reacts with baking soda to prevent the batter from becoming too dense. Small to medium lumps in the batter are fine, but take care not to overmix, or you'll end up with heavy, tough pancakes.

Pancake and Waffle Mix (V)

Weigh or lightly spoon 27 ounces all-purpose flour (about 6 cups) into dry measuring cups; level with a knife. Combine the flour, ½ cup sugar, 2 tablespoons baking powder, 2 teaspoons baking soda, and 1¾ teaspoons salt in a large bowl, stirring with a whisk.
Note: This recipe yields 6¾ cups—enough to make four batches of Buttermilk Pancakes. Store in an airtight container in the pantry for up to 6 months.

SERVES 24 (serving size: 4½ tablespoons): CALORIES 135; FAT 0.3g (sat 0.1g, mono 0g, poly 0.1g); PROTEIN 3g; CARB 29g; FIBER 1g; SUGARS 4g (est. added sugars 4g); CHOL 0mg; IRON 1mg; SODIUM 386mg; CALCIUM 87mg

Gluten-Free Pecan-Oatmeal Waffles GF V

Hands-on: 13 minutes | Total: 23 minutes
Serves 8 (serving size: 1 waffle, ¼ cup berries, and 1 tablespoon maple syrup)

2½ cups Gluten-Free Oatmeal Pancake and Waffle Mix (see opposite)
¼ teaspoon ground cinnamon
1½ cups low-fat buttermilk
¼ cup butter, melted
½ cup plus 2 tablespoons maple syrup
1 teaspoon vanilla extract
2 large egg whites, lightly beaten
⅓ cup chopped toasted pecans
Cooking spray
1 cup fresh blueberries
1 cup fresh raspberries

1. Lightly spoon the mix into dry measuring cups; level with a knife. Combine the mix and cinnamon in a large bowl, stirring with a whisk. Combine the buttermilk, butter, 2 tablespoons maple syrup, vanilla, and egg whites, stirring with a whisk; add to the mix, stirring until smooth. Fold in the pecans. Let stand 10 minutes.
2. Coat a waffle iron with cooking spray; preheat. Spoon about ½ cup batter per waffle onto hot waffle iron, spreading the batter to the edges. Cook 1½ minutes or until steaming stops; repeat the procedure with the remaining batter. Top each waffle with 2 tablespoons blueberries, 2 tablespoons raspberries, and 1 tablespoon maple syrup.

CALORIES 336; FAT 11.7g (sat 4.4g, mono 4.2g, poly 2.1g); PROTEIN 6g; CARB 53g; FIBER 4g; SUGARS 23g (est. added sugars 18g); CHOL 17mg; IRON 1mg; SODIUM 315mg; CALCIUM 159mg

1,300-CALORIE PLAN/1,400-CALORIE PLAN: No changes
1,500-CALORIE PLAN: Add 1 cup fresh strawberries (53 calories).

Keeping Waffles Warm

If you're making waffles for a crowd, or would just rather serve everyone breakfast all at once, preheat your oven to 200°F. After each waffle emerges from the waffle iron, place it on a baking sheet in the oven. The waffles will stay crisper if you line them up in a single layer rather than stacking them.

Gluten-Free Oatmeal Pancakes 

Place 2½ cups Gluten-Free Oatmeal Pancake and Waffle Mix (see opposite) in a bowl. Combine 1½ cups low-fat buttermilk, ¼ cup melted butter, and 2 large egg whites; add to the mix, stirring until smooth.Heat a large nonstick skillet or griddle over medium-high heat. Pour ¼ cup batter per pancake onto the skillet. Cook 1 to 2 minutes or until the tops are covered with bubbles and the edges look cooked. Carefully turn pancakes over; cook 1 to 2 minutes or until bottoms are lightly browned.

SERVES 7 (serving size: 2 pancakes): CALORIES 242; FAT 9.2g (sat 4.6g, mono 2.8g, poly 1.8g); PROTEIN 7g; CARB 33g; FIBER 3g; SUGARS 6g (est. added sugars 4g); CHOL 20mg; IRON 1mg; SODIUM 355mg; CALCIUM 143mg

Gluten-Free Oatmeal Pancake and Waffle Mix GF V

Weigh or lightly spoon 8 ounces oat flour (about 2 cups), 2.1 ounces tapioca flour (about ½ cup), and 5.4 ounces potato starch (about 1 cup) into dry measuring cups; level with a knife. Combine the flours, potato starch, ¼ cup sugar, 2 tablespoons flaxseed meal, 1 tablespoon baking powder, 1 teaspoon baking soda, and ¼ teaspoon salt in a large bowl, stirring well with a whisk. Add 1 cup certified gluten-free old-fashioned rolled oats, stirring with a whisk.

Note: This recipe yields 5 cups—enough to make two batches of Gluten-Free Oatmeal Pancakes. Store in an airtight container in the pantry for up to 2 months or in the freezer for up to 4 months.

SERVES 20 (serving size: ¼ cup): CALORIES 115; FAT 0.9g (sat 0.2g, mono 0.2g, poly 0.2g); PROTEIN 2g; CARB 20g; FIBER 1g; SUGARS 3g (est. added sugars 3g); CHOL 0mg; IRON 0mg; SODIUM 175mg; CALCIUM 23mg

Ginger, Berry,
and Oat Smoothie

Smoothies

Smoothies are an easy way to get a healthy start to your day with multiple fruit and vegetable servings in each glass. Plus, they're quick and easy to make and are ideal when you need a portable meal. Smoothies are open to endless interpretation, so use the recipes below as starting points, and then make substitutions to suit your taste buds and whatever in-season produce you can find.

Ginger, Berry, and Oat Smoothie 

Place ¼ cup prepared oatmeal, ¼ cup 1% low-fat milk, ½ teaspoon grated peeled fresh ginger, 1 cup fresh blackberries, ½ cup sliced strawberries, 1 teaspoon honey, and ½ cup crushed ice in a blender; process until smooth.

SERVES 1: CALORIES 176; FAT 2.4g (sat 0.6g, mono 0.5g, poly 0.8g); PROTEIN 6g; CARB 36g; FIBER 10g; SUGARS 19g (est. added sugars 6g); CHOL 3mg; IRON 5mg; SODIUM 58mg; CALCIUM 179mg

Peanut Butter–Berry Smoothie 

Place ¼ cup 1% low-fat milk, ½ medium-sized ripe banana, 1 tablespoon creamy peanut butter, 1 cup fresh or frozen raspberries, and ½ cup crushed ice in a blender; process until smooth.

SERVES 1: CALORIES 237; FAT 9.8g (sat 2.1g, mono 4.4g, poly 2.5g); PROTEIN 8g; CARB 35g; FIBER 10g; SUGARS 17g (est. added sugars 2g); CHOL 3mg; IRON 1mg; SODIUM 97mg; CALCIUM 118mg

Green Machine Smoothie 

Place 1 cup fresh baby spinach leaves, 1½ cups chopped fresh honeydew melon, and ⅓ cup vanilla fat-free Greek yogurt in a blender; process until smooth.

SERVES 1: CALORIES 169; FAT 0.5g (sat 0.2g, mono 0g, poly 0.1g); PROTEIN 9g; CARB 35g; FIBER 4g; SUGARS 29g (est. added sugars 2g); CHOL 0mg; IRON 2mg; SODIUM 113mg; CALCIUM 135mg

Banana Breakfast Smoothie 

Place ½ cup 1% low-fat milk, ½ cup crushed ice, 1 tablespoon honey, ⅛ teaspoon ground nutmeg, and 1 frozen sliced ripe large banana in a blender; process 2 minutes or until smooth. Add 1 cup plain 2% Greek yogurt; process just until blended. Serve immediately.

SERVES 2 (serving size: 1 cup): CALORIES 151; FAT 0.6g (sat 0.4g, mono 0.2g, poly 0g); PROTEIN 5g; CARB 33g; FIBER 1g; SUGARS 26g (est. added sugars 10g); CHOL 9mg; IRON 0mg; SODIUM 75mg; CALCIUM 200mg

Blackberry-Mango Smoothie  

Place 1½ cups frozen blackberries, 1 cup fresh mango slices, 1 cup (about 6½ ounces) low-fat tofu (such as Silken soft), 1 cup fresh orange juice, and 3 tablespoons honey in a blender; process until smooth.

SERVES 4 (serving size: 1 cup): CALORIES 162; FAT 0.6g (sat 0.1g, mono 0g, poly 0.3g); PROTEIN 4g; CARB 38g; FIBER 3g; SUGARS 33g (est. added sugars 13g); CHOL 0mg; IRON 1mg; SODIUM 45mg; CALCIUM 34mg

Mango Lassi Smoothie 

Place 1½ cups 1% low-fat milk, 1 cup plain low-fat yogurt, 1 tablespoon honey, and a dash of ground cardamom in a blender; pulse to combine. Add 2 cups fresh mango slices to blender; process until smooth.

SERVES 4 (serving size: about 1 cup): CALORIES 143; FAT 2.2g (sat 1.3g, mono 0.6g, poly 0.1g); PROTEIN 7g; CARB 26g; FIBER 1g; SUGARS 24g (est. added sugars 4g); CHOL 8mg; IRON 0mg; SODIUM 84mg; CALCIUM 236mg

Roasted Plum Breakfast Parfaits

Hands-on: 6 minutes | Total: 30 minutes | Serves 6 (serving size: 1 parfait)

Nectarines or peaches would be just as delicious as plums in this recipe. You may need to adjust the roasting time by a few minutes, but otherwise the method is the same. Whichever fruit you choose, it can be made ahead and stored in the refrigerator for up to 3 days.

6 plums, pitted and each cut into 6 wedges
¼ cup fresh orange juice
3 tablespoons light brown sugar
1½ tablespoons butter, melted
⅛ teaspoon salt
2 cups vanilla 2% Greek yogurt
2 cups low-fat granola (without raisins)
1½ tablespoons chopped pistachios

1. Preheat the oven to 400°F.
2. Combine the plums, juice, sugar, butter, and salt in a bowl, tossing gently to coat. Transfer the plums to a 13 x 9-inch broiler-safe glass or ceramic baking dish. Bake at 400°F for 20 minutes or until the plums are very soft.
3. Turn the oven to broil (leave the dish in the oven). Broil the plums 4 minutes or until the pan juices are syrupy. Remove from the oven; cool completely.
4. Place 2 plum wedges in the bottom of each of 6 parfait glasses. Layer with about 2½ tablespoons yogurt and about 2½ tablespoons granola. Repeat the layers once. Top each parfait with 2 more plum wedges, and drizzle each with 1½ tablespoons of the pan juices. Sprinkle evenly with the pistachios.

CALORIES 302; FAT 7.2g (sat 3.2g, mono 1.9g, poly 1g); PROTEIN 12g; CARB 53g; FIBER 5g; SUGARS 31g (est. added sugars 12g); CHOL 16mg; IRON 1mg; SODIUM 166mg; CALCIUM 144mg

1,300-CALORIE PLAN/1,400-CALORIE PLAN: No changes
1,500-CALORIE PLAN: Sprinkle 2 tablespoons low-fat granola over the parfait (48 calories).

Fried Egg and Crunchy Breakfast Salad (V)

Hands-on: 11 minutes | Total: 11 minutes | Serves 1

If you have access to whole-grain rye bread, definitely give it a try here; it's so flavorful on its own and adds a special lift to this salad. You can make the toasted breadcrumbs up to 2 days ahead; just store in an airtight container or zip-top bag until you're ready for them.

1 ounce whole-grain bread
1 tablespoon extra-virgin olive oil, divided
1 large egg
1½ teaspoons white wine vinegar
⅛ teaspoon kosher salt
⅛ teaspoon freshly ground black pepper
1½ cups salad greens
4 radishes, halved

1. Tear the bread into small pieces. Heat a small skillet over medium-high heat. Add 1 teaspoon oil to the pan; swirl to coat the pan. Add the breadcrumbs to the pan; cook 3 minutes or until toasted, stirring occasionally. Remove from the pan.
2. Reduce the heat to medium. Add ½ teaspoon of the oil to the pan. Crack the egg into the pan; cover and cook for 1½ to 2 minutes or until the desired degree of doneness.
3. Combine the remaining 1½ teaspoons oil, vinegar, salt, and pepper in a medium bowl. Add the greens and radishes; toss to coat. Top with the egg and breadcrumbs.

CALORIES 250; FAT 18.9g (sat 3.5g, mono 11.7g, poly 2.5g); PROTEIN 9g; CARB 14g; FIBER 5g; SUGARS 2g (est. added sugars 0g); CHOL 186mg; IRON 2mg; SODIUM 389mg; CALCIUM 163mg

serve with:

- ½ cup orange juice (55 calories)

1,300-CALORIE PLAN/1,400-CALORIE PLAN: No changes
1,500-CALORIE PLAN: Increase the serving of orange juice to 1 cup (110 calories).

Keys to Building a Breakfast Salad

Here are some tips for making a great one:

AVOID OVERLY STRONG FLAVORS
Raw garlic isn't ideal first thing in the morning.

INCLUDE PROTEIN AND FAT FOR SATIETY
That protein can come from an egg, cheese, bacon, nuts, beans, or whole grains. Unsaturated fats (olive and nut oils, avocado, or nuts) help keep you satisfied longer.

CONSIDER TEXTURE
Try to include something crispy-crunchy, creamy-silky, juicy-fresh, and/or meaty-chewy.

VARY THE BASE
Sometimes, go with greens. Other days, try beans, whole grains, or veggies.

Grapefruit, Avocado, and Prosciutto Breakfast Salad DF GF

Hands-on: 10 minutes | Total: 10 minutes | Serves 1

Bright, refreshing grapefruit pairs surprisingly well with nutty-earthy toasted sesame oil. This meal is full of satiating heart-healthy fats that will keep you full until lunch.

1 small Ruby Red grapefruit
¾ teaspoon dark sesame oil
⅛ teaspoon freshly ground black pepper
Dash of kosher salt
1 cup microgreens, baby arugula, or torn lettuce
½ ripe peeled avocado, thinly sliced
1 very thin slice prosciutto

Peel the grapefruit; cut the sections from the grapefruit over a medium bowl. Squeeze the membranes to extract about 1 tablespoon juice. Set the sections aside. Add the oil, pepper, and salt to the juice, stirring with a whisk. Add the greens; toss to coat. Arrange the greens on a plate; top with the grapefruit sections, avocado, and prosciutto.

CALORIES 245; FAT 15.8g (sat 2.5g, mono 8.2g, poly 2.9g); PROTEIN 7g; CARB 24g; FIBER 8g; SUGARS 15g (est. added sugars 0g); CHOL 11mg; IRON 1mg; SODIUM 503mg; CALCIUM 53mg

serve with:

- Coffee with 1 tablespoon half-and-half (22 calories)

1,300-CALORIE PLAN/1,400-CALORIE PLAN: No changes
1,500-CALORIE PLAN: Add an additional ¼ cup thinly sliced avocado to your salad (60 calories).

Sausage, Gravy, and Egg Breakfast Sandwiches

324 TOTAL CALORIES

Hands-on: 32 minutes | Total: 32 minutes
Serves 6 (serving size: 1 sandwich)

This sandwich will rival what you get at the drive-through. Plus, you can freeze these and have them stashed away for easy breakfasts. See note at right to find out how.

½ pound turkey breakfast sausage
2 teaspoons canola oil
1¾ cups 2% reduced-fat milk
5 teaspoons all-purpose flour
1 teaspoon chopped fresh thyme
¼ teaspoon garlic powder
¼ teaspoon onion powder
⅛ teaspoon kosher salt
Dash of ground red pepper
6 large eggs, lightly beaten
6 light multigrain English muffins, split and toasted

1. Divide the sausage into 6 equal portions; pat each portion into a 3-inch patty (about ¼ inch thick). Heat a large skillet over medium-high heat. Add 1 teaspoon of the oil to the pan; swirl to coat the pan. Add the patties; cook 2 minutes on each side or until done. Transfer the patties to a plate. Keep warm. Reserve the drippings in the pan.
2. Combine the milk and the next 6 ingredients (through red pepper), stirring with a whisk until smooth. Add the mixture to the pan; bring to a boil, scraping the pan to loosen browned bits. Cook 3 minutes or until thick and bubbly. Remove from the heat.
3. Heat a large nonstick skillet over medium heat. Add the remaining 1 teaspoon oil to the pan; swirl to coat. Add the eggs; cook 4 minutes, stirring until curds form.
4. Place 1 sausage patty on each of the bottom halves of the muffins. Divide eggs evenly among servings. Top each with 3 tablespoons gravy and top half of muffin.

CALORIES 324; FAT 16.2g (sat 4.6g, mono 5.6g, poly 3.7g); PROTEIN 20g; CARB 32g; FIBER 8g; SUGARS 4g (est. added sugars 0g); CHOL 222mg; IRON 2mg; SODIUM 568mg; CALCIUM 128mg

1,300-CALORIE PLAN/1,400-CALORIE PLAN: No changes
1,500-CALORIE PLAN: Serve with ½ cup grapes (52 calories).

Freezing Breakfast Sandwiches

To freeze, cool the sandwiches and gravy separately to room temperature, and then wrap each sandwich in plastic wrap, place in a large heavy-duty zip-top plastic bag, and freeze. Fill ice-cube molds with the gravy (3 tablespoons per cube), and freeze until solid. Transfer the gravy cubes to a large heavy-duty zip-top plastic bag and return to the freezer. The sandwiches and gravy will keep for up to 3 months in the freezer.

286
TOTAL CALORIES

Egg and Hash Brown Casserole LC

Hands-on: 35 minutes | Total: 9 hours, 10 minutes | Serves 8

This dish is like enjoying an omelet stuffed with spinach, Swiss cheese, and mushrooms, with hearty sides of bacon and hash browns, all in one package. Garnish with fresh basil leaves, if you'd like.

8 slices center-cut bacon
1½ cups chopped onion
8 ounces sliced shiitake mushroom caps
3 garlic cloves, minced
2 cups shredded hash brown potatoes (such as Simply Potatoes)
¼ cup no-salt-added chicken stock (such as Swanson)
5 cups fresh baby spinach
2 tablespoons thinly sliced fresh basil
½ teaspoon kosher salt
½ teaspoon freshly ground black pepper
3 ounces reduced-fat Swiss cheese, finely chopped (about ¾ cup)
Cooking spray
½ cup 1% low-fat milk
6 large eggs, lightly beaten

1. Cook the bacon in a large nonstick skillet over medium heat until crisp. Remove the bacon from the pan; crumble. Increase the heat to medium-high. Add the onion, mushrooms, and garlic to the drippings in the pan; sauté for 6 minutes. Add the potatoes and stock; cook 6 minutes, stirring frequently. Add the spinach, basil, ¼ teaspoon salt, and ¼ teaspoon pepper; cook 2 minutes or until the spinach wilts. Remove from the heat; let stand 10 minutes. Stir in the crumbled bacon and cheese. Place the mushroom mixture in an 11 x 7-inch broiler-safe glass or ceramic baking dish coated with cooking spray. Cover and refrigerate overnight.
2. Preheat the oven to 350°F.
3. Uncover the dish. Combine the remaining ¼ teaspoon salt, ¼ teaspoon pepper, milk, and eggs in a medium bowl. Pour the egg mixture over the mushroom mixture. Bake at 350°F for 28 minutes.
4. Preheat the broiler to high (leave the dish in the oven). Broil for 3 minutes or until the top is browned and just set. Let stand 5 minutes.

CALORIES 286; FAT 18g (sat 6g, mono 7.4g, poly 2.3g); PROTEIN 14g; CARB 17g; FIBER 2g; SUGARS 3g (est. added sugars 0g); CHOL 164mg; IRON 2mg; SODIUM 507mg; CALCIUM 180mg

1,300-CALORIE PLAN/1,400-CALORIE PLAN: No changes
1,500-CALORIE PLAN: Serve with ¼ cup cubed avocado (60 calories) or 1 cup fresh strawberries (53 calories).

Healthy Breakfasts to Buy

Because some days there's just no time to make breakfast

FROM THE FREEZER CASE

Amy's Tofu Scramble is a hefty serving of veggie-tofu scramble and hash browns.

CALORIES 320; FAT 19g (sat 3g); PROTEIN 22g; SUGARS 4g; FIBER 4g; SODIUM 580mg

FROM THE CEREAL AISLE

Grape-Nuts Original has four simple ingredients to enjoy hot or cold.

CALORIES 210; FAT 1g (sat 0g); PROTEIN 6g; SUGARS 5g; FIBER 7g; SODIUM 270mg

FROM THE DRIVE-THROUGH

Starbucks Egg and Cheddar Breakfast Sandwich is a whole-wheat English muffin with egg and cheese.

CALORIES 280; FAT 13g (sat 5g); PROTEIN 12g; SUGARS 2g; FIBER 2g; SODIUM 460mg

Seattle Couple Not Hungry on This Diet Ever. *Ever.*

DARCI AND PAUL ROGOJIN OF SEATTLE reached out to tell us how much they enjoyed the recipes on the Cooking Light Diet, and how they planned to make one a football watching go-to. Darci also mentioned that she was down 10 pounds, while Paul had lost 20*. Darci said that in addition to the meals themselves, she also enjoyed the convenience of the editable online shopping list, and the way the plan has made them think about what they eat.

"It makes me think about my choices when I'm in a restaurant," Darci said. "It's really affected how we think about food. Even at work, there've been days when I don't have time to bring a breakfast. We have a little cafeteria, so I will choose something different because of this diet."

Those restaurant decisions have been aided in part by how much the Rogojins have enjoyed snacking on the Cooking Light Diet.

"I love the snacks," Darci said. "That's the fun little treat part! There's some stuff on there that I'm like, 'No way! I can't believe I get to eat this.' And they fill us up, and they totally work. I'm never hungry on this [diet] ever. Ever."

Darci also said that, unlike other diet plans and services they've tried, the Cooking Light Diet doesn't make you feel like you're being deprived or robbed of the food choices you enjoy. And the amount of food is surprising, to boot.

"You won't feel like you're missing out on anything, which a lot of diets make you feel," Darci said. "You can have anything you want, really. Another thing that's been eye-opening to us is portion control. 'Okay, you're only supposed to have half a cup of this,' whereas before we would load our plates up."

It's all these things that have Darci convinced in the CLD's sustainability.

"It's real food, it's delicious, and it never makes you feel like you're on a diet," Darci said. "It's a sustainable diet. That's the beauty of this."

**Members following The Cooking Light Diet lose more than half a pound per week, on average.*

"The Cooking Light Diet doesn't make you feel like you're being deprived or robbed of the food choices you enjoy."

Herbed Frittata with Vegetables and Goat Cheese LC V

Hands-on: 15 minutes | Total: 15 minutes | Serves 4 (serving size: 1 wedge)

The night before: Blanch the asparagus and stir together the egg mixture. In the morning: Cook the frittata.

6 ounces asparagus, trimmed and cut into 2-inch pieces
¼ cup water
3 tablespoons chopped fresh chives
2 tablespoons chopped fresh dill
⅜ teaspoon salt
¼ teaspoon freshly ground black pepper
7 large eggs, lightly beaten
1 teaspoon olive oil
2 ounces soft goat cheese (about ¼ cup)

1. Combine the asparagus and ¼ cup water in a small microwave-safe bowl; cover and microwave at HIGH 2 minutes or until tender. Rinse with cold water; drain. Combine the chives, dill, salt, pepper, and eggs in a medium bowl; stir with a whisk.
2. Preheat the broiler to high.
3. Heat a small ovenproof skillet over medium heat. Add the oil to the pan; swirl to coat the pan. Add the asparagus and the egg mixture to the pan; cook 3 minutes or until the eggs are partially set, stirring occasionally. Sprinkle with the cheese. Place the pan under the broiler. Broil 2 minutes or until the eggs are set and the top is lightly browned. Remove the pan from the oven. Run a spatula around the edge and under the frittata to loosen from the pan; slide the frittata onto a plate or a cutting board. Cut into 4 wedges.

CALORIES 196; FAT 13.8g (sat 5.8g, mono 5g, poly 1.9g); PROTEIN 15g; CARB 3g; FIBER 1g; SUGARS 2g (est. added sugars 0g); CHOL 337mg; IRON 3mg; SODIUM 420mg; CALCIUM 105mg

serve with:

- 1 small banana (90 calories)

1,300-CALORIE PLAN/1,400-CALORIE PLAN: No changes
1,500-CALORIE PLAN: Add 1 (45-calorie) slice toasted multigrain bread (45 calories) and 1 teaspoon preserves (17 calories).

Quick Breakfast Tacos (V)

Hands-on: 15 minutes | Total: 15 minutes | Serves 4 (serving size: 1 taco)

Don't let the number of ingredients fool you—this recipe is quick and easy to prepare. If you have the time, char the tortillas for crunch. Add a spinach salad with tomatoes and avocados, and this versatile dish can also be enjoyed at lunch.

PICO DE GALLO

1½ cups chopped tomato (about 1 large)
½ cup chopped green onions
½ cup chopped fresh cilantro
2 teaspoons fresh lime juice
⅛ teaspoon salt
⅛ teaspoon freshly ground black pepper
Dash of crushed red pepper

TACOS

¼ teaspoon chopped fresh oregano
⅛ teaspoon salt
⅛ teaspoon freshly ground black pepper
4 large eggs, lightly beaten
Dash of ground red pepper
Cooking spray
¼ cup chopped onion
1 (2-ounce) can diced green chiles, drained
4 (6-inch) corn tortillas
2 ounces shredded colby-Jack cheese (about ½ cup)

1. Make the pico de gallo: Combine the first 7 ingredients in a small bowl.
2. Make the tacos: Combine the oregano and the next 4 ingredients (through ground red pepper) in a small bowl, stirring well with a whisk.
3. Heat a large nonstick skillet over medium heat. Coat the pan with cooking spray. Add the egg mixture, ¼ cup onion, and green chiles to the pan. Cook for 3 minutes or until the eggs are set, stirring frequently. Remove from the heat.
4. Heat the tortillas according to the package directions. Divide the egg mixture evenly among the tortillas. Top each serving with 2 tablespoons shredded cheese and about ⅓ cup pico de gallo.

CALORIES 197; FAT 10.8g (sat 4.5g, mono 3.5g, poly 1.2g); PROTEIN 13g; CARB 14g; FIBER 2g; SUGARS 4g (est. added sugars 0g); CHOL 258mg; IRON 2mg; SODIUM 372mg; CALCIUM 170mg

serve with:

- ½ cup fresh raspberries and ½ cup fresh blueberries (74 calories)
- Coffee with 1 tablespoon half-and-half (22 calories)

1,300-CALORIE PLAN/1,400-CALORIE PLAN: No changes
1,500-CALORIE PLAN: Add ½ medium banana (53 calories).

Spinach and Feta Quiche with Quinoa Crust GF V

Hands-on: 15 minutes | Total: 1 hour, 15 minutes
Serves 4 (serving size: 1 wedge)

Cheesy quiche makes an enjoyable lunch, too—just partner it with a bright, citrusy salad: Whisk together 2 tablespoons canola oil, 1 tablespoon white wine vinegar, 1 teaspoon honey, and ¼ teaspoon kosher salt in a large bowl. Add 3 cups baby kale, ¾ cup grapefruit sections, and ¼ cup sliced red onion; toss to coat.

CRUST

2 cups cooked quinoa, chilled
⅛ teaspoon freshly ground black pepper
1 large egg, beaten
Cooking spray

FILLING

1 teaspoon canola oil
½ onion, thinly sliced
1 (5-ounce) bag baby spinach
½ cup 1% low-fat milk
½ teaspoon kosher salt
¼ teaspoon freshly ground black pepper
¼ teaspoon crushed red pepper
4 large eggs
2 large egg whites
1.5 ounces feta cheese, crumbled (about ⅓ cup)

1. Preheat the oven to 375°F.
2. Make the crust: Combine the quinoa, pepper, and egg in a bowl, stirring well. Press the mixture into the bottom and up the sides of a 9-inch pie plate coated with cooking spray. Bake at 375°F for 20 minutes; cool.
3. Make the filling: Heat a nonstick skillet over medium heat. Add the oil to the pan; swirl to coat the pan. Add the onion; sauté 3 minutes. Add the spinach; sauté 3 minutes. Remove from the heat; cool.
4. Combine milk and next 5 ingredients in a bowl; stir with a whisk. Arrange spinach mixture in crust; pour egg mixture over spinach. Sprinkle with feta. Bake at 375°F for 35 minutes. Let stand 5 minutes; cut into 4 wedges.

CALORIES 282; FAT 11.6g (sat 3.8g, mono 3.6g, poly 1.6g); PROTEIN 17g; CARB 28g; FIBER 5g; SUGARS 4g (est. added sugars 0g); CHOL 243mg; IRON 4mg; SODIUM 552mg; CALCIUM 172mg

serve with:

- ½ cup fresh cantaloupe cubes (27 calories)

1,300-CALORIE PLAN/1,400-CALORIE PLAN: No changes
1,500-CALORIE PLAN: Increase the serving of cantaloupe to 1¼ cups (68 calories).

LUNCH

Tarragon Chicken Salad Sandwiches

Hands-on: 20 minutes | Total: 20 minutes
Serves 4 (serving size: 1 sandwich)

Fresh tarragon infuses this picnic-perfect chicken salad with lovely anise notes. However, feel free to separate part of the salad into a bowl before adding the tarragon for a couple of kid-friendlier servings.

2 cups shredded skinless, boneless rotisserie chicken breast
½ cup canola mayonnaise (such as Hellmann's)
⅓ cup finely chopped celery
¼ cup plain Greek yogurt
3 tablespoons chopped fresh tarragon
2 tablespoons fresh lemon juice
½ teaspoon freshly ground black pepper
4 large green leaf lettuce leaves
8 (1-ounce) slices whole-grain bread, toasted
8 (¼-inch-thick) slices tomato

1. Combine the first 7 ingredients in a large bowl; stir well.
2. Divide the lettuce leaves among 4 bread slices. Top evenly with the chicken mixture, tomato slices, and remaining 4 bread slices.

CALORIES 356; FAT 13.5g (sat 2.2g, mono 6.6g, poly 3.5g); PROTEIN 31g; CARB 27g; FIBER 5g; SUGARS 5g (est. added sugars 0g); CHOL 69mg; IRON 2mg; SODIUM 752mg; CALCIUM 104mg

1,300-CALORIE PLAN: No changes
1,400-CALORIE PLAN/1,500-CALORIE PLAN: Serve with ¾ cup fresh strawberries (40 calories).

339 TOTAL CALORIES

Avocado–Egg Salad Sandwiches with Pickled Celery (V)

Hands-on: 20 minutes | Total: 20 minutes
Serves 4 (serving size: 1 sandwich)

To prevent the avocado from browning in leftover egg salad, place any remaining salad in a bowl and place plastic wrap directly on the surface. Then cover the entire bowl tightly with plastic wrap and store in the refrigerator.

6 large eggs
3 tablespoons water
3 tablespoons cider vinegar
2 teaspoons sugar
¼ cup finely chopped celery
¼ cup mashed ripe avocado
1 tablespoon canola mayonnaise (such as Hellmann's)
1 teaspoon fresh lemon juice
¾ teaspoon Dijon mustard
½ teaspoon black pepper
⅜ teaspoon kosher salt
2 tablespoons dry-roasted salted sunflower seeds
8 (1-ounce) slices whole-grain sunflower bread, toasted
1 cup baby arugula
4 heirloom tomato slices

1. Add water to a large saucepan to a depth of 1 inch; set a large vegetable steamer in the pan. Bring the water to a boil over medium-high heat. Add the eggs to the steamer. Cover and steam the eggs for 16 minutes. Remove from the heat. Place the eggs in a large ice water–filled bowl.
2. While the eggs cook, combine 3 tablespoons water, vinegar, and sugar in a medium microwave-safe bowl; microwave at HIGH for 2 minutes or until boiling. Add the celery; let stand 15 minutes. Drain.
3. Meanwhile, combine the avocado, mayonnaise, juice, mustard, pepper, and salt in a medium bowl, stirring well until smooth.
4. Peel the eggs; discard the shells. Slice the eggs in half lengthwise; reserve 2 yolks for another use. Chop the remaining yolks and egg whites. Gently stir the chopped eggs, pickled celery, and sunflower seeds into the avocado mixture. Top each of 4 bread slices with ¼ cup arugula, about ½ cup egg mixture, and 1 tomato slice. Top with remaining 4 bread slices.

CALORIES 297; FAT 12.3g (sat 2.6g, mono 4.7g, poly 4g); PROTEIN 17g; CARB 29g; FIBER 6g; SUGARS 8g (est. added sugars 2g); CHOL 186mg; IRON 3mg; SODIUM 591mg; CALCIUM 107mg

serve with:

- 1 kiwifruit (42 calories)

1,300-CALORIE PLAN: No changes
1,400-CALORIE PLAN/1,500-CALORIE PLAN: Add ¾ ounce baked light tortilla chips, about 12 chips (98 calories).

Sunflower Seeds

You can find sunflower seeds in most grocery stores in packages and, in some stores, in bulk bins. In addition to this recipe, you can use sunflower seeds in yogurt parfaits and salads, add them to your favorite trail mix, stir them into oatmeal, or use them as a topping for muffins or quick breads.

Avocado, Sprout, and Cashew Spread Sandwich (V)

Hands-on: 20 minutes | Total: 20 minutes | Serves 1

⅓ cup toasted cashews
¼ teaspoon kosher salt
1 garlic clove
1 tablespoon water
1 tablespoon canola mayonnaise
2 (1-ounce) slices whole-wheat bread, toasted
¼ cup baby radish sprouts
3 radishes, very thinly sliced
¼ peeled ripe avocado, sliced
¼ cup arugula leaves
1 teaspoon fresh lemon juice
⅛ teaspoon freshly ground black pepper

1. Place the first 3 ingredients in a mini food processor; pulse until coarsely ground. Add 1 tablespoon water and the mayonnaise; process until smooth. Reserve 2 tablespoons of the cashew spread for another use.
2. Spread 1 tablespoon of the remaining cashew spread over each bread slice; top 1 bread slice with sprouts, radishes, avocado, arugula, juice, pepper, and remaining bread slice.

CALORIES 356; FAT 19.8g (sat 3.3g, mono 11.6g, poly 3.5g); PROTEIN 12g; CARB 36g; FIBER 7g; SUGARS 5g (est. added sugars 0g); CHOL 0mg; IRON 3mg; SODIUM 571mg; CALCIUM 88mg

1300-CALORIE PLAN: No changes
1400-CALORIE PLAN/1500-CALORIE PLAN: Add ¾ cup fresh pineapple chunks (56 calories).

Storing Cashews

Because of their high fat content, cashews won't stay fresh at room temperature for long. Store leftover cashews in an airtight container in the fridge for 4 to 6 months. They can also be frozen for 6 to 8 months.

Apple and Cashew Spread Sandwich (V)

Toast 2 (1-ounce) slices of whole-wheat bread. Prepare the cashew spread as directed in the above recipe. Spread 1 tablespoon cashew spread over each bread slice. Top 1 slice with ½ sliced Fuji apple, 1 teaspoon fresh lemon juice, a dash of freshly ground black pepper, and remaining bread slice.

SERVES 1: CALORIES 324; FAT 14.4g (sat 2.5g, mono 8.3g, poly 2.8g); PROTEIN 11g; CARB 40g; FIBER 5g; SUGARS 11g (est. added sugars 0g); CHOL 0mg; IRON 3mg; SODIUM 563mg; CALCIUM 77mg

serve with:

- ½ cup fresh cantaloupe cubes (27 calories)

1,300-CALORIE PLAN: No changes
1,400-CALORIE PLAN/1,500-CALORIE PLAN: Increase the serving of cantaloupe to 1¼ cups (68 calories).

Turkey and Swiss Wrap with Carrot Salad

Hand-on: 22 minutes | Total: 22 minutes
Serves 1 (serving size: 1 wrap and about ⅓ cup carrot salad)

You can use whatever deli meat and cheese you prefer in this easy, portable sandwich.

DILLY DIJON SPREAD

1½ tablespoons canola mayonnaise (such as Hellmann's)
½ teaspoon Dijon mustard
½ teaspoon minced fresh dill
½ teaspoon grated lemon rind
¼ teaspoon fresh lemon juice
⅛ teaspoon freshly ground black pepper

CARROT SALAD

⅓ cup grated peeled carrot
½ teaspoon minced fresh tarragon
½ teaspoon white wine vinegar
¼ teaspoon sugar

WRAP

1 whole-grain flatbread (such as Flatout)
1 ounce sliced lower-sodium deli oven-roasted turkey (such as Boar's Head)
⅓ ounce thinly sliced Swiss cheese (about 2 slices; such as Sargento)
½ cup chopped red bell pepper
¼ cup baby spinach leaves

1. Make the dilly Dijon spread: Combine the first 6 ingredients in a bowl, stirring with a whisk.
2. Make the wrap: Spread the Dijon spread over the flatbread. Top with the turkey, cheese, bell pepper, and spinach. Starting with the short edge, roll up the flatbread.
3. Make the carrot salad: Combine the carrot, tarragon, vinegar, and sugar in a small bowl; serve with the wrap.

CALORIES 301; FAT 14.6g (sat 3.8g, mono 6.2g, poly 2.7g); PROTEIN 21g; CARB 28g; FIBER 10g; SUGARS 6g (est. added sugars 1g); CHOL 35mg; IRON 1mg; SODIUM 750mg; CALCIUM 216mg

serve with:

- ½ cup grapes (52 calories)

1,300-CALORIE PLAN: No changes
1,400-CALORIE PLAN/1,500-CALORIE PLAN: Increase the serving of grapes to 1 cup (104 calories) or substitute the grapes for 12 sweet potato chips, such as Terra (113 calories).

World Champion BBQ Chef and Wife Start Cooking Light Diet, Lose 115 Pounds

KEN HESS IS NO STRANGER TO GOOD FOOD. A graduate of the Culinary Institute of America, he now plies his trade as a reigning World Champion BBQ pitmaster at Big Bob Gibson BBQ in Decatur, AL. When he's not in the kitchen at work or traveling to compete in various barbecue competitions, he spends time in the kitchen at home with his wife, Jess, and their three young children. With work and family, Ken and Jess were struggling to find time to lose the weight that'd been slowly accumulating over the years.

Luckily for them both, they discovered the Cooking Light Diet. And using it for a full year has taught them new ways to approach their passion for cooking.

"The hardest thing for us was just measuring everything," Ken said. "I never measured seasonings or anything before we started doing this. And now we're measuring everything—oil, seasonings, things like that."

Another thing Ken and Jess are measuring since joining the CLDiet is their incredible weight-loss success.

"January 1st last year when we started I was between 356-357 pounds," Ken said. "The lowest I've gotten was 296, which was right before Thanksgiving. This morning I was 302.7. So I've lost between 50 and 55 pounds*. And Jess has lost 65 pounds*. I'm down two shirt sizes and two pant sizes, too, and she's down also."

The weight-loss benefits and the new way of cooking have prepared Ken and Jess to keep this going for the long haul. Ken knows teaching the kids about portion control and healthy eating now will pay off in the future.

"The way we're eating now is how we want to stay eating as a family," Ken said. "I think that's something—not just as well as my physical health—but I want to be there for my grandchildren. And I also don't want to see my children struggle with weight like I did."

**Members following The Cooking Light Diet lose more than half a pound per week, on average.*

"The hardest thing for us was just measuring everything...I never measured seasonings or anything before we started doing this. And now we're measuring everything—oil, seasonings, things like that."

Grilled Turkey-Plum Sandwiches

Hands-on: 20 minutes | Total: 20 minutes
Serves 4 (serving size: 1 sandwich)

This sandwich skips the cold cuts, and upgrades to hearty grilled turkey cutlets with toppings of sweet plums and fresh basil.

2½ tablespoons canola mayonnaise (such as Hellmann's)
1 teaspoon minced fresh garlic
¼ teaspoon freshly ground black pepper
8 (1-ounce) slices country-style whole-grain bread
Cooking spray
12 ounces turkey cutlets (about ¼ inch thick)
½ teaspoon salt
2 medium-sized ripe black plums, pitted and thinly sliced
16 basil leaves

1. Combine the first 3 ingredients in a small bowl; stir well.
2. Heat a grill pan over medium-high heat. Place 4 bread slices in a single layer on the grill pan; grill 3 minutes on one side or until grill marks appear. Remove the bread from the grill pan. Repeat the procedure with the remaining 4 bread slices.
3. Coat the grill pan with cooking spray. Sprinkle the turkey evenly with salt. Add the turkey to the pan; grill 3 minutes or until done, turning after 1½ minutes.
4. Spread 2 teaspoons mayonnaise mixture over the untoasted side of each of 4 bread slices; top each serving with about 2¼ ounces turkey. Divide the plum slices among the sandwiches; top each serving with 4 basil leaves. Top with the remaining 4 bread slices.

CALORIES 292; FAT 6.1g (sat 0.7g, mono 2.1g, poly 2.2g); PROTEIN 29g; CARB 29g; FIBER 5g; SUGARS 7g (est. added sugars 0g); CHOL 53mg; IRON 3mg; SODIUM 631mg; CALCIUM 74mg

serve with:

- 8 baby carrots (28 calories) and 1 tablespoon hummus (25 calories)

1,300-CALORIE PLAN: No changes
1,400-CALORIE PLAN/1,500-CALORIE PLAN: Increase the serving to 12 baby carrots (42 calories) and 2 tablespoons hummus (50 calories).

345 TOTAL CALORIES

Stash Snacks

To keep your snack-time hunger in check, try stashing some of your favorite healthy snacks at work or in your car or bag. A jar of peanut butter is a shelf-stable friend that's perfect with graham crackers, whole-grain crackers, or apples. If there's a fridge at work, you can start the week with a little more variety: a supply of yogurt, fresh fruit, or a few sticks of string cheese.

Summer Vegetable Sandwich

Hands-on: 20 minutes | Total: 25 minutes
Serves 4 (serving size: 1 piece)

Scooping out part of the bread in this simple sandwich allows for the ideal filling-to-bread ratio. Plus, the bread collects flavorful tomato juices. You can make fresh breadcrumbs or homemade croutons with the scooped-out bread.

8 teaspoons extra-virgin olive oil
1½ teaspoons red wine vinegar
½ teaspoon Dijon mustard
½ teaspoon anchovy paste
¼ teaspoon minced fresh garlic
¼ teaspoon freshly ground black pepper
2 medium-sized ripe tomatoes, seeded and chopped
¾ cup canned artichokes, drained and chopped
¼ cup pitted kalamata olives, coarsely chopped
1 (10-ounce) loaf ciabatta bread
½ small fennel bulb, thinly sliced
2 chilled hard-cooked eggs, sliced
12 basil leaves

1. Combine 2 tablespoons of the oil, vinegar, and the next 4 ingredients (through pepper) in a medium bowl, stirring with a whisk. Add the tomato, artichokes, and olives; toss to coat. Let stand 5 minutes.

2. Cut the ciabatta in half horizontally; remove the insides of the bread, leaving a ½-inch-thick shell. Spoon the tomato mixture over the bottom half, leaving some of the juices in the bowl. Top with the fennel, egg, and basil. Stir the remaining 2 teaspoons oil into the reserved juices; brush the mixture over the cut side of the top half of the bread. Place the top half of the bread on top of the sandwich. Wrap the sandwich tightly in foil; press gently. Unwrap; cut into 4 pieces using a serrated knife.

CALORIES 271; FAT 13.4g (sat 2.2g, mono 8.3g, poly 1.5g); PROTEIN 9g; CARB 29g; FIBER 3g; SUGARS 5g (est. added sugars 0g); CHOL 96mg; IRON 3mg; SODIUM 473mg; CALCIUM 38mg

serve with:

- 1 cup fresh blueberries (84 calories)

1,300-CALORIE PLAN: No changes
1,400-CALORIE PLAN/1,500-CALORIE PLAN: Add a side salad made of 1½ cups fresh spinach (15 calories) drizzled with 2 tablespoons low-fat vinaigrette (30 calories).

Reuben Sandwiches

Hands-on: 18 minutes | Total: 18 minutes
Serves 4 (serving size: 1 sandwich)

With sauerkraut, corned beef, and rye bread, sodium is a serious issue in a traditional Reuben. Add dressing and cheese, and the saturated fat and calories start to climb, too. But this lighter version lets you enjoy this sandwich more often. Chili sauce is a ketchup-based sauce. If you can't find it, substitute ketchup.

DRESSING

¼ cup canola mayonnaise (such as Hellmann's)
1 tablespoon chili sauce
2 teaspoons finely minced dill pickle
1 teaspoon Worcestershire sauce
½ teaspoon grated onion

SANDWICHES

8 (¾-ounce) slices rye bread
3 ounces Swiss cheese, shaved (about ¾ cup)
4 ounces thinly sliced lower-sodium deli corned beef, (such as Boar's Head, top round, cap-off)
1 cup organic sauerkraut, drained well

1. Preheat the broiler to high.
2. Make the dressing: Combine the first 5 ingredients in a small bowl, stirring well.
3. Make the sandwiches: Place the bread slices in a single layer on a heavy baking sheet; broil for 1½ minutes or until toasted. Turn the bread over; broil for 1 minute or until lightly toasted. Remove 4 slices. Divide the cheese among the remaining 4 slices, sprinkling it over the lightly toasted sides. Broil 1 minute or until the cheese melts. Spread about 1½ tablespoons dressing over the cheese-coated side of each bread slice; top each serving with 1 ounce corned beef, ¼ cup sauerkraut, and 1 bread slice. Serve immediately.

CALORIES 336; FAT 19.9g (sat 5.6g, mono 8.1g, poly 3.6g); PROTEIN 15g; CARB 24g; FIBER 3g; SUGARS 2g (est. added sugars 0g); CHOL 40mg; IRON 2mg; SODIUM 790mg; CALCIUM 212mg

serve with:

• ½ cup sliced cucumber (8 calories)

1,300-CALORIE PLAN: No changes
1,400-CALORIE PLAN/1,500-CALORIE PLAN: Add 2 small plums (60 calories).

Roast Beef Sandwiches with Watercress Slaw

Hands-on: 15 minutes | Total: 15 minutes | Serves 4 (serving size: 1 sandwich)

Start with deli roast beef and a package of angel hair slaw to create a hearty roast beef sandwich that's perfect for a portable lunch or even a quick no-cook dinner.

1 cup packaged angel hair slaw
1 cup chopped trimmed watercress
⅓ cup thinly sliced green onions
2 tablespoons minced fresh tarragon
3 tablespoons canola mayonnaise (such as Hellmann's)
¼ teaspoon freshly ground black pepper
1 (8-ounce) French bread baguette
4 teaspoons butter, softened
8 ounces thinly sliced lower-sodium, deli roast beef (such as Boar's Head)
8 (¼-inch-thick) slices tomato

1. Combine the first 6 ingredients in a medium bowl.

2. Cut the baguette crosswise into 4 pieces. Cut each piece in half horizontally using a serrated knife. Spread 1 teaspoon butter on each bottom half of baguette. Top each with 2 ounces roast beef. Arrange about 1 cup of the slaw mixture and 2 tomato slices over each sandwich; top with top halves of baguette.

CALORIES 358; FAT 14.8g (sat 4.2g, mono 6.5g, poly 2.4g); PROTEIN 21g; CARB 38g; FIBER 2g; SUGARS 4g (est. added sugars 0g); CHOL 44mg; IRON 4mg; SODIUM 585mg; CALCIUM 26mg

1,300-CALORIE PLAN: No changes
1,400-CALORIE PLAN/1,500-CALORIE PLAN: Serve with ½ cup mixed fruit (38 calories).

Ham, Cranberry, and Gruyère Sandwiches

Hands-on: 6 minutes | Total: 6 minutes | Serves 2 (serving size: 1 sandwich)

This easy sandwich can be quickly prepped before work in the morning. If you don't have ham or Gruyère, it's also delicious with deli turkey and Swiss cheese.

4 ounces thinly sliced lower-sodium deli ham
4 (1-ounce) slices whole-wheat bread
4 tablespooons prepared whole cranberry relish (such as Stonewall Kitchen)
2 (0.7-ounce) slices Gruyère cheese
⅔ cup alfalfa sprouts

Place 2 ounces of the the ham on each of 2 bread slices; top each with 2 tablespoons of relish, 1 Gruyère slice, and ⅓ cup of the alfalfa sprouts. Top each sandwich with 1 bread slice.

CALORIES 354; FAT 11.6g (sat 5.4g, mono 2.9g, poly 1.2g); PROTEIN 26g; CARB 35g; FIBER 5g; SUGARS 14g (est. added sugars 5g); CHOL 62mg; IRON 2mg; SODIUM 742mg; CALCIUM 343mg

1,300-CALORIE PLAN: No changes
1,400-CALORIE PLAN/1,500-CALORIE PLAN: Serve with 1 cup fresh cantaloupe cubes (54 calories).

Spinach, Hummus, and Bell Pepper Wraps (V)

Hands-on: 10 minutes | Total: 10 minutes | Serves 2 (serving size: 1 wrap)

Make this wrap the night before and store in the fridge—just grab it in the morning on the way out the door. Use Flatout Light whole-grain flatbreads to keep calories in check; you can find them at most supermarkets.

2 (1.9-ounce) whole-grain flatbreads (such as Flatout Light)
½ cup roasted garlic hummus
1 small red bell pepper, thinly sliced
1 cup firmly packed baby spinach
1 ounce crumbled tomato-and-basil feta cheese (about ¼ cup)

1. Spread each flatbread with ¼ cup of the hummus, leaving a ½-inch border around the edge.
2. Divide the bell pepper evenly between the flatbreads; top each with ½ cup of the spinach and 2 tablespoons of the cheese. Starting from one short side, roll up the wraps. Cut each wrap in half.

CALORIES 258; FAT 12.1g (sat 2.9g, mono 5.6g, poly 3g); PROTEIN 15g; CARB 34g; FIBER 13g; SUGARS 7g (est. added sugars 0g); CHOL 10mg; IRON 3mg; SODIUM 793mg; CALCIUM 78mg

serve with:

• 1 medium apple (95 calories)

1,300-CALORIE PLAN: No changes
1,400-CALORIE PLAN/1,500-CALORIE PLAN: Add 3 whole-wheat crackers, such as Back To Nature (60 calories).

Hummus

Hummus delivers a winning combo of protein and healthy fat from chickpeas (garbanzo beans) and tahini (ground sesame seeds). It's available in myriad flavors in grocery stores. Pick your favorite and pair it with filling fresh vegetables or whole-grain pita chips for dipping.

Peanutty Shrimp and Broccoli Rolls DF GF

Hands-on: 15 minutes | Total: 15 minutes
Serves 2 (serving size: 2 rolls and ½ tablespoon dipping sauce)

These rolls are fresh and light, but still satisfying. If you can't find bottled peanut dressing, make your own using 1 tablespoon peanut butter, 1 tablespoon water (omit the water from the recipe), 2 teaspoons rice vinegar, and 2 teaspoons soy sauce.

1½ cups packaged broccoli slaw
¼ cup torn cilantro leaves
¼ cup diagonally sliced scallions (optional)
Hot water
4 (8-inch) round rice paper sheets
4 ounces cooked shrimp, roughly chopped
2 tablespoons bottled peanut sauce
1 tablespoon water

1. Toss together the broccoli slaw, cilantro, and, if using, scallions.
2. Add the hot water to a large, shallow dish to a depth of 1 inch. Place 1 rice paper sheet in dish; let stand just until soft, about 30 seconds. Transfer the sheet to a flat surface. Place about 2 tablespoons of the chopped shrimp on half of the sheet, leaving a ½-inch border; top the shrimp with about ½ cup of the broccoli slaw mixture. Fold in the sides of the wrapper toward the center over the filling; starting with the filled side, roll tightly to enclose. Gently press the seam to seal. Place the roll, seam side down, on a serving platter; cover to keep from drying. Repeat the procedure with the remaining rice paper sheets, chopped shrimp, and broccoli slaw mixture.
3. Whisk together the peanut sauce and 1 tablespoon water in a small bowl; serve with the rolls.

CALORIES 198; FAT 2.9g (sat 0.3g, mono 0.7g, poly 0.5g); PROTEIN 20g; CARB 23g; FIBER 4g; SUGARS 5g (est. added sugars 1g); CHOL 115mg; IRON 4mg; SODIUM 564mg; CALCIUM 90mg

serve with:

- ¾ cup fresh raspberries (48 calories)
- 1½ cups almond milk (90 calories) or ¾ cup plain fat-free yogurt (100 calories)

1,300-CALORIE PLAN: No changes
1,400-CALORIE PLAN/1,500-CALORIE PLAN: Add ½ cup fresh blueberries (42 calories).

Chilled Tomato Soup with Avocado Relish GF V

Hands-on: 10 minutes | Total: 2 hours, 10 minutes
Serves 4 (serving size: 1¼ cups soup and ¼ cup relish)

This easy, no-cook summer soup is a great way to use up lots of tomatoes. Use a high-powered blender to get the soup as smooth as possible. You can make the soup up to 2 days in advance; just wait to prep the avocado relish in the morning before you head to work to prevent it from browning.

3 pounds ripe tomatoes, roughly chopped
6 tablespoons extra-virgin olive oil
1 tablespoon red wine vinegar
¼ teaspoon freshly ground black pepper
¼ teaspoon granulated sugar
2 garlic cloves
½ teaspoon kosher salt
1 ripe avocado, diced
1 ounce queso fresco (fresh Mexican cheese), crumbled (about ¼ cup)
2 tablespoons finely chopped red onion
2 teaspoons fresh lime juice
1 tablespoon finely chopped fresh cilantro (optional)

1. Place the tomatoes, oil, vinegar, pepper, sugar, garlic, and ⅜ teaspoon of the salt in a blender; process until very smooth. Cover and chill at least 2 hours.
2. Gently combine the avocado, queso fresco, onion, lime juice, remaining ⅛ teaspoon salt, and, if using, cilantro. Ladle the chilled tomato soup into 4 bowls; top each with the avocado relish.

CALORIES 265; FAT 11g (sat 2.5g, mono 6.8g, poly 1.3g); PROTEIN 10g; CARB 36g; FIBER 12g; SUGARS 16g (est. added sugars 0g); CHOL 7mg; IRON 3mg; SODIUM 466mg; CALCIUM 99mg

serve with:

- 10 mini gluten-free rice cakes (78 calories) or for a non-gluten-free option, 6 whole-grain saltine crackers (72 calories)

1,300-CALORIE PLAN: No changes
1,400-CALORIE PLAN/1,500-CALORIE PLAN: Add 2 teaspoons peanut butter (63 calories).

Homemade Chicken Noodle Soup DF

Hands-on: 25 minutes | Total: 25 minutes | Serves 6 (serving size: 1¼ cups)

Once you've made your own veggie-packed pot of chicken noodle soup, you won't go back to the canned, supersalty stuff again.

1½ tablespoons canola oil
1½ cups thinly sliced carrot
1 cup finely chopped onion
⅔ cup thinly sliced celery
2 cups water
1 (32-ounce) container unsalted chicken stock (such as Swanson)
1 teaspoon dried thyme or 3 fresh thyme sprigs
6 ounces whole-grain rotini (such as Barilla; about 2 cups)
8 ounces skinless, boneless rotisserie chicken breast, shredded
4 ounces skinless, boneless rotisserie chicken thigh, shredded
¾ teaspoon salt
¼ teaspoon freshly ground black pepper

1. Heat a Dutch oven or large saucepan over medium-high heat. Add the oil to the pan; swirl to coat. Add the carrot, onion, and celery; sauté 5 minutes.

2. While the vegetables cook, pour 2 cups water and stock into a microwave-safe bowl; microwave at HIGH for 5 minutes. (This saves up to 10 minutes in the pot.)

3. Add the hot stock mixture to the pan; bring to a boil. Stir in the thyme and pasta; reduce the heat to medium, and cook 8 minutes.

4. Add the chicken, salt, and pepper to the pan; cook 2 minutes or until thoroughly heated and the pasta is tender.

CALORIES 273; FAT 8.1g (sat 1.2g, mono 3.7g, poly 1.5g); PROTEIN 25g; CARB 26g; FIBER 4g; SUGARS 4g (est. added sugars 0g); CHOL 58mg; IRON 2mg; SODIUM 618mg; CALCIUM 56mg

serve with:

- 10 multigrain crackers, such as Kashi Original 7 Grain (80 calories)

1,300-CALORIE PLAN: No changes
1,400-CALORIE PLAN/1,500-CALORIE PLAN: Increase the serving of soup to 1½ cups.

Rotisserie Chicken

When you pick up a rotisserie chicken from your local deli, what you're really getting is an endless array of mealtime options—use it on sandwiches, in salads, or as a topping for baked potatoes. Consider deboning the meat on the weekend when you have more time so it's ready to go for quick weeknight meals and lunch prep.

Smoky Ham and Split Pea Soup

Hands-on: 15 minutes | Total: 8 hours, 15 minutes
Serves 8 (serving size: 1¼ cups soup and 1 tablespoon sour cream)

Potatoes contribute starchiness and silky thickness to this soup, while sweet carrots and salty ham balance out the light, earthy flavor of the peas. Leftovers fare well in the freezer, so say hello to your new favorite make-ahead soup. Garnish with parsley and additional pepper, if desired.

1 pound dried green split peas, rinsed and drained
1½ cups cubed peeled Yukon gold potatoes
5 garlic cloves, chopped
1 cup chopped onion
1 cup chopped celery
1 cup chopped carrot
1 large bay leaf
1 teaspoon freshly ground black pepper
¾ teaspoon kosher salt
2 pounds smoked ham hocks
6 cups water
½ cup light sour cream

1. Layer the peas and the next 9 ingredients (through ham) in the order listed in a 6-quart electric slow cooker. Gently pour 6 cups water over the top. Cover and cook on LOW for 8 hours.
2. Remove the ham hocks from the slow cooker. Remove the meat from bones, and cut it into bite-sized pieces; discard the skin and bones. Discard the bay leaf.
3. Coarsely mash the soup to the desired consistency, adding additional hot water to thin, if desired. Stir in the chopped ham. Ladle the soup into 8 bowls; top each serving with sour cream.

CALORIES 304; FAT 4.6g (sat 1.9g, mono 0.2g, poly 0.3g); PROTEIN 22g; CARB 45g; FIBER 16g; SUGARS 7g (est. added sugars 0g); CHOL 24mg; IRON 3mg; SODIUM 594mg; CALCIUM 76mg

serve with:

- 1 cup mixed greens (9 calories) tossed with 2 tablespoons reduced-fat balsamic vinaigrette (45 calories)

1,300-CALORIE PLAN: No changes
1,400-CALORIE PLAN/1,500-CALORIE PLAN: Top your side salad with 1 tablespoon sweetened dried cranberries and 1 teaspoon sunflower seeds (47 calories).

Pork, Bean, and Escarole Soup

Hands-on: 25 minutes | Total: 25 minutes
Serves 8 (serving size: 1¾ cups soup and about 1 tablespoon cheese)

Escarole is less bitter than other members of the endive family. It has hearty leaves similar to kale or chard, which you can sub here if you'd like. Use just the leaves for this soup.

1 (1-pound) pork tenderloin, trimmed and cut into bite-sized pieces
1 tablespoon minced fresh rosemary
½ teaspoon freshly ground black pepper
¼ teaspoon kosher salt
¼ teaspoon smoked paprika
¼ teaspoon ground red pepper
2 tablespoons extra-virgin olive oil
1 cup chopped onion
2 garlic cloves, minced
6 cups unsalted chicken stock (such as Swanson)
2 tablespoons tomato paste
2 (15-ounce) cans unsalted cannellini beans, rinsed and drained
8 cups chopped escarole leaves (1 large head)
1.5 ounces Parmesan cheese, grated (about 6 tablespoons)

1. Combine the pork, rosemary, black pepper, salt, paprika, and red pepper in a bowl.

2. Heat a large Dutch oven over medium-high heat. Add the oil to the pan; swirl to coat. Add the pork mixture; sauté 2 minutes. Add the onion and garlic; sauté 4 minutes. Add the stock, tomato paste, and beans; bring to a boil. Reduce the heat and cook, partially covered, for 10 minutes. Mash half of the beans in the pan with a potato masher. Stir in the escarole; cook 2 minutes or until wilted. Ladle the soup into 8 bowls and top with Parmesan cheese.

CALORIES 265; FAT 9g (sat 2.4g, mono 4.5g, poly 0.9g); PROTEIN 28g; CARB 17g; FIBER 6g; SUGARS 3g (est. added sugars 0g); CHOL 55mg; IRON 3mg; SODIUM 441mg; CALCIUM 172mg

serve with:

- 10 multigrain crackers, such as Kashi Original 7 Grain (80 calories)

1,300-CALORIE PLAN: No changes
1,400-CALORIE PLAN/1,500-CALORIE PLAN: Add 1 medium orange (69 calories).

White Cheddar and Chive Potato Soup

Hands-on: 12 minutes | Total: 22 minutes
Serves 4 (serving size: 1 cup soup, about 1 tablespoon sour cream, and 1½ teaspoons minced chives)

This creamy potato soup uses just one pan, making cleanup fast. We love the look and tang of sharp white cheddar.

1 tablespoon canola oil
⅓ cup chopped shallots
2 garlic cloves, minced
2 tablespoons all-purpose flour
3½ cups chopped Yukon gold potatoes (about 1 pound)
1¾ cups 1% low-fat milk
1½ cups organic vegetable broth
⅜ teaspoon kosher salt
¼ teaspoon freshly ground black pepper
2 ounces sharp white cheddar cheese, shredded (about ½ cup)
⅓ cup fat-free sour cream
2 tablespoons minced fresh chives

1. Heat a large saucepan over medium-high heat. Add the oil to the pan; swirl to coat. Add the shallots and garlic; sauté 1½ minutes or until tender. Sprinkle the flour over the vegetables; cook 1 minute, stirring constantly with a whisk.
2. Add the potatoes, milk, broth, salt, and pepper to the pan; bring to a boil. Cover, reduce heat, and simmer 10 minutes or until the potatoes are tender. Remove the pan from the heat. Mash the potato mixture with a potato masher to the desired consistency. Stir in the cheese until it's melted. Stir in 1 tablespoon sour cream. Ladle the soup into 4 bowls. Top each serving with sour cream and chives.

CALORIES 263; FAT 9.6g (sat 4.2g, mono 2.5g, poly 1.1g); PROTEIN 11g; CARB 34g; FIBER 3g; SUGARS 9g (est. added sugars 0g); CHOL 20mg; IRON 1mg; SODIUM 562mg; CALCIUM 286mg

serve with:

- 1⅓ cups Kale Salad with Creamy Peppercorn Dressing, page 203 (66 calories)

1,300-CALORIE PLAN: No changes
1,400-CALORIE PLAN/1,500-CALORIE PLAN: Add 4 whole-grain saltine crackers (48 calories).

Chilled Fresh Corn Soup with Crab DF GF

Hands-on: 25 minutes | Total: 4 hours, 25 minutes
Serves 6 (serving size: about 1 cup soup and 3 tablespoons crab mixture)

The soup can be made up to 2 days in advance, but wait to combine the crabmeat mixture until the day you're serving it. You'll want to be sure the crabmeat is as fresh as possible. You can substitute cooked shrimp or chicken for the crab, or simply top the soup with fresh corn, hot sauce, or chopped fresh parsley.

8 ears fresh corn, husks removed
2 tablespoons canola oil
1 cup chopped yellow onion
¾ teaspoon kosher salt
4 thyme sprigs
1 garlic clove, minced
3 cups organic vegetable broth
8 ounces lump crabmeat, picked to remove any bits of shell
2 tablespoons chopped fresh flat-leaf parsley
1½ tablespoons fresh lemon juice (from 1 lemon)
¼ teaspoon black pepper

1. Cut the kernels from the corn cobs to equal 4 cups. Using the dull side of a knife blade, scrape the milk and remaining pulp from the cobs into the bowl with the kernels; discard the cobs.
2. Heat a large saucepan over medium heat. Add the oil to the pan; swirl to coat. Add the onion, salt, thyme, and garlic; cook, stirring often, until the onion is soft but not brown, about 8 minutes. Add the corn kernels and pulp; cover and cook 5 minutes. Uncover and add the broth. Increase the heat to medium-high, and bring to a boil. Reduce the heat to medium, and cook 5 minutes. Remove from the heat.
3. Process the soup in a blender or with an immersion blender until very smooth. Pour through a fine wire-mesh strainer over a bowl; discard the solids. Cover and chill at least 4 hours.
4. Toss the crabmeat with the parsley, lemon juice, and pepper. Ladle the soup into 6 bowls. Top the servings with the crab mixture.

CALORIES 233; FAT 7.1g (sat 0.8g, mono 3.6g, poly 2g); PROTEIN 14g; CARB 32g; FIBER 4g; SUGARS 10g (est. added sugars 0g); CHOL 40mg; IRON 1mg; SODIUM 575mg; CALCIUM 53mg

serve with:

- 12 multi-seed gluten-free crackers, such as Crunchmaster (112 calories)

1,300-CALORIE PLAN: No changes
1,400-CALORIE PLAN/1,500-CALORIE PLAN: Increase the serving of crackers to 18 (168 calories).

360 TOTAL CALORIES

Vegetarian Niçoise Salad Jar DF GF V

Hands-on: 20 minutes | Total: 20 minutes | Serves 2 (serving size: 1 jar)

Packed in a jar for ease and portability, this unique salad presentation uses traditional Niçoise salad ingredients without tuna or anchovies. You'll save messing up an extra saucepan, as the potatoes and green beans can be cooked together.

8 ounces small red potatoes (about 3 potatoes), cut into 1-inch pieces
4 ounces haricots verts (French green beans), cut into 1-inch pieces
5 teaspoons olive oil
1 tablespoon red wine vinegar
2 teaspoons finely chopped fresh tarragon
1 teaspoon Dijon mustard
¼ teaspoon kosher salt
¼ teaspoon freshly ground black pepper
¾ cup halved cherry tomatoes
¼ cup pitted kalamata olives, halved lengthwise
3 hard-cooked eggs, peeled and quartered

1. Place the potatoes in a medium saucepan with water to cover by 2 inches. Bring to a boil over medium-high heat; cook 5 minutes. Add the haricots verts; cook until the potatoes are tender and the haricots verts are tender-crisp, 3 to 4 minutes. Plunge the vegetables into ice water to stop the cooking process; drain.
2. Whisk together the olive oil, vinegar, tarragon, mustard, salt, and pepper in a small bowl. Divide the mixture between 2 (1-pint) glass jars or other containers with lids. Divide the potatoes and haricots verts evenly between the jars; top each with the tomatoes, olives, and eggs. Seal jars, and chill until ready to serve.
3. Shake the jar gently to distribute the dressing; open the jar, and pour the contents onto a plate—or eat straight out of the jar.

CALORIES 360; FAT 22.5g (sat 4.2g, mono 11.4g, poly 2.8g); PROTEIN 13g; CARB 27g; FIBER 4g; SUGARS 5g (est. added sugars 0g); CHOL 280mg; IRON 3mg; SODIUM 723mg; CALCIUM 112mg

1,300-CALORIE PLAN: No changes
1,400-CALORIE PLAN/1,500-CALORIE PLAN: Serve with 1 cup fresh watermelon cubes (40 calories).

Salmon over Fennel-Grapefruit Salad DF GF

Hands-on: 20 minutes | Total: 20 minutes
Serves 2 (serving size: 1½ cups salad and 4 ounces salmon)

You'll be quite pleased by this salad—it has lots of flavor for so few ingredients. A mandoline is the ideal tool to thinly slice the onion and fennel.

1 tablespoon olive oil
1 (8-ounce) skin-on salmon fillet
⅜ teaspoon kosher salt
¼ teaspoon freshly ground black pepper
1 small fennel bulb
1 red or pink grapefruit
½ cup thinly sliced red onion
1 tablespoon drained capers
1 tablespoon white wine vinegar
1 teaspoon honey
½ teaspoon Dijon mustard

1. Heat a medium skillet over medium heat. Add 1½ teaspoons of the oil; swirl to coat. Heat oil until shimmering, about 1 minute. Sprinkle the salmon with ⅛ teaspoon each of the salt and pepper. Place the salmon in the pan skin side down; cook to desired degree of doneness, 4 to 5 minutes per side. Remove from the pan, and flake into large pieces with a fork or cut in half.
2. Cut the top from fennel bulb, reserving fronds. Cut bulb in half lengthwise; remove the tough center core. Thinly slice the bulb using a mandoline or sharp knife to equal 2 cups. Chop the fronds to equal 2 tablespoons.
3. Cut a ¼-inch-thick slice from each end of the grapefruit using a sharp, thin-bladed knife. Place the fruit, cut side down, on a cutting board. Peel the fruit; cut away the bitter white pith. Slice each fruit between the membranes over a bowl, and gently remove whole segments. Discard the membranes and seeds; reserve the juice in the bowl.
4. Combine the fennel slices, fennel fronds, grapefruit sections, red onion, and capers in a medium bowl. Whisk together 2 tablespoons of the reserved grapefruit juice, vinegar, honey, mustard, and remaining 1½ teaspoons oil, ¼ teaspoon salt, and ⅛ teaspoon pepper in a small bowl. Pour over the fennel mixture; toss to coat. Arrange the fennel mixture on a serving plate; top with the salmon.

CALORIES 343; FAT 14.5 (sat 2.1g, mono 7.4g, poly 3.8g); PROTEIN 25g; CARB 30g; FIBER 6g; SUGARS 15g (est. added sugars 3g); CHOL 62mg; IRON 2mg; SODIUM 629mg; CALCIUM 121mg

1,300-CALORIE PLAN: No changes
1,400-CALORIE PLAN/1,500-CALORIE PLAN: Serve with ½ cup fresh strawberries (53 calories).

Roast Beef and Blue Cheese Panzanella

Hands-on: 20 minutes | Total: 35 minutes | Serves 2 (serving size: 2 cups)

Combine the salad ingredients the night before, and package the dressing separately; toss them together just before serving. If you have leftover steak or chicken on hand, you can use that in place of the deli roast beef.

2 (1.5-ounce) frozen ciabatta rolls (such as Alexia), thawed and cut into 1-inch cubes
1¼ cups halved cherry tomatoes
¾ cup roughly chopped English cucumber
4 ounces lower-sodium cubed deli roast beef
⅓ cup thinly sliced red onion
1 ounce blue cheese, crumbled (about ¼ cup)
1½ tablespoons chopped fresh flat-leaf parsley
1½ tablespoons olive oil
1½ tablespoons balsamic vinegar
¼ teaspoon kosher salt
¼ teaspoon freshly ground black pepper

1. Preheat the oven to 400°F. Place the ciabatta cubes in an even layer on a baking sheet. Bake in preheated oven until toasted and dry, about 10 minutes. Cool 10 minutes.
2. Combine the toasted ciabatta cubes, tomatoes, cucumber, roast beef, red onion, blue cheese, and parsley in a medium bowl.
3. Whisk together the oil, vinegar, salt, and pepper in a small bowl. Drizzle over the ciabatta mixture, and toss gently to coat.

CALORIES 358; FAT 17.9g (sat 5.2g, mono 8.7g, poly 1.7g); PROTEIN 23g; CARB 28g; FIBER 3g; SUGARS 7g (est. added sugars 0g); CHOL 41mg; IRON 3mg; SODIUM 597mg; CALCIUM 105mg

1,300-CALORIE PLAN: No changes
1,400-CALORIE PLAN/1,500-CALORIE PLAN: Serve with 2 fresh plums (60 calories).

Smoked Pork Bánh Mì Lettuce Cups DF GF

Hands-on: 15 minutes | Total: 15 minutes
Serves 2 (serving size: 2 lettuce cups and 1 tablespoon vinegar mixture)

This is a nice low-calorie alternative to a traditional bánh mì sandwich—served in a lettuce cup. If you're making this ahead, wait to drizzle with the vinegar mixture until serving time.

¼ cup water
3 tablespoons unseasoned rice vinegar
1 tablespoon honey
¼ teaspoon kosher salt
¼ teaspoon crushed red pepper
¾ cup matchstick carrots
8 ounces roughly shredded smoked pork, warmed if desired
4 Boston or Bibb lettuce leaves
½ cup thinly sliced English cucumber
2 tablespoons roughly chopped fresh cilantro
2 tablespoons roughly chopped fresh mint (optional)

1. Combine ¼ cup water, vinegar, honey, salt, and red pepper in a small saucepan. Bring to a boil over medium-high heat, stirring to dissolve the salt. Remove from the heat; add the carrots, and let stand 2 minutes. Drain the carrots, reserving the vinegar mixture.
2. Return the vinegar mixture to the saucepan, and return to a boil over medium-high heat. Cook until reduced by half, about 3 minutes.
3. Divide the pork among the lettuce leaves; top with the carrots, cucumber, cilantro, and, if using, mint. Drizzle with the vinegar mixture.

CALORIES 135; FAT 3.8g (sat 1.4g, mono 1.6g, poly 0.4g); PROTEIN 13g; CARB 12g; FIBER 1g; SUGARS 10g (est. added sugars 8g); CHOL 40mg; IRON 2mg; SODIUM 283mg; CALCIUM 27mg

serve with:

- 1½ cups Orange and Almond Salad, page 203 (90 calories)
- 1 large pear (131 calories)

1,300-CALORIE PLAN: No changes
1,400-CALORIE PLAN/1,500-CALORIE PLAN: Add 12 whole almonds (41 calories).

Tart Apple–Hazelnut Chicken Salad DF GF LC

Hands-on: 10 minutes | Total: 10 minutes | Serves 4 (serving size: ½ cup)

Rotisserie chicken makes this recipe a cinch, but feel free to use any leftover cooked chicken you have on hand.

¼ cup canola mayonnaise (such as Hellmann's)
1½ tablespoons chopped fresh tarragon
2 teaspoons water
⅛ teaspoon freshly ground black pepper
2 cups chopped rotisserie chicken breast
½ cup chopped Granny Smith apple
3 tablespoons chopped toasted hazelnuts

Stir together the mayonnaise, tarragon, 2 teaspoons water, and black pepper in a large bowl. Add the chicken, apple, and hazelnuts; toss to combine. Cover and chill until ready to serve.

CALORIES 198; FAT 9.7g (sat 0.9g, mono 5.8g, poly 2.2g); PROTEIN 23g; CARB 5g; FIBER 1g; SUGARS 4g (est. added sugars 0g); CHOL 66mg; IRON 1mg; SODIUM 361mg; CALCIUM 22mg

serve with:

- 10 multi-seed gluten-free crackers, such as Crunchmaster (93 calories) or, for a non-gluten-free option, 12 multigrain crackers, such as Kashi Original 7 Grain (96 calories).
- 2 teaspoons peanut butter (63 calories)

1,300-CALORIE PLAN: No changes
1,400-CALORIE PLAN/1,500-CALORIE PLAN: Increase the serving of peanut butter to 1 tablespoon (95 calories).

Take the Challenge

Challenge yourself to exercise for 30 minutes, 3 times a week—or the equivalent. If you're at that level now, increase to 5 times per week, or up the intensity.

Tortellini Salad with Zucchini and Peas

Hands-on: 20 minutes | Total: 20 minutes | Serves 4 (serving size: 1 cup)

This easy lunch can be prepared in advance; just keep it refrigerated until mealtime.

1 (9-ounce) package refrigerated whole-wheat three-cheese tortellini (such as Buitoni)
⅔ cup frozen peas
2 medium zucchini
2 tablespoons olive oil
2 garlic cloves, minced
1 teaspoon lemon zest plus 1 tablespoon fresh juice (from 1 lemon)
½ teaspoon kosher salt
¼ teaspoon freshly ground black pepper
Basil leaves (optional)

1. Cook the pasta according to package directions, omitting the salt and fat; add the peas after the water boils and cook 6 minutes. Drain and cool 10 minutes; place the pasta and peas in a medium bowl.
2. Using a vegetable peeler, shave the peel from the zucchini in a very thin layer. (Do not peel away the darker green color from the zucchini.) Discard the peel. Shave the zucchini into ribbons.
3. Heat a medium skillet over medium heat. Add 1½ teaspoons of the oil to the pan; swirl to coat. Heat the oil until shimmering, about 1 minute. Add the garlic; cook, stirring constantly, 30 seconds. Remove from the heat. Add the zucchini ribbons; stir constantly until the zucchini is slightly softened, about 1 minute. Add the zucchini mixture to the tortellini mixture in the bowl.
4. Combine the zest, juice, salt, pepper, and remaining 1½ tablespoons oil. Drizzle over the tortellini mixture; toss gently to coat. Sprinkle with the basil, if desired.

CALORIES 302; FAT 14g (sat 3.2g, mono 6.8g, poly 1.6g); PROTEIN 12g; CARB 34g; FIBER 7g; SUGARS 5g (est. added sugars 0g); CHOL 39mg; IRON 2mg; SODIUM 561mg; CALCIUM 115mg

serve with:

- 1 fresh medium tangerine (47 calories)

1,300-CALORIE PLAN: No changes
1,400-CALORIE PLAN/1,500-CALORIE PLAN: Serve with ½ cup plain 2% Greek yogurt (87 calories).

Wheat Berry Salad with Goat Cheese Ⓥ

Hands-on: 15 minutes | Total: 9 hours, 45 minutes
Serves 6 (serving size: about 1⅓ cups)

Taking a cue from traditional tabbouleh, this dish uses lots of peak-season vegetables, tart lemon juice, and pungent fresh herbs.

1¼ cups wheat berries
2½ cups chopped English cucumber
⅔ cup thinly sliced green onions
1½ cups loosely packed chopped arugula
6 tablespoons minced fresh flat-leaf parsley
1 pint grape tomatoes, halved
1 tablespoon grated lemon rind
3 tablespoons fresh lemon juice
1 teaspoon kosher salt
½ teaspoon freshly ground black pepper
½ teaspoon sugar
2 tablespoons extra-virgin olive oil
3 ounces goat cheese, crumbled (about ¾ cup)

1. Place the wheat berries in a medium bowl; cover with water to 2 inches above the wheat berries. Cover and let stand 8 hours. Drain.
2. Place the wheat berries in a medium saucepan; cover with water to 2 inches above wheat berries. Bring to a boil, reduce heat, and cook, uncovered, 1 hour or until tender. Drain and rinse with cold water; drain well. Place the wheat berries in a large bowl; add the cucumber and next 4 ingredients (through tomatoes).
3. Combine the rind and the next 4 ingredients (through sugar) in a bowl; gradually add the oil, stirring constantly with a whisk. Drizzle the dressing over the salad; toss well to coat. Stir in the cheese. Let stand at least 30 minutes; serve at room temperature.

CALORIES 253; FAT 9.7g (sat 3.7g, mono 4.4g, poly 0.9g); PROTEIN 9g; CARB 36g; FIBER 7g; SUGARS 5g (est. added sugars 0g); CHOL 11mg; IRON 1mg; SODIUM 401mg; CALCIUM 79mg

serve with:

- Pita wedges made from ½ (6-inch) pita bread, split and toasted (85 calories)

1,300-CALORIE PLAN: No changes
1,400-CALORIE PLAN/1,500-CALORIE PLAN: Add 1 medium tangerine (47 calories).

Wheat Berries

Nutty, chewy wheat berries work well in hearty salads, stir-fries, soups, and stews. Cook them as you would pasta, in a large pot of boiling water that gives them plenty of space. Check for doneness after 30 minutes, but know they may take as long as an hour to reach the desired tenderness. One cup uncooked yields about 2 cups cooked.

Mother of 3 Saves $400 a Month on Groceries

STEPHANIE ATWELL WAS A BIT SKEPTICAL when she joined the CLDiet. As a mother to three children all under the age of 7, she had no way of knowing what to expect out of the meal plan.

"I thought I'd have to cook two meals," she said. "I thought I was going to have to cook for me and my husband, and I thought I was going to have to cook for the kids. I didn't know serving-wise if it would be enough for everybody, and I also didn't know if they would eat it."

The verdict?

"They eat it. They love it! I get the thumbs up at dinner every day, and they even eat leftovers at lunch," Stephanie said. "It's been nice. I get to cook real food and they get to try real food."

Something else the Atwells love is the effect the Cooking Light Diet has had on their monthly grocery spending, which Stephanie says has gone way down.

"It's about a $400 difference for a month," she said. "$400 less. Just food-wise. I'm not doing drive-thrus, I'm not going into the store and just randomly shopping. So my husband said it's a $400 food difference. ...And my fridge is full of food right now. Real food!"

> "I'm not doing drive-thrus, I'm not going into the store and just randomly shopping...And my fridge is full of food right now. Real food!"

There have been added benefits beyond the checkbook, too. The whole Atwell family has come together around a newly planted herb garden, courtesy of all the recipes calling for fresh ingredients.

"I now have this herb garden on my porch," Stephanie said. "I just use so much basil, rosemary and thyme, and cilantro, and parsley I was like, 'You know, I'm just going to quit buying this and grow it.' So I do! The kids love it. They watch me pick it off the plant and come in and prepare it. And they know what certain vegetables look like now that they've never seen before. It's really great."

**Members following The Cooking Light Diet lose more than half a pound per week, on average.*

Orzo Salad with Spicy Buttermilk Dressing Ⓥ

Hands-on: 27 minutes | Total: 27 minutes
Serves 6 (serving size: about 1 cup orzo mixture, about 1 tablespoon feta cheese, 2 avocado wedges, ½ teaspoon cilantro, and ½ teaspoon parsley)

This tasty and colorful salad gets a spicy kick from the dressing, which includes chili powder and ground red pepper.

1 cup uncooked orzo
1 cup frozen whole-kernel corn, thawed and drained
12 cherry tomatoes, quartered
3 green onions, sliced
1 (15-ounce) can black beans, rinsed and drained
¼ cup low-fat buttermilk
3 tablespoons chopped fresh cilantro
3 tablespoons fresh lime juice
2 tablespoons light sour cream
2 tablespoons canola mayonnaise (such as Hellmann's)
1 teaspoon chili powder
½ teaspoon kosher salt
¼ teaspoon freshly ground black pepper
¼ teaspoon ground red pepper
2 garlic cloves, crushed
1.5 ounces feta cheese, crumbled (about 6 tablespoons)
1 peeled avocado, cut into 12 wedges
1 tablespoon chopped fresh parsley

1. Cook the orzo according to the package directions, omitting the salt and fat. Drain and rinse; drain well. Place the orzo, corn, and the next 3 ingredients (through beans) in a large bowl; toss.
2. Combine the buttermilk, 2 tablespoons of the cilantro, and the next 8 ingredients (through garlic) in a small bowl, stirring well with a whisk. Drizzle over the orzo mixture; toss. Sprinkle the feta cheese over the mixture. Top with the avocado; garnish with the remaining 1 tablespoon cilantro and parsley.

CALORIES 307; FAT 12.3g (sat 2.9g, mono 5.6g, poly 1.8g); PROTEIN 10g; CARB 43g; FIBER 7g; SUGARS 5g (est. added sugars 0g); CHOL 10mg; IRON 2mg; SODIUM 493mg; CALCIUM 100mg

serve with:

• 7 whole almonds (48 calories)

1,300-CALORIE PLAN: No changes
1,400-CALORIE PLAN/1,500-CALORIE PLAN: Increase the serving of almonds to 14 (96 calories).

345
TOTAL CALORIES

Greek Tomato and Cucumber Salad with Farro (V)

Hands-on: 20 minutes | Total: 20 minutes
Serves 4 (serving size: 1 cup salad and about 1 ounce feta)

Whole-grain farro bulks up this hearty Mediterranean salad. If you like the crunch of fresh red onion but not the full pungency, give the slices a 30-second dip in ice water to tame the flavor; drain and toss in the salad.

½ teaspoon grated lemon rind
3 tablespoons fresh lemon juice
3 tablespoons extra-virgin olive oil
2 tablespoons red wine vinegar
2 teaspoons finely chopped fresh oregano
½ teaspoon kosher salt
¼ teaspoon freshly ground black pepper
2 cups cooked farro
⅓ cup kalamata olives, pitted and halved lengthwise
⅓ cup thinly sliced red onion
1½ pounds cherry tomatoes, halved
1½ pounds small pickling cucumbers, halved lengthwise and cut into ½-inch-thick slices
4 ounces feta cheese, crumbled (about ½ cup)

Combine the first 7 ingredients in a large bowl, stirring well with a whisk. Stir in the farro and the next 4 ingredients (through cucumbers), and toss gently to combine. Top with the feta cheese.

CALORIES 325; FAT 18.3g (sat 5.7g, mono 9.3g, poly 2.7g); PROTEIN 11g; CARB 39g; FIBER 7g; SUGARS 9g (est. added sugars 0g); CHOL 25mg; IRON 1mg; SODIUM 626mg; CALCIUM 191mg

serve with:

- ½ cup fresh watermelon cubes (20 calories)

1,300-CALORIE PLAN: No changes
1,400-CALORIE PLAN/1,500-CALORIE PLAN: Increase the watermelon to 1 cup (40 calories) and add ½ cup fresh blueberries (42 calories).

Chicken Taco Salad

Hands-on: 25 minutes | Total: 25 minutes | Serves 6

Using rotisserie chicken helps this convenient dish come together in a flash.

6 (6-inch) corn tortillas
Cooking spray
⅜ teaspoon ground chipotle chile pepper
1 cup salsa verde
3 ounces ⅓-less-fat cream cheese (about ⅓ cup)
1½ cups shredded skinless, boneless rotisserie chicken breast
1½ cups chopped skinless, boneless rotisserie chicken thigh or drumstick
½ cup sliced green onions
2 tablespoons fresh lime juice
5 teaspoons extra-virgin olive oil
⅔ cup organic black beans, rinsed and drained
⅔ cup frozen corn kernels, thawed
⅔ cup chopped red bell pepper
¼ cup chopped fresh cilantro
6 cups chopped romaine lettuce
3 radishes, very thinly sliced

1. Preheat the oven to 450°F.
2. Cut the tortillas into ¼-inch-thick strips. Place the tortilla strips on a jelly-roll pan. Lightly coat with cooking spray; sprinkle with the chipotle pepper. Bake at 450°F for 10 minutes, stirring after 5 minutes. Cool.
3. Heat a medium skillet over medium heat. Add the salsa and cheese to the pan; cook 4 minutes or until the cheese melts, stirring to combine. Stir in the chicken; cook 1 minute. Stir in the onions and 1 tablespoon of the lime juice. Remove the chicken mixture from the pan; keep warm. Rinse the pan with water. Return the pan to medium-high heat. Add 2 teaspoons of the oil to the pan; swirl to coat. Add the beans, corn, and red bell pepper to the pan; sauté 2 minutes. Stir in the cilantro.
4. Combine the remaining 1 tablespoon lime juice and the remaining 1 tablespoon oil in a large bowl; stir with a whisk. Add the lettuce to the bowl; toss to coat. Place about 1 cup lettuce mixture on each of 6 plates; top each serving with about ¾ cup chicken mixture and ⅓ cup corn mixture. Sprinkle with tortilla strips and radishes.

CALORIES 295; FAT 13.4g (sat 3.6g, mono 5.9g, poly 1.6g); PROTEIN 23g; CARB 23g; FIBER 5g; SUGARS 6g (est. added sugars 0g); CHOL 82mg; IRON 2mg; SODIUM 665mg; CALCIUM 73mg

serve with:

• 1 cup fresh cantaloupe cubes (54 calories)

1,300-CALORIE PLAN: No changes
1,400-CALORIE PLAN/1,500-CALORIE PLAN: Add ¼ cup sliced black olives to your salad (50 calories).

Tuna, Olive, and Wheat Berry Salad DF

Hands-on: 9 minutes | Total: 9 minutes | Serves 4

Be sure to seek out a sustainable type of tuna. We like Wild Planet's wild albacore tuna in extra-virgin olive oil; a 5-ounce can, once drained, gives you the correct amount here.

2 tablespoons chopped fresh parsley
2 tablespoons extra-virgin olive oil
2 tablespoons fresh lemon juice
2 teaspoons chopped fresh thyme
½ teaspoon freshly ground black pepper
¼ teaspoon kosher salt
2½ cups cooked wheat berries
½ cup thinly vertically sliced red onion
10 pitted Castelvetrano olives, sliced
4 ounces canned or jarred white tuna packed in oil, drained

Combine the first 6 ingredients in a medium bowl, stirring well with a whisk. Stir in the wheat berries and onion; toss to coat. Place about ¾ cup of the wheat berry mixture on each of 4 plates. Sprinkle evenly with the olives; top evenly with the tuna.

CALORIES 348; FAT 12.8g (sat 1.6g, mono 6.4g, poly 1.9g); PROTEIN 15g; CARB 46g; FIBER 8g; SUGARS 1g (est. added sugars 0g); CHOL 9mg; IRON 0mg; SODIUM 535mg; CALCIUM 10mg

1,300-CALORIE PLAN: No changes
1,400-CALORIE PLAN/1,500-CALORIE PLAN: Serve with 6 multigrain crackers, such as Kashi Original 7 Grain (48 calories).

Arugula, Italian Tuna, and White Bean Salad

Hands-on: 12 minutes | Total: 12 minutes | Serves 4 (serving size: 2¼ cups)

This no-cook recipe is packed with colorful vegetables and gets a flavor kick from zesty vinaigrette.

3 tablespoons fresh lemon juice
1½ tablespoons extra-virgin olive oil
½ teaspoon minced fresh garlic
¼ teaspoon kosher salt
¼ teaspoon freshly ground black pepper
¼ teaspoon Dijon mustard
1 cup grape tomatoes, halved
1 cup thinly vertically sliced red onion
2 (6-ounce) cans Italian tuna packed in olive oil, drained and broken into chunks
1 (15-ounce) can cannellini beans, rinsed and drained
1 (5-ounce) package fresh baby arugula
2 ounces Parmigiano-Reggiano cheese, shaved (about ½ cup)

Whisk together the first 6 ingredients in a large bowl. Add the tomatoes and the next 4 ingredients (through arugula); toss. Top with the cheese.

CALORIES 301; FAT 14.5g (sat 4.1g, mono 6.7g, poly 2.8g); PROTEIN 28g; CARB 15g; FIBER 4g; SUGARS 4g (est. added sugars 0g); CHOL 21mg; IRON 3mg; SODIUM 709mg; CALCIUM 263mg

serve with:

- 1 (¾-ounce) slice French bread (54 calories)

1,300-CALORIE PLAN: No changes
1,400-CALORIE PLAN/1,500-CALORIE PLAN: Combine 1 teaspoon extra-virgin olive oil and a dash of dried oregano (42 calories), and drizzle it over your slice of French bread.

Canned Tuna

Fresh seafood isn't the only way to get more fish into your diet. Great canned tuna packed in oil works just as well and brings with it healthy omega-3s in the tuna oil. Bumble Bee and Wild Planet make versions we like. Be sure to check the sodium on any can you buy.

Feta-Herb Edamame Succotash GF V

Hands-on: 15 minutes | Total: 20 minutes
Serves 4 (serving size: about 1 cup)

Edamame replaces lima beans in traditional succotash to boost protein for a main dish. This comes together very quickly for easy lunch prep, but it can also be cooked the night before and refrigerated until lunchtime.

1 tablespoon olive oil
1 medium-sized yellow onion, chopped (about 1 cup)
2 cups frozen shelled edamame, thawed
1½ cups frozen corn kernels, thawed
1 cup grape tomatoes, halved lengthwise
1 ounce feta cheese, crumbled (about ¼ cup)
2 tablespoons chopped fresh dill
2 tablespoons chopped fresh flat-leaf parsley
2 tablespoons sherry vinegar
½ teaspoon kosher salt
¼ teaspoon freshly ground black pepper

1. Heat a large nonstick skillet over medium-high heat. Add the oil to the pan; swirl to coat. Add the onion, and cook, stirring constantly, until tender, about 4 minutes.
2. Add the edamame; cook, stirring constantly, 2 minutes. Add the corn; cook, stirring constantly, 2 minutes. Remove from the heat. Transfer to a bowl, and cool 10 minutes. Stir in the tomatoes, feta, dill, parsley, vinegar, salt, and pepper.

CALORIES 218; FAT 8.6g (sat 1.3g, mono 3.5g, poly 3.3g); PROTEIN 14g; CARB 23g; FIBER 7g; SUGARS 7g (est. added sugars 0g); CHOL 8mg; IRON 3mg; SODIUM 318mg; CALCIUM 85mg

serve with:

- 6 baby carrots and 3 celery sticks (29 calories)
- 1 (100-calorie) package gluten-free pretzels, such as Snyders (100 calories) or for a non-gluten-free option, 18 mini pretzels (100 calories)

1,300-CALORIE PLAN: No changes
1,400-CALORIE PLAN/1,500-CALORIE PLAN: Add 2 tablespoons hummus (50 calories).

Quinoa–Brown Rice Pilaf with Goat Cheese and Watercress (V)

342 TOTAL CALORIES

Hands-on: 10 minutes | Total: 10 minutes | Serves 2 (serving size: 1 cup)

This comes together really quickly, but it can be made up to 2 days in advance and refrigerated. Plus, it's portable to take with you for lunch. The pine nuts give it a nice surprising crunch. The sweetness of the sherry vinegar and creamy goat cheese balance the bitterness from the watercress. Substitute arugula or spinach for watercress, if you'd like.

1 (8.5-ounce) pouch microwaveable organic precooked quinoa and brown rice with garlic mix (such as Seeds of Change)
2 cups firmly packed watercress, coarsely chopped
1 ounce garlic-and-herb goat cheese, crumbled (about ¼ cup)
2 tablespoons toasted pine nuts
2 teaspoons olive oil
2 teaspoons sherry vinegar
¼ teaspoon freshly ground black pepper
⅛ teaspoon kosher salt

1. Microwave the quinoa and brown rice mix according to the package directions. Place in a medium bowl; cool 5 minutes.
2. Stir in the watercress, goat cheese, pine nuts, oil, vinegar, pepper, and salt.

CALORIES 342; FAT 16.5g (sat 3.5g, mono 4.9g, poly 3.6g); PROTEIN 10g; CARB 42g; FIBER 3g; SUGARS 2g (est. added sugars 0g); CHOL 5mg; IRON 2mg; SODIUM 567mg; CALCIUM 60mg

1,300-CALORIE PLAN: No changes
1,400-CALORIE PLAN/1,500-CALORIE PLAN: Serve with ½ cup fresh pineapple chunks (41 calories).

Orange-Almond Chicken and Cabbage Bowl

Hands-on: 12 minutes | Total: 12 minutes
Serves 2 (serving size: about 2 cups)

Look for Marzetti's Simply Dressed ginger-sesame salad dressing in your grocer's produce section with other refrigerated dressings. Select thin-skinned navel oranges; they are juicier than the thick-skinned ones.

2 navel oranges
3 cups bagged shredded coleslaw mix
1 cup shredded rotisserie chicken breast
3 tablespoons sliced toasted almonds
3 tablespoons ginger-sesame salad refrigerated dressing (such as Marzetti's Simply Dressed)
Sliced scallions (optional)

1. Cut a ¼-inch-thick slice from each end of the oranges using a sharp, thin-bladed knife. Place the oranges, cut sides down, on a cutting board. Peel the oranges; cut away the bitter white pith. Slice each orange between the membranes, and gently remove whole segments. Discard the membranes and seeds.
2. Combine the orange sections, coleslaw mix, chicken, and almonds in a medium bowl. Drizzle with the dressing; toss to combine. Top with the scallions, if desired.

CALORIES 246; FAT 8.4g (sat 1g, mono 3.7g, poly 1.4g); PROTEIN 26g; CARB 21g; FIBER 6g; SUGARS 13g (est. added sugars 3g); CHOL 66mg; IRON 1mg; SODIUM 587mg; CALCIUM 51mg

serve with:

- 7 multigrain baked pita chips, such as Stacy's (108 calories)

1,300-CALORIE PLAN: No changes
1,400-CALORIE PLAN/1,500-CALORIE PLAN: Increase the serving of baked pita chips to 10 chips (155 calories).

Chilled Soy-Lime Rice Noodles with Tofu DF V

Hands-on: 20 minutes | Total: 1 hour, 50 minutes
Serves 6 (serving size: about 1¼ cups noodles and 1 tofu slice)

1 (14-ounce) package water-packed extra-firm tofu, drained
¼ cup fresh lime juice (from 3 limes)
¼ cup lower-sodium soy sauce
2 tablespoons sambal oelek (ground fresh chile paste)
1 tablespoon light brown sugar
3 tablespoons canola oil
7 ounces uncooked rice noodles
1½ cups (about 6 ounces) snow peas
1 large red bell pepper, thinly sliced (about 1½ cups)
Crushed red pepper (optional)
Cilantro leaves (optional)

1. Cut the tofu into 6 slices. Arrange the tofu slices in a single layer on several layers of paper towels. Top with several more layers of paper towels; top with a cast-iron skillet or other heavy pan. Let stand 30 minutes. Combine the tofu slices, lime juice, soy sauce, sambal oelek, brown sugar, and 2 tablespoons of the oil in a large zip-top plastic freezer bag. Seal the bag, and let stand at room temperature for 1 hour, turning the bag occasionally.
2. Meanwhile, cook the rice noodles according to the package directions; drain. Rinse under cold running water; drain well.
3. Remove the tofu from the marinade, reserving the marinade. Heat a large nonstick skillet over medium-high heat. Add the remaining 1 tablespoon oil to the pan; swirl to coat. Add the tofu slices in a single layer; cook until browned, about 2½ minutes per side. Remove the tofu from the pan. Add the snow peas and bell pepper slices; cook, stirring constantly, until slightly softened, 2 to 3 minutes. Remove from the heat. Add the noodles and the reserved marinade; toss to coat. Divide the noodle mixture among 6 bowls; top with tofu slices. Sprinkle with the crushed red pepper and cilantro, if desired.

CALORIES 275; FAT 10.4g (sat 0.9g, mono 4.4g, poly 2g); PROTEIN 10g; CARB 36g; FIBER 2g; SUGARS 4g (est. added sugars 2g); CHOL 0mg; IRON 3mg; SODIUM 639mg; CALCIUM 142mg

serve with:

• ⅔ cup Miso Mixed Vegetable Salad, page 203 (65 calories)

1,300-CALORIE PLAN: No changes
1,400-CALORIE PLAN/1,500-CALORIE PLAN: Add 2 small plums (60 calories).

Tofu

Cooking with tofu is really easy. You'll want to purchase water-packed varieties so you can season the tofu to your liking—this helps keep calories and sodium in check, as some vacuum-packed varieties come already seasoned. Be sure to press the tofu between paper towels before cooking it. This removes some of the water it was soaked in, making for a crisper, browner crust.

Bacon, Tomato, and Quinoa-Stuffed Avocado DF GF

Hands-on: 8 minutes | Total: 8 minutes
Serves 1 (serving size: 2 stuffed avocado halves)

Cook the quinoa and bacon in advance (or use leftovers for both). It's best to cut the avocado and mix the ingredients the morning you plan to eat this for lunch.

1 small ripe avocado
½ cup cooked quinoa, cooled to room temperature
⅓ cup chopped tomato
1 teaspoon olive oil
¼ teaspoon lemon zest plus 2 teaspoons fresh lemon juice (from 1 lemon)
¼ teaspoon kosher salt
⅛ teaspoon freshly ground black pepper
1 bacon slice, cooked and crumbled
Chopped fresh flat-leaf parsley (optional)

1. Cut the avocado in half lengthwise; remove the pit. Scoop the avocado flesh from the peels; reserve the peels. Roughly chop half of the avocado flesh; reserve the remaining avocado flesh for another use.
2. Gently stir together the chopped avocado, quinoa, tomato, oil, zest, juice, salt, and pepper; spoon mixture into avocado peels. Sprinkle with bacon and, if desired, parsley.

CALORIES 351; FAT 23.3g (sat 4g, mono 13.7g, poly 3.5g); PROTEIN 10g; CARB 32g; FIBER 10g; SUGARS 3g (est. added sugars 0g); CHOL 8mg; IRON 2mg; SODIUM 583mg; CALCIUM 36mg

1,300-CALORIE PLAN: No changes
1,400-CALORIE PLAN/1,500-CALORIE PLAN: Serve with ½ cup grapes (52 calories).

Black Bean Tostadas (V)

Hands-on: 10 minutes | Total: 10 minutes | Serves 2 (serving size: 1 tostada)

You can measure and prep the ingredients ahead, storing all except the tostada shells in individual containers in the fridge. Then build the tostadas just before serving. For quick substitutions, you can use pinto beans instead of black beans and shredded iceberg instead of romaine.

1 cup canned reduced-sodium black beans, drained
1 tablespoon olive oil
⅛ teaspoon freshly ground black pepper
2 (½-ounce) tostada shells
1 cup shredded romaine lettuce
6 tablespoons store-bought pico de gallo or fresh salsa
1 ounce Cotija cheese, crumbled (about ¼ cup)
2 lime wedges (optional)

1. Combine the beans, oil, and pepper in a small bowl; mash to desired consistency.
2. Spread the bean mixture on the tostada shells. Top each with ½ cup lettuce, 3 tablespoons pico de gallo, and 2 tablespoons cheese. Serve with lime wedges, if desired.

CALORIES 295; FAT 10.6g (sat 3.5g, mono 4.3g, poly 1g); PROTEIN 13g; CARB 30g; FIBER 8g; SUGARS 2g (est. added sugars 0g); CHOL 15mg; IRON 2mg; SODIUM 518mg; CALCIUM 290mg

serve with:

- ¼ cup cubed avocado (45 calories)

1,300-CALORIE PLAN: No changes
1,400-CALORIE PLAN/1,500-CALORIE PLAN: Increase the serving of cubed avocado to ½ cup (90 calories).

Cotija

This fresh Mexican cheese—pronounced ko-TEE-hah—is a cow's milk cheese named after the city in Michoacán. Versions available in the U.S. are a softer cheese, similar to feta, which can be used as a substitute if your grocery store doesn't carry Cotija. You can use it crumbled or grated over tacos, beans, or soups.

Pancetta and Kale Frittata GF LC

Hands-on: 15 minutes | Total: 15 minutes | Serves 4 (serving size: 2 wedges)

Many supermarkets sell packages of prediced pancetta to save time. (Our favorite is Boar's Head.) Or substitute bacon for the pancetta, if you like.

6 large eggs
¼ teaspoon kosher salt
¼ teaspoon freshly ground black pepper
1 ounce diced pancetta
½ cup chopped yellow onion
2 cups firmly packed baby kale
1 ounce Parmigiano-Reggiano cheese, shredded (about ¼ cup)

1. Preheat the broiler with oven rack 3 to 4 inches from the heat. Whisk together the eggs, salt, and pepper until well blended.
2. Heat a medium-sized ovenproof skillet over medium heat. Add the pancetta; cook until almost crisp, about 4 minutes. Add the onion; cook until the onion is tender and the pancetta is crisp, about 4 minutes. Add the kale, and cook until wilted, about 30 seconds. Add the egg mixture, and cook until the eggs are partially set, about 5 minutes, lifting up the edges to allow the uncooked egg to drip to the bottom. Sprinkle with the cheese. Broil until the top is lightly browned and the eggs are set, about 2 minutes. Cut the frittata into 8 wedges.

CALORIES 182; FAT 11.6g (sat 4.5g, mono 4.3g, poly 1.8g); PROTEIN 14g; CARB 4g; FIBER 1g; SUGARS 1g (est. added sugars 0g); CHOL 289mg; IRON 2mg; SODIUM 488mg; CALCIUM 185mg

serve with:

- 2 cups fresh baby salad greens (18 calories), 2 tablespoons reduced-fat dressing (45 calories), 2 tablespoons sweetened dried cranberries (60 calories), and 7 whole almonds (48 calories)

1,300-CALORIE PLAN: No changes
1,400-CALORIE PLAN/1,500-CALORIE PLAN: Add ½ cup fat-free cottage cheese (52 calories).

Asparagus and Mushroom Quiche LC V

Hands-on: 30 minutes | Total: 1 hour, 35 minutes
Serves 8 (serving size: 1 wedge)

Quiche is a great make-ahead meal. Bake on Sunday night and enjoy it for lunch throughout the week. You can use Gruyère or Swiss in place of fontina cheese, and green beans can substitute for the asparagus.

½ (14.1-ounce) package refrigerated piecrusts
Cooking spray
2 tablespoons olive oil
1 (8-ounce) container sliced cremini mushrooms
8 ounces asparagus, trimmed and cut into 1½-inch pieces
1 shallot, finely chopped
1 cup 2% reduced-fat milk
½ teaspoon kosher salt
¼ teaspoon freshly ground black pepper
4 large eggs
3 ounces fontina cheese, shredded (about ¾ cup)

1. Preheat the oven to 425°F. Fit the piecrust into a 9-inch metal pie pan lightly coated with cooking spray. Fold the edges under and crimp. Line the crust with aluminum foil or parchment paper; fill with pie weights or dried beans. Bake at 425°F until set, about 10 minutes. Remove the pie weights and foil; bake until the crust is lightly browned, about 10 minutes. Remove from the oven, and cool 20 minutes. Reduce the oven temperature to 350°F.
2. Heat a large nonstick skillet over medium-high heat. Add the oil to the pan; swirl to coat. Add the mushrooms, and cook until just beginning to brown, about 8 minutes. Add the asparagus and shallots; cook until the asparagus is just tender, 2 to 3 minutes. Remove from the heat; cool 5 minutes. Transfer the mixture to the piecrust.
3. Whisk together the milk, salt, pepper, and eggs in a medium bowl; stir in the fontina. Pour evenly over mushroom mixture in piecrust. Bake at 350°F until set, 30 to 40 minutes. Cool 10 minutes; cut into 8 wedges.

CALORIES 258; FAT 17.5g (sat 6.9g, mono 5g, poly 1.4g); PROTEIN 11g; CARB 16g; FIBER 1g; SUGARS 3g (est. added sugars 0g); CHOL 157mg; IRON 1mg; SODIUM 405mg; CALCIUM 130mg

serve with:

- 1½ cups fresh spinach (15 calories), 2 tablespoons reduced-fat vinaigrette (35 calories), and 7 whole almonds (48 calories)

1,300-CALORIE PLAN: No changes
1,400-CALORIE PLAN/1,500-CALORIE PLAN: Add 1 tablespoon toasted pine nuts (57 calories) to your salad.

DINNER

Crispy Fish with Lemon-Dill Sauce

Hands-on: 25 minutes | Total: 25 minutes
Serves 4 (serving size: 1 fillet, about 2 tablespoons sauce, and 1 lemon wedge)

Panko is the secret ingredient that makes these oven-fried fish fillets crispy. The lemon-dill sauce is the perfect complement in flavor and texture.

2 large egg whites, lightly beaten
1 cup panko (Japanese breadcrumbs)
½ teaspoon paprika
¾ teaspoon onion powder
¾ teaspoon garlic powder
4 (6-ounce) skinless cod fillets
1 teaspoon freshly ground black pepper
⅜ teaspoon salt
Cooking spray
¼ cup canola mayonnaise (such as Hellmann's)
2 tablespoons finely chopped dill pickle
1 teaspoon fresh lemon juice
1 teaspoon chopped fresh dill
4 lemon wedges

1. Preheat the broiler to high.
2. Place the egg whites in a shallow dish. Combine the panko, paprika, onion powder, and garlic powder in a shallow dish. Sprinkle the fish with the pepper and salt. Dip each fillet in the egg whites, and then dredge in the panko mixture; place on a broiler pan coated with cooking spray. Broil 4 minutes on each side or until desired degree of doneness.
3. Combine the mayonnaise, pickle, lemon juice, and dill. Serve with the fish and lemon wedges.

CALORIES 245; FAT 5.2g (sat 0.2g, mono 2.7g, poly 1.4g); PROTEIN 35g; CARB 12g; FIBER 1g; SUGARS 1g (est. added sugars 0g); CHOL 63mg; IRON 1mg; SODIUM 580mg; CALCIUM 18mg

serve with:

- ½ cup cooked brown rice and ½ cup steamed green beans (160 calories)

1,300-CALORIE PLAN: Increase the serving of brown rice to ¾ cup (209 calories).

1,400-CALORIE PLAN/1,500-CALORIE PLAN: Serve with 1 cup cooked brown rice and 1 serving of Ginger-Garlic Green Beans, page 202 (260 calories).

Seared Tilapia with Spinach and White Bean Orzo DF

Hands-on: 15 minutes | Total: 15 minutes
Serves 4 (serving size: 1¼ cups pasta mixture and 1 fillet)

Feel free to sub another fish, such as flounder or red snapper, for the tilapia in this versatile dish.

¾ cup uncooked orzo pasta
4 (6-ounce) tilapia fillets
½ teaspoon salt
½ teaspoon freshly ground black pepper
1½ tablespoons olive oil
½ teaspoon crushed red pepper
3 garlic cloves, minced
1 (5-ounce) package fresh baby spinach
1 cup halved grape tomatoes
1 (15-ounce) can unsalted cannellini beans, rinsed and drained
4 lemon wedges (optional)

1. Cook the orzo according to the package directions, omitting the salt and fat.
2. While the pasta cooks, sprinkle the fish with ¼ teaspoon each of the salt and black pepper. Heat a large nonstick skillet over medium-high heat. Add 1 tablespoon of the oil to the pan; swirl to coat. Add the fish to the pan; cook 3 minutes on each side or until the desired degree of doneness. Remove the fish from the pan; keep warm.
3. Add the remaining 1½ teaspoons oil to the pan. Add the crushed red pepper and garlic; sauté 30 seconds. Add the spinach; sauté 1 minute or just until the spinach wilts. Stir in the tomatoes, beans, remaining ¼ teaspoon salt, and remaining ¼ teaspoon black pepper; cook 1 minute or just until thoroughly heated. Remove the pan from the heat. Add the pasta to the pan; toss to coat. Divide the pasta mixture among 4 plates, and top with the fish fillets. Serve with the lemon wedges, if desired.

CALORIES 399; FAT 9g (sat 1.7g, mono 4.6g, poly 1.2g); PROTEIN 42g; CARB 38g; FIBER 6g; SUGARS 3g (est. added sugars 0g); CHOL 85mg; IRON 3mg; SODIUM 455mg; CALCIUM 71mg

1,300-CALORIE PLAN: Serve with 1 cup fresh strawberries (53 calories).
1,400-CALORIE PLAN/1,500-CALORIE PLAN: Drizzle the 1 cup fresh strawberries with 2 teaspoons of honey (95 calories).

Buy In-Season Produce

Fresh fruit is a no-brainer when it comes to adding a healthful dessert or snack to your meals. But it's easy to get stuck in the rut of buying the same fruits again and again. Avoid this habit by shopping for what's in season. You'll enjoy ephemeral flavors plus nutritional variety as your choices change naturally throughout the year. Plus, you'll have the extra benefit of a dessert that's skinny on the calories!

Indiana Man Changes Eating Habits, Loses Over 30 Pounds

PATRICK MOORE OF SCHERERVILLE, IN, is a fanatical guitar player. When he's not at work providing software support and development, he's probably at home or at church, strumming some tunes. He'd also be the first to tell you he used to be a fanatical eater.

"My eating style before the Cooking Light Diet was 'anything that got in my way,'" Patrick said. "I was just eating like a cow, constantly."

Given his penchant for excessive eating, Patrick had seen many diets, and knew how hard they were to sustain. He says that's not the case with the CLDiet, and its nonrestrictive menu structure has surprised him.

"I've seen a lot of bad diets," Patrick said. "I've seen people struggle and go on a bad diet and lose a bunch of weight real fast and then be fat two weeks later. The CLDiet isn't like that at all. What's surprised me the most is that we haven't had to totally cut anything out of our diets. I still eat steak, I still eat bacon, I still eat butter, but my wife does it according to the portions suggested. So instead of putting a whole stick of butter in something, she'll put in half a tablespoon. You still get the flavor, and it still tastes good, and you still get to eat the food you like. You don't have to eat a bunch of stuff that's totally tasteless and leaves you wanting for more when you're done eating. So that was the biggest surprise for me."

"What's surprised me the most is that we haven't had to totally cut anything out of our diets. I still eat steak. I still eat bacon...but my wife does it according to the portions suggested."

Patrick says that once he mastered the mental aspect of changing his eating habits, embracing the CLDiet was a snap, and he was able to lose over 30 pounds*.

"I think a small part of trying to lose a lot of weight...the diet is one of the smaller issues. The biggest issue is the mental aspect. You know, 'What am I going to do right now? Because normally this time of day I'd sit down with a bag of potato chips.' You find something else to do. You go outside and cut the grass or go for a walk or something. So there are a lot of aspects to a good diet. And this one is a good one."

**Members following The Cooking Light Diet lose more than half a pound per week, on average.*

Tilapia with Lemon-Garlic Sauce LC

Hands-on: 15 minutes | Total: 15 minutes
Serves 4 (serving size: 1 fillet and about 2 tablespoons sauce)

Incredibly simple, remarkably delicious—this is an entrée that's elegant enough for entertaining and fast enough to brighten weeknight dinner doldrums.

4 (6-ounce) tilapia fillets
¼ teaspoon salt
¼ teaspoon black pepper
3 tablespoons quick-mixing flour (such as Wondra)
2 tablespoons unsalted butter
1 tablespoon olive oil
1 tablespoon minced fresh garlic
⅓ cup dry white wine
⅓ cup unsalted chicken stock (such as Swanson)
2 tablespoons chopped fresh parsley
1 tablespoon fresh lemon juice

1. Sprinkle the fish with the salt and pepper. Place the flour in a shallow dish. Dredge both sides of the fish in the flour; reserve the unused flour. Heat a large skillet over medium-high heat. Add 1 tablespoon of the butter and the oil to the pan; swirl until the butter melts. Add the fish to the pan; cook 2 minutes on each side or until the fish flakes easily when tested with a fork. Remove from the pan; keep warm.
2. Add the reserved flour and garlic to the pan; cook 90 seconds or until lightly browned, stirring constantly. Add the wine and stock, stirring with a whisk; bring to a boil. Cook 2 minutes or until slightly thickened. Remove the pan from the heat; stir in the parsley, lemon juice, and remaining 1 tablespoon butter. Serve the fish with the sauce.

CALORIES 295; FAT 12.4g (sat 5.1g, mono 4.8g, poly 1.2g); PROTEIN 35g; CARB 6g; FIBER 0g; SUGARS 0g (est. added sugars 0g); CHOL 100mg; IRON 1mg; SODIUM 248mg; CALCIUM 26mg

serve with:

- ½ cup Sautéed Broccolini, page 202 (73 calories)
- 1 cup fresh spinach tossed with 1½ tablespoons reduced-fat vinaigrette (36 calories)

1,300-CALORIE PLAN: Add 1 tablespoon feta cheese and 1 teaspoon sunflower seeds to your salad and increase the reduced-fat vinaigrette to 2 tablespoons (76 calories).
1,400-CALORIE PLAN/1,500-CALORIE PLAN: Add 1 tablespoon feta cheese to your salad and increase the reduced-fat vinaigrette to 2 tablespoons (76 calories). Also, add 1 small multigrain roll (70 calories).

Creamy Tuna Noodle Casserole with Peas and Breadcrumbs

Hands-on: 20 minutes | Total: 20 minutes
Serves 4 (serving size: about 1½ cups)

We love the old-school feel of this skillet supper. If you can't find whole-wheat panko, sauté fresh whole-wheat crumbs until crisp.

6 ounces uncooked no-yolk egg noodles
1 tablespoon olive oil
1 tablespoon unsalted butter
1 cup finely chopped onion
1 cup thinly sliced celery
3 tablespoons all-purpose flour
2¼ cups 1% low-fat milk
½ cup frozen green peas, thawed
1½ tablespoons chopped fresh dill
1 teaspoon finely grated lemon rind
1 tablespoon fresh lemon juice
1 teaspoon dry mustard (such as Colman's)
½ teaspoon kosher salt
¼ teaspoon freshly ground black pepper
1 (5-ounce) can solid white albacore tuna packed in water, drained and broken into chunks
¼ cup whole-wheat panko (Japanese breadcrumbs)
1.5 ounces Parmesan cheese, grated (about ⅓ cup)

1. Preheat the broiler to low.
2. Fill a large saucepan with water; bring to a boil. Add the noodles; cook 3 minutes or until al dente. Drain. Heat a 10-inch ovenproof skillet over medium heat. Add the oil and butter; swirl until the butter melts. Add the onion and celery; sauté 6 minutes or until tender. Sprinkle the flour over the vegetables; cook 45 seconds. Add the milk, stirring constantly. Stir in the peas and next 7 ingredients (through tuna). Remove the pan from the heat; gently stir in the noodles. Sprinkle the breadcrumbs and cheese over the top. Broil 2 minutes or until the topping is lightly browned.

CALORIES 436; FAT 11.9g (sat 5.2g, mono 4.6g, poly 0.8g); PROTEIN 27g; CARB 54g; FIBER 5g; SUGARS 12g (est. added sugars 0g); CHOL 34mg; IRON 3mg; SODIUM 550mg; CALCIUM 322mg

1,300-CALORIE PLAN: No changes
1,400-CALORIE PLAN/1,500-CALORIE PLAN: Serve with 1 cup mixed greens, ¼ cup fresh orange sections, and 2 teaspoons sliced almonds (51 calories).

Thai Shrimp Scampi DF

Hands-on: 15 minutes | Total: 15 minutes
Serves 4 (serving size: about 1½ cups)

There are lots of sustainable shrimp options available; ask at the seafood counter to ensure you're making the right choice. If you have trouble finding lemongrass, substitute ½ teaspoon grated lemon rind.

8 ounces uncooked multigrain spaghetti
8 ounces asparagus, trimmed and cut diagonally into 1½-inch pieces
2 teaspoons canola oil
2 tablespoons minced fresh lemongrass
3 garlic cloves, minced
⅔ cup light coconut milk
⅓ cup unsalted chicken stock (such as Swanson)
1 tablespoon Thai green curry paste (such as Thai Kitchen)
¾ teaspoon kosher salt
12 ounces medium shrimp, peeled and deveined
1 cup chopped fresh cilantro
1 cup chopped fresh mint

1. Cook the pasta according to the package directions, omitting the salt and fat. Add the asparagus during the last 2 minutes of cooking. Drain; return to the pan.
2. Heat a large skillet over medium-high heat. Add the oil to the pan; swirl to coat. Add the lemongrass and garlic; sauté 30 seconds. Stir in the coconut milk, stock, curry paste, salt, and shrimp; bring to a boil. Reduce the heat; simmer 3 minutes or until the shrimp are done, stirring occasionally. Stir the shrimp mixture, cilantro, and mint into the pasta mixture.

CALORIES 354; FAT 7.4g (sat 2.2g, mono 1.6g, poly 0.8g); PROTEIN 24g; CARB 49g; FIBER 6g; SUGARS 3g (est. added sugars 0g); CHOL 107mg; IRON 2mg; SODIUM 604mg; CALCIUM 81mg

serve with:

- 1 cup baby salad greens tossed with 1½ tablespoons reduced-fat Asian sesame dressing (43 calories)

1,300-CALORIE PLAN: Top your salad with 1 tablespoon chopped peanuts (54 calories).
1,400-CALORIE PLAN/1,500-CALORIE PLAN: Add a mandarin orange to your salad or serve it on its own (35 calories).

Quick Fried Brown Rice with Shrimp and Snap Peas DF

Hands-on: 20 minutes | Total: 20 minutes
Serves 4 (serving size: 1½ cups)

Stir up your weeknight meal routine by serving this quick 20-minute meal.

1½ (8.8-ounce) pouches precooked brown rice (such as Uncle Ben's)
2 tablespoons lower-sodium soy sauce
1 tablespoon sambal oelek (ground fresh chile paste)
1 tablespoon honey
2 tablespoons peanut oil
10 ounces medium shrimp, peeled and deveined
3 large eggs, lightly beaten
1½ cups sugar snap peas, diagonally sliced
⅓ cup unsalted, dry-roasted peanuts
⅛ teaspoon salt
3 garlic cloves, crushed

1. Heat the rice according to the package directions.
2. Combine the soy sauce, sambal oelek, and honey in a large bowl. Combine 1 teaspoon of the peanut oil and the shrimp in a medium bowl; toss to coat. Heat a wok or large skillet over high heat. Add the shrimp to the pan, and stir-fry 2 minutes. Add the shrimp to the soy sauce mixture; toss to coat the shrimp. Add 1 teaspoon peanut oil to the pan; swirl to coat. Add the eggs to the pan; cook 45 seconds or until set. Remove the eggs from the pan; cut into bite-sized pieces.
3. Add 1 tablespoon oil to the pan; swirl to coat. Add the rice; stir-fry 4 minutes. Add the rice to the shrimp mixture. Add the remaining 1 teaspoon oil to the pan; swirl to coat. Add the sugar snap peas, peanuts, salt, and garlic to the pan; stir-fry for 2 minutes or until the peanuts begin to brown. Add the shrimp mixture and the egg to the pan, and cook for 2 minutes or until thoroughly heated.

CALORIES 418; FAT 19.8g (sat 3.6g, mono 8.5g, poly 5.9g); PROTEIN 22g; CARB 39g; FIBER 3g; SUGARS 6g (est. added sugars 4g); CHOL 229mg; IRON 2mg; SODIUM 587mg; CALCIUM 82mg

1,300-CALORIE PLAN: Serve with 1 cup steamed broccoli or add it into your stir-fry (20 calories).
1,400-CALORIE PLAN/1,500-CALORIE PLAN: Serve with 1½ cups Orange and Almond Salad, page 203 (90 calories).

Spiced Sirloin, Butternut, and Tomato Stew

Hands-on: 25 minutes | Total: 25 minutes | Serves 4 (serving size: 2 cups)

These tender meatballs have a mild, warm spice. Chopped cilantro at the end adds a nice freshness. You can substitute ground chicken for the sirloin, if you'd like.

⅓ cup 2% reduced-fat milk
1½ whole-wheat bread slices (such as Arnold), cubed
1 pound ground sirloin
½ teaspoon ground cumin
½ teaspoon ground coriander
½ teaspoon freshly ground black pepper
½ cup finely chopped fresh cilantro
⅝ teaspoon kosher salt
2 tablespoons olive oil
1 cup chopped butternut squash
¾ cup chopped yellow onion
1 tablespoon finely chopped garlic
1¼ cups unsalted beef stock
2 cups chopped tomatoes
¾ cup unsalted tomato sauce
1½ cups cauliflower florets

1. Pour the milk over the bread cubes in a bowl. Let stand 5 minutes.
2. Combine the soaked bread cubes, beef, cumin, coriander, pepper, ¼ cup cilantro, and ⅛ teaspoon salt. Gently shape into 12 (1½-inch) meatballs.
3. Heat a Dutch oven over medium-high heat. Add the oil; swirl to coat the pan. Add the meatballs in a single layer; cook, turning to brown on all sides, about 4 minutes. Transfer the meatballs to a plate. Add the squash, onion, and garlic to the pan; cook, stirring occasionally, 3 minutes. Add the stock, scraping the bottom of the pan to loosen any browned bits. Add the remaining ½ teaspoon salt; cook 6 minutes or until the liquid is reduced by half. Add the tomatoes and tomato sauce; bring to a simmer. Cook, stirring occasionally, 6 to 8 minutes or until slightly thickened. Stir in the cauliflower; cover and cook 3 minutes. Return the meatballs to the pan; cover and cook just until the meatballs are cooked through, 6 to 8 minutes. Sprinkle with the remaining ¼ cup cilantro.

CALORIES 335; FAT 13.1g (sat 3.3g, mono 7.1g, poly 1.6g); PROTEIN 29g; CARB 29g; FIBER 7g; SUGARS 10g (est. added sugars 1g); CHOL 62mg; IRON 5mg; SODIUM 556mg; CALCIUM 120mg

serve with:

- 1 (1-ounce) slice French bread (82 calories)

1,300-CALORIE PLAN: Increase the serving of French bread to 1½ ounces (123 calories).

1,400-CALORIE PLAN/1,500-CALORIE PLAN: Increase the serving of French bread to 1½ ounces and drizzle with 1 teaspoon olive oil (163 calories).

Slow Down

It's almost a cliché, but, like many clichés, it's true: Because it takes a few minutes for your stomach to relay signals of satiety to your brain, eating too fast means you pile on calories without being aware. Eat more slowly, and you'll feel your body's signals sooner and eat less. When you sit down for a meal, make an eat-slower pledge.

Beef and Black Bean Enchiladas GF

Hands-on: 60 minutes | Total: 1 hour, 30 minutes
Serves 6 (serving size: 2 enchiladas and 1 tablespoon crema)

You can make all the components ahead and simply assemble the enchiladas just before baking.

Mexican Crema

Thick and slightly tangy Mexican crema adds a cooling finish to enchiladas and tacos. If you can't find it at the grocery store, substitute reduced-fat sour cream thinned with a little lime juice.

SAUCE

2 dried ancho chiles, stemmed
3 cups fat-free, lower-sodium chicken broth
1 (6-inch) corn tortilla*, torn into small pieces
⅓ cup cilantro leaves
2 teaspoons minced fresh garlic
2 green onions, coarsely chopped

ENCHILADAS

8 ounces ground sirloin
2 teaspoons olive oil
2 cups chopped onion
4 teaspoons minced fresh garlic
1 teaspoon dried Mexican oregano
½ teaspoon ground cumin
¼ teaspoon kosher salt
1 tablespoon no-salt-added tomato paste
⅔ cup canned organic black beans, rinsed and drained
½ cup fat-free, lower-sodium chicken broth
1 tablespoon fresh lime juice
4 cups water
12 (6-inch) corn tortillas*, at room temperature
Cooking spray
2½ ounces shredded sharp cheddar cheese (about ⅔ cup)
2 ounces shredded Monterey Jack cheese (about ½ cup)
3 green onions, thinly sliced
6 tablespoons Mexican crema

1. Preheat the oven to 400°F.
2. Make the sauce: Place the ancho chiles in a medium saucepan. Add 3 cups broth; bring to a boil. Reduce the heat, and simmer for 5 minutes. Stir in 1 torn tortilla; simmer 5 minutes, stirring occasionally. Pour the chile mixture into a blender; let stand 10 minutes. Add the cilantro, 2 teaspoons garlic, and 2 coarsely chopped green onions to the blender; process until smooth. Return the mixture to the pan; bring to a boil over medium heat. Cook until reduced to 2 cups (about 7 minutes), stirring occasionally. Remove the sauce from the heat.
3. Make the enchiladas: Heat a large skillet over medium-high heat. Add the beef; sauté 5 minutes or until browned. Remove the beef from the pan using a slotted spoon; drain on paper towels. Wipe the pan with paper towels. Return the pan to medium heat. Add the oil to the pan; swirl to coat. Add the onion; cook 8 minutes or until tender, stirring occasionally.

Add the garlic and next 3 ingredients (through salt); cook 2 minutes, stirring constantly. Stir in the tomato paste; cook 1 minute, stirring frequently. Stir in the drained beef, beans, and ½ cup broth; bring to a boil, scraping the pan to loosen the browned bits. Cook 1 minute, stirring occasionally. Remove from the heat; stir in the lime juice.

4. Place 4 cups water in a saucepan over medium-high heat; bring to a simmer. Working with 1 tortilla at a time, dip the tortillas in the simmering water 2 to 3 seconds each or until softened. Place 1 tortilla on a flat work surface; spoon 3 tablespoons of the beef mixture onto 1 end of each tortilla. Roll the enchiladas up jelly-roll style. Repeat the procedure with the remaining tortillas and beef mixture. Spread ½ cup sauce in the bottom of a 13 x 9-inch glass or ceramic baking dish coated with cooking spray. Arrange the enchiladas, seam sides down, in the prepared dish. Pour the remaining sauce over the enchiladas. Top with the cheeses. Bake at 400°F for 20 minutes or until lightly browned and bubbly. Let stand 10 minutes. Sprinkle with 3 sliced green onions; serve with the crema.

*Make sure the corn tortillas are certified gluten free.

CALORIES 343; FAT 15.4g (sat 5.8g, mono 5.1g, poly 1.4g); PROTEIN 18g; CARB 36g; FIBER 7g; SUGARS 5g (est. added sugars 0g); CHOL 48mg; IRON 3mg; SODIUM 540mg; CALCIUM 236mg

serve with:

- ¾ cup fresh pineapple chunks (62 calories)

1,300-CALORIE PLAN: Decrease the serving of fresh pineapple chunks to ½ cup (41 calories) and add one-fourth of an avocado, sliced (80 calories).

1,400-CALORIE PLAN/1,500-CALORIE PLAN: Increase the serving of fresh pineapple chunks to 1 cup (82 calories) and add one-fourth of an avocado, sliced (80 calories)

394
TOTAL CALORIES

Classic Lasagna with Meat Sauce

Hands-on: 16 minutes | Total: 66 minutes
Serves 6 (serving size: 1 piece)

Extra-lean ground beef (which sometimes cooks up dry) works well here because it's combined with marinara to keep it moist.

12 ounces fat-free ricotta cheese (about 1½ cups)
6 ounces part-skim mozzarella cheese, shredded (about 1½ cups)
¼ cup flat-leaf parsley leaves
1½ tablespoons unsalted butter, melted
1 tablespoon finely chopped fresh oregano
5 garlic cloves, minced
1 large egg, lightly beaten
12 ounces extra-lean ground beef (93% lean)
½ teaspoon freshly ground black pepper
¼ teaspoon crushed red pepper
1 (25-ounce) jar lower-sodium marinara sauce
Cooking spray
6 lasagna noodles, cooked
1 ounce Parmigiano-Reggiano cheese, grated (about ¼ cup)

1. Preheat the oven to 375°F.
2. Combine the ricotta, 2 ounces (about ½ cup) mozzarella, 2 tablespoons parsley, butter, oregano, 1 garlic clove, and egg; set aside.
3. Heat a large nonstick skillet over medium-high heat. Add the ground beef; sprinkle with the peppers and the remaining 4 garlic cloves. Cook for 9 minutes or until the beef is browned, stirring to crumble; drain. Return the beef mixture to the pan; stir in the marinara sauce, and remove from the heat.
4. Spread ½ cup of the meat sauce in the bottom of a broiler-safe 11 x 7-inch glass or ceramic baking dish coated with cooking spray. Cut the bottom third off each noodle to form 6 long and 6 short noodles; cut the short noodles in half to form 12 pieces. Arrange 2 long noodles along outside the edges of the dish; arrange 4 short noodle pieces along the center of the dish. Top the noodles with 1 cup meat sauce. Top with 2 long noodles and 4 short noodle pieces, all of the ricotta mixture, and 1 cup of the meat sauce. Arrange the remaining 2 long noodles and 4 short noodle pieces on the top. Spread the remaining meat sauce over the top of the noodles. Sprinkle with the remaining 4 ounces (1 cup) mozzarella cheese and the Parmigiano-Reggiano cheese. Cover with foil coated with cooking spray. Bake at 375°F for 30 minutes. Uncover and bake for an additional 10 minutes or until bubbly.
5. Preheat the broiler to high. (Keep the lasagna in the oven.)
6. Broil the lasagna for 1 to 2 minutes or until the cheese is golden brown

and the sauce is bubbly. Remove from the oven; let stand 10 minutes. Sprinkle with the remaining 2 tablespoons parsley; cut into 6 pieces.

CALORIES 350; FAT 14g (sat 6g, mono 3.3g, poly 0.6g); PROTEIN 25g; CARB 28g; FIBER 2g; SUGARS 7g (est. added sugars 2g); CHOL 89mg; IRON 2mg; SODIUM 625mg; CALCIUM 410mg

serve with:

- 1½ cups chopped romaine lettuce tossed with 2 tablespoons reduced-fat Caesar dressing (44 calories)

1,300-CALORIE PLAN: Toss your salad with ½ ounce plain croutons (58 calories).

1,400-CALORIE PLAN/1,500-CALORIE PLAN: Toss your salad with ½ ounce plain croutons (58 calories) and add 1 small multigrain dinner roll (60 calories).

Beef Flatbread Tacos with Cucumber and Yogurt Sauce

378 TOTAL CALORIES

Hands-on: 18 minutes | Total: 18 minutes | Serves 4 (serving size: 2 tacos)

Ground lamb would be equally delicious in these fun gyro-inspired tacos. If you can't find the flatbreads we call for, you can use corn tortillas instead.

1 (6-ounce) container plain 2% Greek yogurt
1 tablespoon olive oil
¾ teaspoon freshly ground black pepper
¼ teaspoon kosher salt
4 multigrain flatbreads (such as Foldit 5 Grain Flax)
1 English cucumber
12 ounces lean ground beef (90% lean)
1 (14.5-ounce) can unsalted Italian-style diced tomatoes

1. Preheat the broiler to high.
2. Combine the yogurt, olive oil, ¼ teaspoon pepper, and ⅛ teaspoon salt.
3. Cut each flatbread in half at the fold. Broil 1 minute or until toasted, turning after 30 seconds.
4. Cut the cucumber in half lengthwise. Place, cut side down, on a cutting board, and cut into ¼-inch slices.
5. Heat a nonstick skillet over medium-high heat. Add the beef to the pan, stirring to crumble. Add the tomatoes to the pan; cook 6 minutes. Stir in the remaining ½ teaspoon pepper and remaining ⅛ teaspoon salt.
6. Spread 1 tablespoon of the yogurt mixture on each flatbread half; divide the beef mixture among the flatbreads. Top with the cucumber slices and remaining yogurt mixture.

CALORIES 378; FAT 14.8g (sat 4.5g, mono 6.2g, poly 0.7g); PROTEIN 30g; CARB 32g; FIBER 4g; SUGARS 6g (est. added sugars 0g); CHOL 58mg; IRON 4mg; SODIUM 583mg; CALCIUM 103mg

1,300-CALORIE PLAN: Serve with 3 large green olives, sliced (30 calories) and 2 tablespoons crumbled feta cheese (50 calories) on the side or as a taco topping.

1,400-CALORIE PLAN/1,500-CALORIE PLAN: Serve with 3 large green olives, sliced (30 calories) and 2 tablespoons crumbled feta cheese (50 calories) on the side or as a topping. Add 5 baked pita chips, such as Stacy's Simply Naked (65 calories).

423
TOTAL CALORIES

Whole-Grain Mini Meat Loaves

Hands-on: 30 minutes | Total: 45 minutes | Serves 4 (serving size: 2 loaves)

Quinoa and vegetables bulk up meat loaf to a hefty portion; freeze leftover meat loaf for up to 2 months.

1½ teaspoons olive oil
½ cup grated carrot (about 2 ounces)
1½ tablespoons minced fresh garlic
1 tablespoon chopped fresh thyme
½ medium-sized red onion, finely chopped
1 (8-ounce) package sliced cremini mushrooms, finely chopped
½ cup unsalted chicken stock (such as Swanson)
½ teaspoon kosher salt
½ teaspoon freshly ground black pepper
2 demi baguette slices
1½ cups cooked quinoa
1 pound ground sirloin
2 large eggs, lightly beaten
2 ounces goat cheese, crumbled (about ½ cup)
½ cup unsalted ketchup

1. Preheat the oven to 450°F. Line a baking sheet with parchment paper.
2. Heat a large skillet over medium-high heat. Add the oil; swirl to coat. Add the carrot, garlic, thyme, and onion; sauté 3 minutes. Add the mushrooms; sauté 6 minutes. Add the stock, salt, and pepper; bring to a boil. Cook 3 minutes or until the liquid evaporates, stirring frequently. Cool completely.
3. Place the bread in a mini food processor; process until coarse crumbs form. Combine the breadcrumbs, quinoa, beef, and eggs. Stir in the mushroom mixture and cheese. Shape the beef mixture into 8 (4 x 2-inch) free-form loaves; place on prepared baking sheet. Bake at 450°F for 15 minutes or until done. Top each loaf with 1 tablespoon ketchup.

CALORIES 395; FAT 13.5g (sat 5.3g, mono 5.3g, poly 2g); PROTEIN 34g; CARB 36g; FIBER 3g; SUGARS 12g (est. added sugars 7g); CHOL 160mg; IRON 4mg; SODIUM 461mg; CALCIUM 74mg

serve with:

- ½ cup sautéed Brussels sprouts (28 calories)

1,300-CALORIE PLAN: Increase the serving of sautéed Brussels sprouts to 1 cup (56 calories).

1,400-CALORIE PLAN/1,500-CALORIE PLAN: Add ½ cup mashed potatoes (108 calories).

Downsize Your Dishes

Our dinner plates have gotten larger over the years, ballooning up to 11 or 12 inches in diameter. Studies have shown that bigger plates lead to people unconsciously doling out larger portions—22% more. So keep your plates to 10 inches to help keep portion sizes in check.

Mother of 2 Makes Time to Eat Healthy, Shed Baby Weight

AFTER GIVING BIRTH TO HER SECOND CHILD, Kristen Zawitz decided it was time to start setting a good example for her kids. But the 33-year-old Ohio resident still needed a way to decide what healthy meals to eat.

"I was looking to lose some baby weight," Kristen said. "I used to sit down and try to go through cookbooks or *Cooking Light* magazines and pick healthy meals, but it was time consuming and overwhelming because there were so many options. I would just get frustrated or run out of time, so I would only make a couple of recipes. Other times we were filling it in with eating out, and I think that was part of the problem with how we gained weight to begin with."

"We definitely intend to stick with this even after we reach our goal weight... The Cooking Light Diet saves time, and it's helped us lose weight. What's not to love?"

Fortunately for Kristen, the Cooking Light Diet proved to be the answer she and her husband Chris had been looking to find for a long, long time.

"We've kind of yo-yo dieted off and on our whole lives, but we both say that this time it feels different," Kristen said. "I'd joined [other diets] in the past. We've tried just counting calories before. We would get more food, and it didn't taste as good. Obviously if it doesn't taste good, you're not going to keep it up."

Not only have she and her husband kept it up, but both have also managed to lose a significant amount of weight in the process.

"I'm down 25 pounds* now, and my husband is down 28 pounds*," Kristen said. We're definitely eating everything we're making, and the CLDiet really helped us cut back on food waste. I think this meal plan has helped us want to improve our overall health. It takes a couple of weeks to find your rhythm if you're not used to cooking all the time, so just stick with it and you'll find a way to make it work for you. We definitely intend to stick with this even after we reach our goal weight. ...[I mean] The Cooking Light Diet saves time and it's helped us lose weight. What's not to love?"

**Members following The Cooking Light Diet lose more than half a pound per week, on average.*

Sweet and Tangy Glazed Pork Tenderloin with Potato Mash GF

Hands-on: 12 minutes | Total: 35 minutes
Serves 4 (serving size: 3 ounces pork and about ½ cup potatoes)

Using jelly rather than preserves in the glaze helps maintain a smooth texture, but you can use either. Instead of grape, try strawberry, cherry, or red currant.

1 pound small red potatoes
⅓ cup 2% reduced-fat milk
1½ tablespoons butter
¾ teaspoon kosher salt
¾ teaspoon black pepper
2 teaspoons olive oil
1 teaspoon chopped fresh thyme
1 small garlic clove, grated
1 (1-pound) pork tenderloin, trimmed
Cooking spray
2 tablespoons grape jelly
2 tablespoons red wine vinegar
1 tablespoon minced shallots

1. Preheat the oven to 500°F.
2. Place the potatoes in a large saucepan; fill with water to 1 inch above the potatoes. Bring to a boil; cook 10 minutes or until the potatoes are tender. Drain; return to the pan. Mash the potatoes to the desired consistency with a potato masher. Stir in the milk, butter, ¼ teaspoon salt, and ¼ teaspoon pepper.
3. Combine 1 teaspoon of the oil, thyme, garlic, remaining ½ teaspoon salt, and remaining ½ teaspoon pepper; rub the mixture over the pork. Place the pork on a jelly-roll pan coated with cooking spray; bake at 500°F for 10 minutes. Combine the jelly, vinegar, shallots, and remaining 1 teaspoon oil in a small saucepan; bring to a boil. Cook 1 minute, stirring occasionally. Brush half of the jelly mixture over the pork; bake at 500°F for 5 minutes. Turn the pork; brush with the remaining half of the jelly mixture. Bake 5 to 8 minutes or until a thermometer registers 145°F. Place the pork on a cutting board; let stand 5 minutes. Cut across the grain into thin slices. Serve with the mashed potatoes.

CALORIES 327; FAT 9.9g (sat 4.1g, mono 3.9g, poly 0.9g); PROTEIN 27g; CARB 31g; FIBER 2g; SUGARS 9g (est. added sugars 5g); CHOL 87mg; IRON 2mg; SODIUM 482mg; CALCIUM 47mg

serve with:

- 1 serving Sautéed Broccolini, page 202 (73 calories)

1,300-CALORIE PLAN: Add 1 small whole-grain dinner roll (75 calories).
1,400-CALORIE PLAN/1,500-CALORIE PLAN: Add 1 small whole-grain dinner roll (75 calories) and spread with 1 teaspoon butter (34 calories).

375 TOTAL CALORIES

Pork Medallions with Scallions and Magic Green Sauce DF GF LC

Hands-on: 20 minutes | Total: 20 minutes
Serves 4 (serving size: 1 pork chop)

Green onions are used three ways: in a sauce, as a vegetable, and as a garnish. You can make the sauce a day ahead. It magically transforms the simplest food into something spectacular; try it on chicken or steak, too, or as a spread in a sandwich.

1 small jar capers
1 cup packed chopped fresh cilantro (1 bunch)
¼ cup extra-virgin olive oil
1 tablespoon water
2 bunches green onions
4 (4-ounce) boneless center-cut loin pork chops
⅜ teaspoon salt
¼ teaspoon black pepper
16 heirloom cherry tomatoes (red and yellow), halved

1. Spoon 1 tablespoon caper brine and 2 tablespoons drained capers into the bowl of a mini food processor. Add the cilantro, 3 tablespoons oil, and 1 tablespoon water. Chop the green onions to measure 3 tablespoons. Add 3 tablespoons green onions to the cilantro mixture; process until smooth.
2. Cut the remaining onions diagonally into 2-inch pieces. Cut 8 pieces lengthwise into slivers; set aside.
3. Heat a large skillet over medium-high heat. Sprinkle the pork with ¼ teaspoon of the salt and pepper. Add the remaining 1 tablespoon oil to the pan; swirl to coat. Add the pork and 2-inch onion pieces; cover and cook 4 minutes. Turn the pork over. Add the tomatoes; cook 2 minutes. Sprinkle with the remaining ⅛ teaspoon salt. Arrange the pork mixture on a platter. Drizzle with the sauce; sprinkle with the slivered onions.

CALORIES 316; FAT 21.6g (sat 4.8g, mono 13.4g, poly 2.2g); PROTEIN 24g; CARB 7g; FIBER 2g; SUGARS 3g (est. added sugars 0g); CHOL 62mg; IRON 2mg; SODIUM 436mg; CALCIUM 67mg

serve with:

- 1 cup sautéed or roasted zucchini cooked with 1 teaspoon olive oil (59 calories)

1,300-CALORIE PLAN: Add 1 cup mixed greens (9 calories) tossed with 2 tablespoons reduced-fat dressing (45 calories).
1,400-CALORIE PLAN/1,500-CALORIE PLAN: Add 1½ cups mixed greens (14 calories), 1 tablespoon toasted pecans (47 calories), and 2 tablespoons reduced-fat dressing (45 calories).

Staying-on-Track Strategies

DELAY GRATIFICATION

When a craving hits, slip your mind into rational gear by saying, "not now, maybe tomorrow." Saying "later" rather than "never" may help decrease the frequency of cravings.

KEEP IT REAL

Eating an apple isn't likely to satisfy a yen for chocolate. Instead, enjoy what you really want in moderation.

EAT REGULARLY

Waiting too long between meals can turn normal hunger pangs into an out-of-control craving. Keep healthful options—energy bars, fat-free milk, even a peanut butter and jelly sandwich—on hand to keep hunger in check.

Roasted Pork Chops with Cabbage and Carrots GF

Hands-on: 18 minutes | Total: 30 minutes
Serves 4 (serving size: 1 pork chop, ¾ cup cabbage mixture, and 1½ tablespoons sauce)

This is a classic combination of German flavors with apple, caraway, and cabbage paired with pork. The same pan is used to prepare this meal from start to finish so cleanup is easy.

4 (6-ounce) bone-in, center-cut pork chops
¾ teaspoon kosher salt
¾ teaspoon black pepper
1 tablespoon unsalted butter
2 cups chopped green and red cabbage
1½ cups diagonally sliced carrots
½ teaspoon caraway seeds
⅓ cup unsalted chicken stock (such as Swanson)
4 tablespoons apple cider vinegar
3 tablespoons apple jelly
2 tablespoons olive oil

1. Preheat the oven to 400°F. Sprinkle the pork chops with ½ teaspoon each of the salt and pepper. Melt the butter in a large ovenproof skillet over medium-high. Add the pork chops; cook to the desired degree of doneness, about 4 minutes per side. Remove from the pan; cover to keep warm.
2. Add the cabbage, carrots, caraway seeds, and remaining ¼ teaspoon each salt and pepper to the pan. Stir in the stock, scraping the bottom of the pan to loosen any browned bits. Return the pork chops to the pan. Cover and transfer the pan to the oven. Bake at 400°F until the carrots are tender, about 12 minutes.
3. Remove the cabbage mixture from the pan; cover to keep warm. Add the vinegar, jelly, and oil to the pan; bring to a boil over medium-high heat. Cook, whisking often, until slightly reduced and smooth, about 3 minutes. Divide the pork chops and cabbage mixture among 4 plates. Drizzle with the vinegar mixture.

CALORIES 310; FAT 16g (sat 4.6g, mono 7.9g, poly 1.6g); PROTEIN 24g; CARB 17g; FIBER 2g; SUGARS 12g (est. added sugars 9g); CHOL 78mg; IRON 1mg; SODIUM 459mg; CALCIUM 57mg

serve with:

- ½ cup cooked wild rice (83 calories)

1,300-CALORIE PLAN: Add 1 kiwifruit (42 calories).
1,400-CALORIE PLAN/1,500-CALORIE PLAN: Increase the serving of wild rice to 1 cup (166 calories) and add 1 kiwifruit (42 calories).

Pork Chops with Balsamic Roasted Vegetables GF LC

Hands-on: 20 minutes | Total: 55 minutes
Serves 4 (serving size: 1 cup vegetable mixture, 1 pork chop, 2 teaspoons balsamic vinegar mixture, 1½ teaspoons parsley, and 1 tablespoon Gorgonzola cheese)

4 (4-ounce) boneless center-cut loin pork chops
½ teaspoon kosher salt
¾ teaspoon black pepper
¼ cup extra-virgin olive oil
12 ounces small red potatoes, halved
3 tablespoons balsamic vinegar
1 teaspoon tomato paste
1 tablespoon chopped fresh thyme
1 medium-sized red onion, peeled and cut into 8 wedges
1 (8-ounce) package cremini mushrooms, halved
2 tablespoons chopped fresh flat-leaf parsley
1 ounce Gorgonzola cheese, crumbled (about ¼ cup)

1. Preheat the oven to 425°F.
2. Heat a large heavy roasting pan over high heat. Sprinkle the pork with ¼ teaspoon each of the salt pepper. Add 2 tablespoons of the oil to the pan; swirl to coat. Add the pork to the pan; cook 3 minutes on each side or until browned. Place the pork on a plate (pork will not be cooked through). Reduce the heat to medium-high. Add the potatoes to the pan, cut sides down; cook 2 minutes. Remove the pan from the heat.
3. Combine the vinegar, tomato paste, remaining ½ teaspoon pepper, and remaining 2 tablespoons oil in a bowl, stirring with a whisk. Combine 2 tablespoons balsamic mixture, thyme, onion, and mushrooms in a bowl, tossing to coat. Add mushroom mixture to the pan. Bake at 425°F for 25 minutes, stirring after 10 minutes. Arrange pork chops over the vegetables; bake 10 minutes or until a thermometer registers 145°F. Remove the pork from the pan. Sprinkle vegetable mixture with remaining ¼ teaspoon salt. Divide vegetable mixture among 4 plates. Top each serving with pork chops, remaining balsamic vinegar mixture, parsley, and Gorgonzola cheese.

CALORIES 385; FAT 21.7g (sat 5.2g, mono 12g, poly 2.2g); PROTEIN 27g; CARB 21g; FIBER 3g; SUGARS 5g (est. added sugars 0g); CHOL 73mg; IRON 2mg; SODIUM 415mg; CALCIUM 83mg

1,300-CALORIE PLAN: Serve with ½ cup Braised Brussels Sprouts with Mustard and Thyme, page 202 (93 calories).
1,400-CALORIE PLAN/1,500-CALORIE PLAN: Increase the serving of Braised Brussels Sprouts with Mustard and Thyme to ¾ cup (140 calories).

Double-Duty Sauces

In this recipe, the balsamic vinaigrette doubles as a marinade for the vegetables and a sauce for the pork. If you plan to marinate meat, poultry, or seafood first and then use the leftover mixture as a sauce, it's important to bring the mixture to a boil to kill any bacteria that might have been transferred from the raw meat. Just place the marinade in a saucepan, bring it to a boil, and boil for at least 1 minute.

One-Pan Broccoli-Bacon Mac 'n' Cheese

Hands-on: 25 minutes | Total: 25 minutes
Serves 6 (serving size: about 1⅓ cups)

Butternut squash puree enhances the color here without distracting from the cheesy flavor, and it sneaks in another serving of vegetables. If you can't find frozen butternut puree, swap in an equal amount of mashed sweet potato or canned unsweetened pumpkin.

2 slices center-cut bacon, chopped
3 garlic cloves, minced
2 cups unsalted chicken stock (such as Swanson)
1 cup 1% low-fat milk
1 (10-ounce) package frozen butternut squash puree, thawed
10 ounces uncooked large elbow macaroni
3 cups chopped broccoli florets
½ teaspoon salt
½ teaspoon freshly ground black pepper
5 ounces sharp cheddar cheese, shredded (about 1¼ cups)

1. Heat a large skillet over medium-high heat. Add the bacon; cook 4 minutes or until crisp, stirring occasionally. Remove the bacon from the pan.
2. Remove all but 2 teaspoons of the bacon drippings from the pan. Add the garlic to the drippings in the pan; sauté 30 seconds. Add the stock, milk, and squash to the pan; bring to a boil, stirring occasionally. Add the pasta; cover, reduce the heat, and simmer 5 minutes, stirring occasionally. Stir in the broccoli; cover and cook 3 minutes or until the pasta is done and the sauce is thickened. Stir in the salt, pepper, and 4 ounces of the cheese. Sprinkle the bacon and the remaining 1 ounce cheese on top. Cover; let stand 1 minute.

CALORIES 339; FAT 10g (sat 5.7g, mono 2.8g, poly 0.7g); PROTEIN 18g; CARB 45g; FIBER 4g; SUGARS 5g (est. added sugars 0g); CHOL 29mg; IRON 3mg; SODIUM 566mg; CALCIUM 267mg

serve with:

• 1 cup Orange and Almond Salad, page 203 (60 calories)

1,300-CALORIE PLAN: Increase the serving of Orange and Almond Salad to 1½ cups (90 calories) and add 1 small plum or half a small apple (30 calories).
1,400-CALORIE PLAN/1,500-CALORIE PLAN: Increase the serving of Orange and Almond Salad to 1½ cups (90 calories) and add 1 small apple (60 calories).

412
TOTAL CALORIES

Mushroom and Bacon Casserole

Hands-on: 35 minutes | Total: 65 minutes
Serves 8 (serving size: about 1 cup)

Very few things embody comfort food like this hearty, warming casserole with the familiar flavors of bacon and cheese.

4 cups unsalted beef stock (such as Swanson)
3 cups water
8 slices center-cut bacon, chopped
1 cup chopped onion
1 tablespoon chopped fresh thyme
6 garlic cloves, minced
8 ounces sliced cremini mushrooms
8 ounces sliced shiitake mushroom caps
½ teaspoon kosher salt
2 cups uncooked pearl barley
⅓ cup Madeira wine
4 ounces Gruyère cheese, shredded (about 1 cup)
½ cup chopped drained oil-packed sun-dried tomato halves
2 teaspoons lower-sodium soy sauce
¼ teaspoon freshly ground black pepper
1 (10-ounce) package frozen chopped spinach, thawed, drained, and squeezed dry
Cooking spray

1. Preheat the oven to 375°F.
2. Bring the stock and 3 cups water to a simmer in a large saucepan (do not boil). Keep the mixture warm.
3. Cook the bacon in a Dutch oven over medium-high heat until crisp. Remove the bacon from the pan, reserving 1 tablespoon drippings in the pan; set the bacon aside.
4. Return the pan to medium-high heat. Add the onion, thyme, and garlic to the drippings in the pan; sauté 3 minutes or until tender. Add the mushrooms and salt; cook 10 minutes or until browned, stirring occasionally. Stir in the barley; cook 1 minute, stirring frequently. Add the Madeira; cook 1 minute or until the liquid is absorbed. Reduce the heat to medium. Stir in 2 cups of the broth mixture; cook 4 minutes or until the liquid is nearly absorbed, stirring frequently. Add the remaining broth mixture, 1 cup at a time, stirring frequently until each portion of the broth mixture is absorbed before adding the next (about 30 minutes total). Stir in 2 ounces Gruyère, tomatoes, soy sauce, pepper, spinach, and bacon.
5. Place the barley mixture in a 2-quart glass or ceramic baking dish coated with cooking spray; sprinkle with the remaining 2 ounces cheese. Cover with aluminum foil coated with cooking spray. Bake at 375°F for 15 minutes. Remove the foil, and bake 10 minutes or until the cheese melts. Let stand 5 minutes.

Give In

Given the universal nature of food cravings, experts agree that if you rarely enjoy a food you crave, you're more likely to go overboard when you finally do give in. The key to successful weight management, experts say, is learning to address cravings rather than to always deny them. A Tufts University study found people who occasionally give in to hankerings manage their weight most successfully.

CALORIES 352; FAT 10.2g (sat 4.3g, mono 2.8g, poly 1g); PROTEIN 16g; CARB 49g; FIBER 10g; SUGARS 5g (est. added sugars 1g); CHOL 24mg; IRON 3mg; SODIUM 435mg; CALCIUM 220mg

serve with:

- 1 small whole-wheat dinner roll (60 calories)

1,300-CALORIE PLAN: Add 1 cup steamed or roasted broccoli (55 calories).

1,400-CALORIE PLAN/1,500-CALORIE PLAN: Add 1 cup steamed or roasted broccoli (55 calories) and drizzle your dinner roll with 1 teaspoon olive oil (40 calories).

Chicken Parmesan with Zucchini Noodles LC

Hands-on: 25 minutes | Total: 1 hour, 15 minutes
Serves 4 (serving size: ¾ cup zucchini noodles and 1 chicken cutlet)

A julienne peeler creates lovely "zoodles," but may we suggest a spiralizer? It works like a pencil sharpener, turning veggies into noodles. (Look for them at kitchen stores and amazon.com.)

2 tablespoons olive oil
1 tablespoon chopped fresh thyme
6 garlic cloves, thinly sliced
1 shallot, thinly sliced
1 pound heirloom tomatoes, chopped
½ cup dry white wine
½ teaspoon kosher salt
½ teaspoon freshly ground black pepper
3 tablespoons 2% Greek yogurt
1 ounce grated Parmesan cheese (about ¼ cup)
4 (4-ounce) skinless, boneless chicken breast cutlets
½ cup whole-wheat panko (Japanese breadcrumbs)
1 teaspoon garlic powder
Cooking spray
4 medium zucchini
2 ounces fresh mozzarella cheese, very thinly sliced
½ cup torn basil leaves

1. Preheat the oven to 425°F.
2. Heat a large skillet over medium heat. Add 1 tablespoon oil to the pan; swirl to coat. Add the thyme, 4 garlic cloves, and shallots; cook 2 minutes. Add the tomatoes, wine, ¼ teaspoon salt, and pepper; cook 8 minutes or until the liquid is reduced by half.
3. Combine the yogurt and Parmesan; spread over both sides of the cutlets. Combine the panko and garlic powder. Dredge the cutlets in the panko mixture. Place the cutlets on a wire rack coated with cooking spray. Place the rack on a baking sheet. Bake at 425°F for 12 minutes or until done.
4. Using a julienne peeler, peel the zucchini lengthwise into strips, stopping at the inside part containing the seeds; discard seeds.
5. Preheat the broiler to high. Top each cutlet with 2 tablespoons of the sauce; top the sauce evenly with the mozzarella. Broil 2 minutes or until the cheese is bubbly.
6. Heat a large nonstick skillet over medium-high heat. Add the remaining 1 tablespoon oil to the pan; swirl to coat. Add the remaining 2 garlic cloves; cook 1 minute. Add the zucchini; cook 2 minutes. Remove from the heat. Toss with the remaining sauce, remaining ¼ teaspoon salt, and half of the basil.

7. Arrange the zucchini noodles on each of 4 plates. Serve with the chicken cutlets; sprinkle with the remaining half of the basil.

CALORIES 400; FAT 16.6g (sat 5.1g, mono 6.5g, poly 1.6g); PROTEIN 36g; CARB 23g; FIBER 5g; SUGARS 9g (est. added sugars 0g); CHOL 91mg; IRON 3mg; SODIUM 529mg; CALCIUM 163mg

1300-CALORIE PLAN: To keep this meal low carb, serve it with 1 cup roasted broccoli (55 calories).

1400-CALORIE PLAN/1500-CALORIE PLAN: Serve with 1 cup roasted broccoli topped with 1 tablespoon grated Parmesan cheese (77 calories).

Baked Chicken Moussaka GF

Hands-on: 20 minutes | Total: 32 minutes | Serves 4 (serving size: 1¾ cups)

1 tablespoon olive oil
10 ounces ground chicken
2 cups cubed eggplant
1 cup chopped red bell pepper
½ cup chopped yellow onion
1 tablespoon chopped fresh thyme
1 tablespoon finely chopped garlic
1 cup canned unsalted white beans, rinsed, drained, and slightly mashed
1 cup chopped tomato (about 1 medium tomato)
1 cup unsalted tomato sauce (such as Muir Glen)
¼ cup unsalted chicken stock (such as Swanson)
1¼ teaspoons kosher salt
1 teaspoon freshly ground black pepper
¾ cup plain low-fat Greek yogurt
2 large eggs, lightly beaten
¼ cup chopped fresh flat-leaf parsley
2 tablespoons toasted pine nuts

1. Preheat the oven to 400°F. Heat a large skillet over medium-high heat. Add the oil to the pan; swirl to coat. Add the chicken; cook, stirring often, until browned, about 5 minutes. Add the eggplant, bell pepper, onion, thyme, and garlic. Cook, stirring often, until the vegetables are tender and beginning to brown, about 6 minutes. Add the beans, tomato, tomato sauce, stock, salt, and black pepper; bring to a simmer. Reduce the heat to medium; simmer, stirring occasionally, 5 minutes. Transfer the mixture to an 8-inch square glass or ceramic baking dish.
2. Stir together the yogurt and eggs in a bowl. Pour the mixture over the chicken mixture. (The yogurt mixture will not fully cover the chicken mixture; you still want to see vegetables poking through.) Bake at 400°F until the yogurt mixture is set and the liquid is bubbling, 12 to 14 minutes. Sprinkle with the parsley and pine nuts.

CALORIES 339; FAT 16.2g (sat 3.7g, mono 7g, poly 3.5g); PROTEIN 26g; CARB 25g; FIBER 7g; SUGARS 10g (est. added sugars 0g); CHOL 157mg; IRON 4mg; SODIUM 735mg; CALCIUM 105mg

serve with:

- 1 cup chopped romaine, ¼ cup cherry tomatoes, 1 tablespoon chopped kalamata olives, and 1 tablespoon light olive oil vinaigrette (58 calories)

1,300-CALORIE PLAN: Top your salad with 2 tablespoons crumbled feta cheese (50 calories).
1,400-CALORIE PLAN/1,500-CALORIE PLAN: Top your salad with 2 tablespoons crumbled feta cheese (50 calories) and serve with half of a warm 6-inch pita (80 calories).

397 TOTAL CALORIES

Moussaka

This Greek dish is similiar to lasagna, but it's traditionally layered with eggplant, tomatoes, ground beef or lamb, and a rich béchamel sauce. In this lightened recipe, we opted for ground chicken, using a mix of light and dark meat for added richness. Browning the chicken well is important here, since most of the rich, meaty flavor is going to come from that step. Don't be tempted to rush it.

Skillet Chicken and Couscous with Pomegranate Sauce DF

Hands-on: 22 minutes | Total: 22 minutes
Serves 4 (serving size: about 5 ounces chicken, ¼ of the couscous mixture, and 2 tablespoons sauce)

The pomegranate sauce contributes to a sweet-and-sour flavor with the balsamic vinegar. Using rotisserie chicken helps speed up prep and cook time.

3 (7-ounce) boneless, skinless chicken breasts halves
1 teaspoon kosher salt
1 teaspoon black pepper
2 tablespoons olive oil
¼ cup pomegranate juice
2 tablespoons balsamic vinegar
1½ teaspoons granulated sugar
1 cup unsalted chicken stock (such as Swanson)
10 ounces fresh baby spinach
½ cup uncooked couscous
½ cup sliced red onion
¼ cup pomegranate arils
3 tablespoons chopped fresh flat-leaf parsley

1. Sprinkle the chicken with ½ teaspoon each of the salt and pepper. Heat a large skillet over medium-high heat. Add the oil to the pan; swirl to coat. Add the chicken to the pan; cook until a meat thermometer inserted in the thickest portion registers 160°F, 5 to 6 minutes per side. Remove the chicken from the pan. Add the pomegranate juice, vinegar, sugar, and ¼ cup of the stock to the pan; bring to a boil. Cook until syrupy and reduced by half, about 1 minute and 30 seconds, scraping to loosen any browned bits from the bottom of the pan. Add ½ cup of the stock; cook, stirring occasionally, until slightly syrupy, about 3 minutes.
2. Heat the remaining ¼ cup stock in a medium saucepan over medium heat. Stir in the spinach, couscous, and onion; cover and cook until the spinach is wilted and the couscous is done, about 5 minutes. Stir in the remaining ½ teaspoon each salt and pepper.
3. Cut the chicken into bite-sized pieces. Divide the chicken and couscous mixture among 4 bowls. Drizzle the sauce over the mixture. Sprinkle with the pomegranate arils and parsley.

CALORIES 410; FAT 13.2g (sat 2g, mono 6.4g, poly 3.1g); PROTEIN 38g; CARB 35g; FIBER 5g; SUGARS 6g (est. added sugars 3g); CHOL 95mg; IRON 4mg; SODIUM 806mg; CALCIUM 85mg

1,300-CALORIE PLAN: Serve with 1 (½-ounce) slice whole-grain bread (40 calories).

1,400-CALORIE PLAN/1,500-CALORIE PLAN: Serve with 1 (1-ounce) slice whole-grain bread (80 calories).

Fast Skillet Chicken Cacciatore DF GF

Hands-on: 13 minutes | Total: 28 minutes
Serves 4 (serving size: 1 chicken breast half and about 1 cup sauce)

Lean chicken breasts cook quickly—in just 15 minutes compared to the hour-long braise in most cacciatore recipes. If you'd like more heat in the sauce, kick up the crushed red pepper to ½ teaspoon.

1½ tablespoons olive oil
1½ teaspoons finely chopped fresh rosemary
1 teaspoon finely chopped garlic
¼ teaspoon kosher salt
¼ teaspoon freshly ground black pepper
4 (6-ounce) skinless, boneless chicken breast halves
Cooking spray
1 cup thinly sliced onion
1 cup thinly sliced red bell pepper
½ cup thinly sliced green bell pepper
1 (8-ounce) package presliced cremini mushrooms
½ cup dry red wine (such as Chianti)
½ cup coarsely chopped fresh basil
¼ teaspoon crushed red pepper
1 (15-ounce) can crushed tomatoes

1. Combine 1½ teaspoons oil, rosemary, garlic, salt, and black pepper in a small bowl, stirring with a whisk. Rub the oil mixture over the chicken. Heat a large skillet over medium-high heat. Coat the pan with cooking spray. Add the chicken to the pan; cook 2 minutes on each side (chicken will not be cooked through). Remove the chicken from the pan.
2. Add the remaining 1 tablespoon oil to the pan; swirl to coat. Add the onion, bell peppers, and mushrooms; cook 4 minutes, stirring occasionally. Add the wine; cook 1 minute or until the liquid is reduced by half. Stir in ¼ cup of the basil, crushed red pepper, and tomatoes; cook 1 minute. Return the chicken to the pan; turn to coat. Reduce the heat; cover and simmer 15 minutes or until the chicken is done. Sprinkle with the remaining ¼ cup basil.

CALORIES 337; FAT 10.3g (sat 1.8g, mono 5.1g, poly 1.5g); PROTEIN 41g; CARB 16g; FIBER 4g; SUGARS 9g (est. added sugars 0g); CHOL 109mg; IRON 3mg; SODIUM 465mg; CALCIUM 71mg

serve with:

- 1 serving Parmesan Polenta Rounds, page 202 (90 calories)

1,300-CALORIE PLAN: Add ½ cup grapes (52 calories).
1,400-CALORIE PLAN/1,500-CALORIE PLAN: Add ¾ cup grapes (78 calories).

Know Your Cues

Are you aware of what prompts you to eat? In addition to hunger, you may be eating in response to emotions such as frustration, boredom, stress, worry, or many other things. Keep a food diary that lists not only when and what you eat—but also how you feel as you're starting your meal. You may discover that it's an emotional cue that's pulling you to the table.

Weeknight Lemon Chicken Skillet Dinner

Hands-on: 20 minutes | Total: 30 minutes
Serves 4 (serving size: 1 chicken breast half and ¾ cup potato mixture)

12 ounces baby red potatoes, halved
1 tablespoon olive oil
4 (6-ounce) skinless, boneless chicken breast halves, pounded to ¾-inch thickness
¾ teaspoon kosher salt
½ teaspoon black pepper
2 thyme sprigs
4 ounces cremini mushrooms, quartered
1 tablespoon chopped fresh thyme
¼ cup whole milk
5 teaspoons all-purpose flour
1¾ cups unsalted chicken stock (such as Swanson)
8 very thin lemon slices
1 (8-ounce) package trimmed haricots verts
2 tablespoons chopped fresh flat-leaf parsley

1. Preheat the oven to 450°F.
2. Place the potatoes in a medium saucepan; cover with water. Bring to a boil, and simmer 12 minutes or until tender. Drain.
3. Heat a large ovenproof skillet over medium-high heat. Add 1 teaspoon oil to the pan; swirl to coat. Sprinkle chicken with ¼ teaspoon each of salt and pepper. Add chicken and thyme sprigs to pan; cook 5 minutes or until the chicken is browned. Turn chicken over. Place the pan in the oven; bake at 450°F for 10 minutes or until chicken is done. Remove chicken from pan.
4. Return pan to medium-high heat. Add remaining 2 teaspoons oil to the pan; swirl. Add potatoes, cut sides down; mushrooms; and 1 tablespoon thyme. Cook 3 minutes or until browned, stirring once. Combine milk and flour in a bowl, stirring with a whisk. Add flour mixture, stock, lemon, beans, remaining ½ teaspoon salt, and remaining ¼ teaspoon pepper to pan; simmer 1 minute or until slightly thickened. Add chicken; cover, reduce heat, and simmer 3 minutes or until beans are crisp-tender. Sprinkle with parsley.

CALORIES 342; FAT 8.6g (sat 1.8g, mono 3.9g, poly 1.2g); PROTEIN 43g; CARB 23g; FIBER 4g; SUGARS 4g (est. added sugars 0g); CHOL 110mg; IRON 3mg; SODIUM 642mg; CALCIUM 77mg

serve with:

- 1 small whole-grain dinner roll (60 calories)

1,300-CALORIE PLAN: Spread the roll with 1 teaspoon butter (34 calories).
1,400-CALORIE PLAN/1,500-CALORIE PLAN: Serve with 1 (5-ounce) glass wine (116 calories).

Pounding Chicken Breasts

Pounded chicken cooks more evenly and quickly in the pan. Place the chicken breasts between two sheets of plastic wrap or in a zip-top plastic bag and pound them to an even thinness using a meat mallet or heavy skillet.

Chicken Thighs with Cilantro Sauce DF GF

Hands-on: 20 minutes | Total: 20 minutes
Serves 4 (serving size: 2 thighs and 1 tablespoon sauce)

As a variation, you could grill the chicken thighs—a little charring would complement the sauce. No mortar and pestle? Process the paste base in a mini chopper.

Cooking spray
8 skinless, boneless chicken thighs (about 2 pounds)
½ teaspoon kosher salt
2 tablespoons finely chopped shallots
1 large garlic clove, minced
⅓ cup finely chopped fresh cilantro
1½ tablespoons dark sesame oil
1 tablespoon lower-sodium soy sauce
½ teaspoon Sriracha (hot chile sauce)
½ teaspoon grated lime rind

1. Heat a large skillet over medium-high heat. Coat the pan with cooking spray. Sprinkle the chicken with ¼ teaspoon of the salt. Add the chicken to the pan; sauté 6 minutes or until browned. Turn; sauté 4 minutes or until the chicken is done. Place the chicken on a platter; keep warm.
2. Combine the shallots, garlic, and remaining ¼ teaspoon salt in a mortar and pestle; smash the mixture to a paste. Combine the garlic mixture, cilantro, and remaining ingredients. Spread 1½ teaspoons cilantro mixture over each chicken thigh.

CALORIES 260; FAT 14.8g (sat 3.4g, mono 6g, poly 4.1g); PROTEIN 29g; CARB 2g; FIBER 0g; SUGARS 1g (est. added sugars 0g); CHOL 159mg; IRON 1mg; SODIUM 489mg; CALCIUM 16mg

serve with:

- 1 cup stir-fried or roasted broccoli (55 calories)
- ½ cup roasted potatoes (70 calories)

1,300-CALORIE PLAN: Increase the serving of potatoes to ¾ cup (105 calories).

1,400-CALORIE PLAN/1,500-CALORIE PLAN: Serve with 1 (5-ounce) glass wine (116 calories).

Enjoy Exercise More

If exercise is something you struggle with, you may want to try mixing what you like with what you loathe. Find an activity you can't live without, such as talking on the phone, watching your favorite show, or shopping or surfing online, and then only allow yourself to do it as you exercise—or immediately afterwards. Spending 20 minutes exercising will go by a lot faster when your mind is distracted by something you enjoy.

Quick Chicken Piccata GF LC

Hands-on: 20 minutes | Total: 20 minutes
Serves 4 (serving size: 2 chicken thighs and about ¼ cup sauce)

Chicken piccata is typically made with sliced chicken breasts, but we find chicken "thighcatta" to be even more flavorful.

8 skinless, boneless chicken thighs (about 1½ pounds)
½ teaspoon kosher salt
½ teaspoon freshly ground black pepper
3 tablespoons olive oil
½ cup dry white wine
2 tablespoons capers, drained
4 garlic cloves, crushed
1 thyme sprig
¾ cup unsalted chicken stock (such as Swanson)
1½ tablespoons fresh lemon juice
1 tablespoon unsalted butter
2 tablespoons chopped fresh flat-leaf parsley

Sprinkle the chicken with ¼ teaspoon of the salt and ½ teaspoon pepper. Heat a skillet over medium-high heat. Add 1 tablespoon of the oil to the pan; swirl to coat. Add the chicken to the pan; cook 5 minutes. Turn the chicken over. Add the wine, capers, garlic, and thyme to the pan; cook 2 minutes. Add the stock, remaining ¼ teaspoon salt, and remaining 2 tablespoons oil to the pan; bring to a boil. Reduce the heat to medium; cook 8 minutes. Remove the pan from the heat. Stir in the lemon juice and butter. Sprinkle with the parsley.

CALORIES 360; FAT 22.8g (sat 5.9g, mono 12.1g, poly 3.1g); PROTEIN 30g; CARB 3g; FIBER 0g; SUGARS 1g (est. added sugars 0g); CHOL 166mg; IRON 2mg; SODIUM 498mg; CALCIUM 31mg

serve with:

- 1 cup roasted or steamed asparagus, about 10 medium spears (30 calories)

1,300-CALORIE PLAN: Add ½ cup couscous (88 calories).
1,400-CALORIE PLAN/1,500-CALORIE PLAN: Add ⅔ cup couscous (118 calories).

Roasted Chicken Thighs with Brussels Sprouts GF LC

Hands-on: 15 minutes | Total: 45 minutes
Serves 4 (serving size: 1 chicken thigh, 1 cup Brussels sprouts, and 2 tablespoons sauce)

1 tablespoon olive oil
1 tablespoon minced fresh garlic
2 teaspoons chopped fresh thyme
½ teaspoon kosher salt
½ teaspoon black pepper
4 (6-ounce) bone-in chicken thighs
1 lemon, cut into wedges
¼ cup dry white wine
2 teaspoons butter
¼ cup thinly sliced onion
1 pound Brussels sprouts, halved
⅓ cup unsalted chicken stock

1. Preheat oven to 425°F. Combine 1 teaspoon oil, garlic, 1 teaspoon thyme, and ¼ teaspoon each of the salt and pepper. Loosen skin on the thighs by inserting your fingers, gently pushing between skin and meat. Rub garlic mixture under loosened skin. Heat a large ovenproof skillet over medium-high heat. Add 1 teaspoon oil; swirl to coat. Add chicken to the pan, skin sides down; cook 4 minutes. Turn chicken over; top with lemon wedges. Place pan in oven; bake at 425°F for 18 minutes or until done. Remove chicken and lemon from pan; discard lemon. Discard drippings (do not wipe out pan). Return pan to medium-high heat. Add wine; cook 2 minutes, scraping pan to loosen browned bits. Remove from heat; add butter, swirling until melted.
2. Heat a large skillet over medium-high heat. Add remaining 1 teaspoon oil; swirl. Add onion; sauté 1 minute. Add Brussels sprouts, remaining ¼ teaspoon salt, and remaining ¼ teaspoon pepper; cook 8 minutes or until crisp-tender. Add stock; cover and cook 2 minutes. Serve chicken with Brussels sprouts and sauce. Sprinkle servings with remaining 1 teaspoon thyme.

CALORIES 343; FAT 20.4g (sat 5.8g, mono 9.2g, poly 3.5g); PROTEIN 27g; CARB 13g; FIBER 5g; SUGARS 3g (est. added sugars 0g); CHOL 140mg; IRON 23mg; SODIUM 420mg; CALCIUM 72mg

serve with:

- 1½ cups spinach and 2 tablespoons reduced-fat dressing (59 calories)

1,300-CALORIE PLAN: Add 2 tablespoons sliced toasted almonds to your salad (66 calories).

1,400-CALORIE PLAN/1,500-CALORIE PLAN: If you're following a low-carb diet, add 2 tablespoons sliced toasted almonds and 1 tablespoon grated Parmesan to your salad (88 calories). If not, you can serve this with ½ cup hot cooked brown rice (109 calories).

Chicken Thighs

Thighs have a deeper, meatier flavor than chicken breasts. The little bit of extra fat they contain keeps them wonderfully moist and juicy. Why is dark meat dark? Muscles that move more get more oxygen flow and are darker and richer in nutrients (a reason ducks have no white meat). Chickens don't fly—they use their legs and thighs to get around—which makes these parts darker than the breast and wings.

Ginger-Soy Chicken Thighs with Scallion Rice DF

Hands-on: 18 minutes | Total: 18 minutes
Serves: 4 (serving size: 2 thighs, about ½ cup rice, and about 1½ tablespoons sauce)

If you can't find ginger preserves, you can substitute ½ cup apricot preserves plus 2 teaspoons grated peeled fresh ginger.

1 (3½-ounce) bag boil-in-bag long-grain rice
2 tablespoons thinly sliced green onions
1 tablespoon olive oil
8 (2-ounce) skinless, boneless chicken thighs
½ cup ginger preserves
2 tablespoons lower-sodium soy sauce
2 garlic cloves, minced

1. Prepare the rice according to the package directions. Drain; fluff the rice with a fork. Gently stir in the green onions.
2. While the rice cooks, heat a large skillet over medium-high heat. Add the oil to the pan; swirl to coat. Add the chicken; cook 5 minutes on each side or until done. Remove from the pan; keep warm. Add the preserves, soy sauce, and garlic to the pan; bring to a boil. Cook the sauce 2 minutes or until reduced to ⅓ cup, stirring occasionally. Return the chicken to the pan; turn to coat with the sauce. Serve the rice with the chicken.

CALORIES 355; FAT 7.8g (sat 1.6g, mono 3.8g, poly 1.5g); PROTEIN 25g; CARB 47g; FIBER 0g; SUGARS 26g (est. added sugars 26g); CHOL 94mg; IRON 2mg; SODIUM 366mg; CALCIUM 18mg

serve with:

- ½ cup Cucumber-Peanut Salad, page 203 (52 calories)

1,300-CALORIE PLAN: Add ½ cup fresh mango slices (50 calories).
1,400-CALORIE PLAN/1,500-CALORIE PLAN: Add 1 cup fresh mango slices (100 calories).

It's OK to Fidget

One study showed that fidgeters may burn several hundred extra calories a day, simply by shifting in their chairs, bouncing their legs, and doing random movements throughout the day. You can use this to your advantage. To relax, take a stroll instead of curling up with a book. When watching TV, clean the room or fold laundry during the commercials. If you have a desk job, stand up and move around at least twice each hour. Or modify your desk with a standing desk option that allows you to switch back and forth from sitting to standing.

Cauliflower Grits with Barbecue Rotisserie Chicken GF LC

Hands-on: 23 minutes | Total: 23 minutes | Serves 4 (serving size: ¾ cup grits, ¾ cup chicken mixture, and about 1 tablespoon green onions)

Don't rush processing the cauliflower; it's key to get it to the consistency of grits.

12 ounces cauliflower florets
1 cup unsalted chicken stock
½ cup coarsely ground cornmeal
3 ounces sharp cheddar cheese, shredded (about ¾ cup)
½ teaspoon black pepper
⅛ teaspoon kosher salt
½ cup unsalted tomato sauce
3 tablespoons water
2 tablespoons yellow mustard
1 tablespoon unsalted ketchup
¾ teaspoon garlic powder
½ teaspoon chipotle chile powder
½ teaspoon onion powder
6 ounces shredded rotisserie chicken breast
6 ounces shredded rotisserie chicken thigh
¼ cup sliced green onions

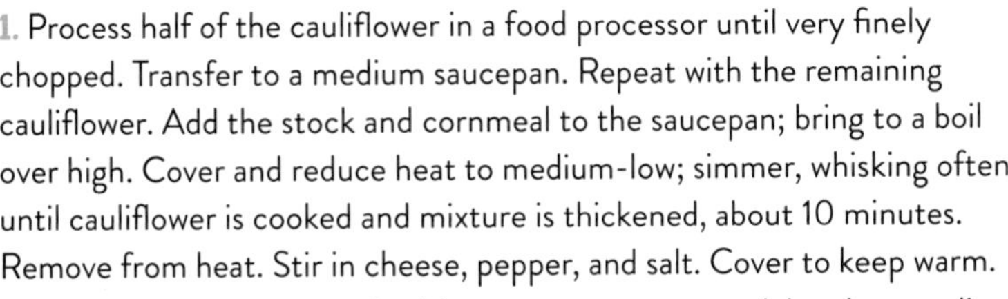

1. Process half of the cauliflower in a food processor until very finely chopped. Transfer to a medium saucepan. Repeat with the remaining cauliflower. Add the stock and cornmeal to the saucepan; bring to a boil over high. Cover and reduce heat to medium-low; simmer, whisking often, until cauliflower is cooked and mixture is thickened, about 10 minutes. Remove from heat. Stir in cheese, pepper, and salt. Cover to keep warm.
2. Combine tomato sauce, 3 tablespoons water, mustard, ketchup, garlic powder, chile powder, and onion powder in a small saucepan. Bring to a simmer over medium heat. Simmer, stirring often, until slightly thickened, about 6 minutes. Stir in the shredded chicken. Divide cauliflower mixture among 4 bowls. Top with chicken mixture. Sprinkle with green onions.

CALORIES 347; FAT 15g (sat 6.3g, mono 3g, poly 1.3g); PROTEIN 32g; CARB 22g; FIBER 4g; SUGARS 4g (est. added sugars 1g); CHOL 116mg; IRON 2mg; SODIUM 650mg; CALCIUM 204mg

serve with:

- 1½ cups mixed greens tossed with 1½ tablespoons light vinaigrette (53 calories)

1,300-CALORIE PLAN: Add ¼ cup fresh orange sections and 1 tablespoon chopped toasted walnuts to your salad (66 calories).
1,400-CALORIE PLAN/1,500-CALORIE PLAN: Add ¼ cup fresh orange sections, 1 tablespoon toasted chopped walnuts, and 1 tablespoon Gorgonzola cheese to your salad (91 calories).

383 TOTAL CALORIES

Ground Chicken Wraps with Chili Sauce DF LC

Hands-on: 33 minutes | Total: 33 minutes
Serves 4 (serving size: 3 wraps and ¼ of the bok choy mixture)

2 tablespoons Asian sweet chili sauce
1½ tablespoons lower-sodium soy sauce
1 teaspoon finely chopped garlic
5 tablespoons unsalted vegetable stock
2 tablespoons toasted sesame oil
1 pound ground chicken
1 cup shiitake mushroom caps, finely chopped
½ cup finely chopped green onions
⅓ cup finely chopped fresh cilantro
2 tablespoons fresh lime juice (from 2 limes)
⅜ teaspoon kosher salt
4 medium baby bok choy (about 12 ounces), quartered
1 cup sliced red bell pepper
1 tablespoon hoisin sauce
12 Bibb lettuce leaves
¾ cup grated carrot
7 tablespoons unsalted, dry-roasted peanuts, chopped

1. Combine the chili sauce, soy sauce, garlic, 3 tablespoons of the stock, and 2 teaspoons oil in a small microwave-safe bowl. Microwave at HIGH until the mixture bubbles and is slightly thickened, about 45 seconds.
2. Heat a large skillet over medium-high heat. Add 2 teaspoons oil to pan; swirl. Add chicken; cook, stirring often, until browned, about 5 minutes. Add mushrooms, green onions, and cilantro; cook, stirring occasionally, 2 minutes. Stir in lime juice and ¼ teaspoon salt. Remove from pan; cover to keep warm. Wipe pan clean with a paper towel. Add remaining 2 teaspoons oil; swirl. Add bok choy and bell pepper; cook, stirring often, until bok choy is lightly browned, 2 to 3 minutes. Add hoisin and remaining 2 tablespoons stock and ⅛ teaspoon salt; cook, stirring often, until vegetables are well coated and liquid is mostly evaporated, 1 to 2 minutes.
3. Divide the chicken mixture among the lettuce leaves. Top each with 1 tablespoon grated carrot, about 2 teaspoons sauce, and about 1½ teaspoons peanuts. Serve with the bok choy mixture.

CALORIES 383; FAT 24.7g (sat 4.8g, mono 11.1g, poly 7.5g); PROTEIN 28g; CARB 17g; FIBER 5g; SUGARS 6g (est. added sugars 1g); CHOL 98mg; IRON 3mg; SODIUM 603mg; CALCIUM 141mg

1,300-CALORIE PLAN: Serve with 1 (5-ounce) glass wine (116 calories).
1,400-CALORIE PLAN/1,500-CALORIE PLAN: Serve with 1 (5-ounce) glass wine (116 calories) or, if you're not on a low-carb plan, add ½ cup hot cooked brown rice (109 calories).

Bok Choy

You can find bok choy in either mature or baby form. Mature bok choy has white stems and dark-green leaves, while baby bok choy is smaller, light green, and can be cooked whole. It has a mild flavor similar to chard. You can find it in most conventional grocery stores.

Tamale Chicken Potpies GF

Hands-on: 20 minutes | Total: 35 minutes | Serves 4

This individually sized twist on potpie offers two perks: Vibrant south-of-the-border flavor and portion control.

2 teaspoons canola oil
1 cup chopped onion
12 ounces ground chicken
1 tablespoon ground cumin
½ teaspoon chili powder
½ teaspoon salt
1 cup chopped zucchini
¾ cup fresh corn kernels
1 (10-ounce) can diced tomatoes and green chiles, undrained
1 (8-ounce) can unsalted tomato sauce (such as Muir Glen)
Cooking spray
½ cup coarsely ground yellow cornmeal
1½ cups water
3 ounces Monterey Jack cheese, shredded (about ¾ cup)

1. Preheat the oven to 400°F.
2. Heat a large skillet over medium-high heat. Add oil to pan; swirl. Add onion; sauté 3 minutes. Add chicken; cook 3 minutes, stirring to crumble. Stir in cumin, chili powder, and ¼ teaspoon salt; cook 1 minute. Add zucchini, corn, tomatoes, and tomato sauce; bring to a boil. Reduce heat; simmer 8 minutes, stirring occasionally. Divide chicken mixture among 4 (10-ounce) ramekins coated with cooking spray. Place ramekins on a jelly-roll pan.
3. Place cornmeal, ½ cup water, and remaining ¼ teaspoon salt in a medium bowl, stirring to combine. Bring remaining 1 cup water to a boil in a medium saucepan. Gradually add cornmeal mixture to pan; cook 3 minutes or until thickened, stirring frequently. Stir in 2 ounces of the cheese. Divide cornmeal mixture among ramekins. Sprinkle with remaining 1 ounce cheese. Bake at 400°F for 15 minutes or until light golden brown.

CALORIES 355; FAT 16.8g (sat 6.4g, mono 6.6g, poly 2.5g); PROTEIN 24g; CARB 28g; FIBER 3g; SUGARS 6g (est. added sugars 0g); CHOL 92mg; IRON 3mg; SODIUM 493mg; CALCIUM 194mg

serve with:

- ½ cup fresh mango slices (50 calories)

1,300-CALORIE PLAN: Instead of the mango slices, serve this with a side of ½ cup black beans spiked with garlic, fresh lime juice, and crushed red pepper (105 calories).

1,400-CALORIE PLAN/1,500-CALORIE PLAN: Serve with a side of ½ cup black beans spiked with garlic, fresh lime juice, and crushed red pepper (105 calories).

Quick Sides Under 100 Calories

Parmesan Polenta Rounds

Preheat the broiler to high. Heat an ovenproof skillet over medium-high heat. Coat the pan with cooking spray. Add 8 ounces of prepared polenta that's been cut into 8 (½-inch-thick) slices to the pan; cook 2 minutes on each side or until golden. Sprinkle evenly with 2 tablespoons of finely grated Parmesan cheese and 1½ tablespoons melted unsalted butter. Broil 2 to 3 minutes or until the cheese melts.

SERVES 4 (serving size: 2 polenta rounds): CALORIES 90; FAT 5.2g (sat 3.2g, mono 1.3g, poly 0.2g); PROTEIN 2g; CARB 8g; FIBER 1g; SUGARS 0g (est. added sugars 0g); CHOL 14mg; IRON 0mg; SODIUM 138mg; CALCIUM 29mg

Roasted Asparagus and Shiitake Mushrooms

Preheat the oven to 425°F. Combine 1 tablespoon olive oil, ½ teaspoon freshly ground black pepper, 12 ounces trimmed asparagus, and 4 ounces sliced shiitake mushroom caps on a foil-lined baking sheet; toss to coat. Bake at 425°F for 10 minutes or until the asparagus is crisp-tender. Drizzle with 1½ teaspoons lower-sodium soy sauce.

SERVES 4 (serving size: about 1 cup): CALORIES 59; FAT 3.7g (sat 0.5g, mono 2.5g, poly 0.4g); PROTEIN 3g; CARB 5g; FIBER 2g; SUGARS 2g (est. added sugars 0g); CHOL 0mg; IRON 1mg; SODIUM 14mg; CALCIUM 20mg

Braised Brussels Sprouts with Mustard and Thyme

Melt 1 tablespoon butter in a large nonstick skillet over medium heat. Add 1 pound trimmed and halved Brussels sprouts to the pan, cut sides down; cook 2 minutes without stirring. Add 2 large thinly sliced shallots to the pan; toss to combine. Cook 2 minutes. Sprinkle with ¼ teaspoon each kosher salt and freshly ground black pepper. Add ¼ cup unsalted chicken stock to pan; cover partially, and cook 3 minutes or until Brussels sprouts are crisp-tender. Combine 2 tablespoons unsalted chicken stock, 2½ teaspoons Dijon mustard, and 1 teaspoon honey in a bowl; stir into sprouts mixture. Sprinkle with 1½ teaspoons chopped fresh thyme. Cook 1 minute, stirring well.

SERVES 4 (serving size: ½ cup): CALORIES 93; FAT 3.2g (sat 1.9g, mono 0.8g, poly 0.3g); PROTEIN 4g; CARB 14g; FIBER 5g; SUGARS 5g (est. added sugars 1g); CHOL 9mg; IRON 2mg; SODIUM 237mg; CALCIUM 56mg

Sautéed Broccolini

Heat a large skillet over medium-high heat. Add 2 teaspoons canola oil to pan; swirl to coat. Add 1 pound trimmed Broccolini to the pan; cook 5 minutes, stirring occasionally. Add ½ cup unsalted chicken stock. Cover, reduce the heat to low, and cook 6 minutes or until the Broccolini is crisp-tender. Stir in 2 teaspoons balsamic vinegar, ¼ teaspoon kosher salt, and ¼ teapoon freshly ground black pepper.

SERVES 4 (serving size: about 4 ounces): CALORIES 73; FAT 2.3g (sat 0.2g, mono 1.3g, poly 0.6g); PROTEIN 5g; CARB 9g; FIBER 1g; SUGARS 3g (est. added sugars 0g); CHOL 0mg; IRON 1mg; SODIUM 170mg; CALCIUM 84mg

Ginger-Garlic Green Beans

Cook 12 ounces trimmed green beans in boiling water 5 minutes or until crisp-tender. Drain and plunge beans into ice water; drain. Heat a large skillet over medium-high heat. Add 1 teaspoon canola oil to the pan; swirl to coat. Add 2 teaspoons minced peeled fresh ginger and 1 teaspoon minced fresh garlic; sauté 1 minute. Add the beans, ¼ teaspoon salt, and ¼ teaspoon freshly ground black pepper; cook 2 minutes or until heated.

SERVES 4 (serving size: about 3 ounces): CALORIES 42; FAT 1.4g (sat 0.1g, mono 0.8g, poly 0.4g); PROTEIN 2g; CARB 6g; FIBER 2g; SUGARS 3g (est. added sugars 0g); CHOL 0mg; IRON 1mg; SODIUM 151mg; CALCIUM 32mg

Shaved Carrot and Parsley Salad

Combine 1½ tablespoons white wine vinegar, 1½ tablespoons extra-virgin olive oil, ¼ teaspoon kosher salt, and ¼ teaspoon freshly ground black pepper in a medium bowl, stirring with a whisk. Add 3 cups thinly shaved carrot and 1½ cups flat-leaf parsley leaves to the vinaigrette; toss to coat.

SERVES 4 (serving size: ¾ cup): CALORIES 91; FAT 5.6g (sat 0.8g, mono 3.8g, poly 0.9g); PROTEIN 2g; CARB 10g; FIBER 3g; SUGARS 5g (est. added sugars 0g); CHOL 0mg; IRON 2mg; SODIUM 196mg; CALCIUM 62mg

Kale Salad with Creamy Peppercorn Dressing

Combine ⅓ cup low-fat buttermilk, 1 tablespoon canola mayonnaise, ½ teaspoon white wine vinegar, ½ teaspoon minced fresh garlic, ½ teaspoon cracked black pepper, and ¼ teaspoon kosher salt in a medium bowl, stirring with a whisk. Add ½ cup cored and very thinly sliced fennel and 3 ounces baby kale leaves (about 3 cups); toss to coat.

SERVES 4 (serving size: about ⅔ cup): CALORIES 33; FAT 1.3g (sat 0.1g, mono 0.6g, poly 0.4g); PROTEIN 2g; CARB 4g; FIBER 1g; SUGARS 1g (est. added sugars 0g); CHOL 1mg; IRON 0mg; SODIUM 183mg; CALCIUM 60mg

Raspberry and Blue Cheese Salad

Combine 1½ tablespoons olive oil, 1½ teaspoons red wine vinegar, ¼ teaspoon Dijon mustard, ⅛ teaspoon salt, and ⅛ teaspoon black pepper. Add 5 cups mixed baby greens; toss. Top with ½ cup fresh raspberries, ¼ cup chopped toasted pecans, and 1 ounce blue cheese.

SERVES 6 (serving size: 1 cup): CALORIES 88; FAT 8.1g (sat 1.6g, mono 4.7g, poly 1.4g); PROTEIN 2g; CARB 3g; FIBER 1g; SUGARS 1g (est. added sugars 0g); CHOL 4mg; IRON 0mg; SODIUM 129mg; CALCIUM 41mg

Cucumber-Peanut Salad

Combine 2 cups thinly sliced English cucumber, ½ cup vertically sliced red onion, 3 tablespoons fresh lime juice, 2 teaspoons light brown sugar, and ¼ teaspoon salt in a medium bowl; toss to coat. Sprinkle with 2 tablespoons chopped unsalted, dry-roasted peanuts.

SERVES 4 (serving size: ½ cup): CALORIES 52; FAT 2.4g (sat 0.3g, mono 1.1g, poly 0.7g); PROTEIN 2g; CARB 7g; FIBER 1g; SUGARS 4g (est. added sugars 2g); CHOL 0mg; IRON 0mg; SODIUM 150mg; CALCIUM 18mg

Orange and Almond Salad

Peel and section 2 navel oranges. Combine orange sections, 5 cups mixed baby greens, 2 tablespoons sliced toasted almonds, 4 teaspoons olive oil, and 1 tablespoon rice vinegar; toss to coat. Sprinkle with ⅛ teaspoon kosher salt and a dash of freshly ground black pepper.

SERVES 4 (serving size: about 1½ cups): CALORIES 90; FAT 6g (sat 0.7g, mono 4.1g, poly 0.9g); PROTEIN 2g; CARB 9g; FIBER 3g; SUGARS 6g (est. added sugars 0g); CHOL 0mg; IRON 1mg; SODIUM 85mg; CALCIUM 26mg

Miso Mixed Vegetable Salad

Steam 1 cup sugar snap peas for 3 minutes or until crisp-tender; rinse with cold water, and drain. Combine the peas, ¼ cup sliced radishes, and ¼ cup finely chopped bell pepper. Combine 2 teaspoons rice vinegar, 1 teaspoon white miso, 1 teaspoon canola oil, and ¼ teaspoon dark sesame oil; toss with salad.

SERVES 2 (serving size: about ⅔ cup): CALORIES 65; FAT 3.1g (sat 0.3g, mono 1.8g, poly 1g); PROTEIN 2g; CARB 7g; FIBER 2g; SUGARS 4g (est. added sugars 0g); CHOL 0mg; IRON 1mg; SODIUM 85mg; CALCIUM 35mg

Lemony Green Beans

Bring a large pot of water to a boil. Add 1 pound trimmed green beans; cook 4 minutes or until crisp-tender. Drain. Toss the beans with 1 tablespoon butter, 2 teaspoons fresh lemon juice, ¼ teaspoon kosher salt, and ¼ teaspoon freshly ground black pepper.

SERVES 4 (serving size: 4 ounces): CALORIES 62; FAT 3.1g (sat 1.9g, mono 0.8g, poly 0.2g); PROTEIN 2g; CARB 8g; FIBER 3g; SUGARS 4g (est. added sugars 0g); CHOL 28mg; IRON 1mg; SODIUM 152mg; CALCIUM 44mg

Asparagus and Lemon Microwave Risotto Ⓥ

Hands-on: 15 minutes | Total: 32 minutes | Serves 4 (serving size: 1 cup)

This risotto is not covered while microwaving. Be sure you are using at least a 2-quart bowl to allow plenty of room for the liquid to boil.

¾ cup chopped onion
2 tablespoons butter
1 tablespoon olive oil
2 garlic cloves, minced
1 cup uncooked Arborio rice or other medium-grain rice
3 cups unsalted vegetable stock
⅓ cup dry white wine
1 pound asparagus, trimmed and cut into ½-inch pieces
½ teaspoon grated lemon rind
1½ tablespoons fresh lemon juice
½ teaspoon salt
¼ teaspoon freshly ground black pepper
1½ ounces vegetarian Parmesan cheese, shaved (about ⅓ cup; such as BelGioioso)

Combine the first 4 ingredients in a 2-quart microwave-safe glass bowl. Microwave at HIGH 3 minutes. Stir in the rice; microwave at HIGH 3 minutes. Stir in the stock and wine; microwave at HIGH 16 minutes, stirring for 30 seconds every 4 minutes. Add the asparagus; microwave at HIGH 2 minutes. Stir in the rind, juice, salt, pepper, and half of the cheese. Top with the remaining cheese.

CALORIES 349; FAT 11.7g (sat 5.3g, mono 4.5g, poly 0.7g); PROTEIN 13g; CARB 48g; FIBER 5g; SUGARS 5g (est. added sugars 0g); CHOL 21mg; IRON 3mg; SODIUM 550mg; CALCIUM 130mg

serve with:

- 1½ cups spinach tossed with 1½ tablespoons light vinaigrette (60 calories)

1,300-CALORIE PLAN: Top your salad with 1 tablespoon toasted walnuts (48 calories).

1,400-CALORIE PLAN/1,500-CALORIE PLAN: Serve with 1 (5-ounce) glass wine (116 calories).

Storing Grains

Store grains in airtight containers in a cool, dark place. If you live in a hot, humid climate, keep them in the refrigerator. In general, you can store cooked grains, tightly covered, in the refrigerator for up to five days. Grains with a chewy texture (wild, brown, and black rice, barley, and bulgur) can be frozen without turning mushy.

Butternut Squash and Swiss Chard Tart

Hands-on: 15 minutes | Total: 55 minutes | Serves 6 (serving size: 1 wedge)

To speed up prep time, roast the squash and par-bake the crust simultaneously.

CRUST

6 ounces whole-wheat pastry flour (about 1½ cups)
3 tablespoons pine nuts, toasted and chopped
¼ teaspoon kosher salt
¼ teaspoon freshly ground black pepper
¼ teaspoon baking powder
¼ cup extra-virgin olive oil
3 tablespoons ice water
Cooking spray

TART

3 cups cubed peeled butternut squash
4 teaspoons extra-virgin olive oil
¾ cup chopped onion
4 garlic cloves, thinly sliced
1 bunch Swiss chard, trimmed and thinly sliced (about 5 cups)
1 tablespoon balsamic vinegar
½ teaspoon kosher salt
¼ teaspoon freshly ground black pepper
2 large eggs, lightly beaten
2.5 ounces cave-aged Gruyère cheese, finely grated

1. Preheat the oven to 400°F.
2. Make the crust: Weigh or lightly spoon flour into dry measuring cups; level with a knife. Place the flour, 1½ tablespoons nuts, ¼ teaspoon salt, ¼ teaspoon pepper, and baking powder in a food processor; pulse 3 times to combine. Combine ¼ cup oil and 3 tablespoons ice water in a small bowl. With the processor on, slowly add the oil mixture through the food chute; process until the dough is crumbly. Sprinkle the dough into a 9-inch pie plate coated with cooking spray. Press the dough evenly into bottom and up the sides of the pie plate. Bake at 400°F for 23 minutes or until lightly browned.
3. Make the tart: Combine the squash and 1 teaspoon of the oil on a baking sheet coated with cooking spray; toss. Bake at 400°F for 25 minutes, stirring once.
4. Heat a large nonstick skillet over medium heat. Add the remaining 1 tablespoon oil to the pan; swirl to coat. Add the onion and garlic; sauté 7 minutes. Add the chard, vinegar, ½ teaspoon salt, and ¼ teaspoon pepper; cook 3 minutes or until the chard wilts. Combine the chard mixture, eggs, and 2 ounces of the cheese in a large bowl. Add the squash and remaining 1½ tablespoons nuts; toss gently to coat.

5. Pour the squash mixture into the crust, and sprinkle with the remaining cheese. Bake at 400°F for 23 minutes or until the filling is set.

CALORIES 363; FAT 21.1g (sat 4.7g, mono 11.4g, poly 3.3g); PROTEIN 11g; CARB 35g; FIBER 6g; SUGARS 3g (est. added sugars 0g); CHOL 75mg; IRON 3mg; SODIUM 389mg; CALCIUM 217mg

serve with:

- ½ cup fresh strawberries (27 calories)

1,300-CALORIE PLAN: Increase the serving of fresh strawberries to 1 cup (54 calories).
1,400-CALORIE PLAN/1,500-CALORIE PLAN: Increase the serving of fresh strawberries to 1 cup and drizzle with 2 teaspoons honey (96 calories).

Vegetable "Meat" Loaf

Hands-on: 60 minutes | Total: 1 hour, 47 minutes
Serves 6 (serving size: 1 slice)

Vegetarians and carnivores alike will love this ingenious twist on meat loaf. The meaty-flavored, umami-rich recipe received our Test Kitchen's highest rating. Ordinarily you wouldn't pack a meat loaf into the pan, but since we're using a vegetable mixture, you will to make sure it holds together.

"MEAT" LOAF

1 large red bell pepper
1 large green bell pepper
2 pounds cremini mushrooms, coarsely chopped
1 tablespoon olive oil
1 cup ½-inch asparagus pieces
½ cup chopped red onion
1 cup panko (Japanese breadcrumbs)
1 cup chopped toasted walnuts
2 tablespoons chopped fresh basil
1 tablespoon ketchup
1 teaspoon Dijon mustard
½ teaspoon kosher salt
½ teaspoon freshly ground black pepper
4 ounces vegetarian Parmesan cheese, grated (about 1 cup; such as BelGioioso)
2 large eggs, lightly beaten
Cooking spray

TOPPING

2 tablespoons ketchup
1 tablespoon vodka or vegetable stock
¼ teaspoon Dijon mustard

1. Preheat the broiler to high.
2. Make the "meat" loaf: Cut the bell peppers in half lengthwise; discard the seeds and membranes. Place the pepper halves, skin sides up, on a foil-lined baking sheet; flatten with hand. Broil 12 minutes or until blackened. Place in a paper bag; fold to close tightly. Let stand for 10 minutes. Peel and finely chop. Place the bell peppers in a large bowl.
3. Reduce the oven temperature to 350°F.
4. Place about one-fourth of the mushrooms in a food processor; pulse 10 times or until finely chopped. Transfer the chopped mushrooms to a bowl. Repeat the procedure 3 times with the remaining mushrooms.
5. Heat a large nonstick skillet over medium-high heat. Add the oil to the pan; swirl to coat. Add the mushrooms to the pan; sauté 15 minutes or until the liquid evaporates, stirring occasionally. Add the mushrooms to the bell peppers. Wipe the pan with paper towels. Add the asparagus and onion to the pan; sauté 6 minutes or until just tender, stirring occasionally. Add the onion mixture to the mushroom mixture.
6. Arrange the breadcrumbs in an even layer on a baking sheet; bake at 350°F for 10 minutes or until golden. Add the breadcrumbs and the next

8 ingredients (through eggs) to the mushroom mixture, stirring well. Spoon the mixture into a 9 x 5-inch loaf pan coated with cooking spray; press gently to pack. Bake at 350°F for 45 minutes or until a thermometer registers 155°F.

7. Make the topping: Combine 2 tablespoons ketchup, vodka, and mustard in a small bowl; brush the ketchup mixture over the "meat" loaf. Bake an additional 10 minutes. Let stand 10 minutes; cut into 6 slices.

CALORIES 354; FAT 20.8g (sat 2.5g, mono 4.6g, poly 10.3g); PROTEIN 20g; CARB 25g; FIBER 5g; SUGARS 9g (est. added sugars 2g); CHOL 128mg; IRON 3mg; SODIUM 655mg; CALCIUM 284mg

serve with:

- 1 cup steamed green beans (31 calories)

1,300-CALORIE PLAN: Top the green beans with 1½ tablespoons vegetarian Parmesan cheese (42 calories).

1,400-CALORIE PLAN/1,500-CALORIE PLAN: Add ½ cup mashed potatoes, such as Simply Potatoes (100 calories).

Chipotle-Bean Burritos

Hands-on: 15 minutes | Total: 15 minutes | Serves 6 (serving size: 1 burrito)

Refrigerated fresh salsa or pico de gallo has a bright, zippy taste. In place of the chipotle chile powder, you can use ½ teaspoon regular chili powder plus ⅛ teaspoon ground red pepper.

1 tablespoon canola oil
1 garlic clove, minced
½ teaspoon chipotle chile powder
¼ teaspoon salt
⅓ cup water
1 (15-ounce) can organic black beans, rinsed and drained
1 (15-ounce) can organic kidney beans, rinsed and drained
3 tablespoons refrigerated fresh salsa
6 (10-inch) reduced-fat flour tortillas (such as Mission)
4 ounces preshredded reduced-fat 4-cheese Mexican blend cheese (about 1 cup)
1½ cups chopped plum tomato (about 3)
1½ cups shredded romaine lettuce
6 tablespoons thinly sliced green onions
6 tablespoons reduced-fat sour cream

1. Heat a large nonstick skillet over medium heat. Add the oil to the pan; swirl to coat. Add the garlic to the pan; cook 1 minute, stirring frequently. Stir in the chile powder and salt; cook 30 seconds, stirring constantly. Stir in ⅓ cup water and the beans; bring to a boil. Reduce the heat, and simmer 10 minutes. Remove from the heat; stir in the salsa. Partially mash the bean mixture with a fork.
2. Warm the tortillas according to the package directions. Spoon about ⅓ cup of the bean mixture into the center of each tortilla. Top each serving with about 2½ tablespoons cheese, ¼ cup tomato, ¼ cup lettuce, 1 tablespoon onions, and 1 tablespoon sour cream; roll up.

CALORIES 386; FAT 10.1g (sat 4.1g, mono 2.5g, poly 0.9g); PROTEIN 18g; CARB 57g; FIBER 14g; SUGARS 5g (est. added sugars 0g); CHOL 19mg; IRON 2mg; SODIUM 749mg; CALCIUM 300mg

1,300-CALORIE PLAN: Serve with 2 tablespoons guacamole (46 calories).
1,400-CALORIE PLAN/1,500-CALORIE PLAN: Serve with 2 tablespoons

Szechuan-Style Tofu with Peanuts DF V

Hands-on: 20 minutes | Total: 20 minutes | Serves 4 (serving size: ¾ cup rice, about ¾ cup tofu mixture, and 1 tablespoon peanuts)

Spice up your supper with this Asian-flavored vegetarian dish. For meat-eaters, feel free to substitute chicken for the tofu.

2 (3½-ounce) bags boil-in-bag jasmine rice
1 (14-ounce) package water-packed firm tofu, drained and cut into 1-inch pieces
Cooking spray
½ cup fat-free, less-sodium vegetable broth
1 tablespoon sambal oelek (ground fresh chile paste)
1 tablespoon lower-sodium soy sauce
1 teaspoon cornstarch
2 teaspoons black bean garlic sauce
1 tablespoon canola oil
¼ teaspoon salt
1 (8-ounce) package presliced mushrooms
½ cup matchstick-cut carrots
1 tablespoon bottled ground fresh ginger (such as Spice World)
½ cup chopped green onions
¼ cup unsalted, dry-roasted peanuts, chopped

1. Preheat the broiler to high.
2. Cook the rice according to the package directions, omitting the salt and fat.
3. Arrange the tofu in a single layer on a foil-lined jelly-roll pan coated with cooking spray; broil 14 minutes or until golden.
4. While the tofu cooks, combine the broth and next 4 ingredients (through black bean sauce), stirring with a whisk; set aside.
5. Heat a large nonstick skillet over medium-high heat. Add the oil to the pan; swirl to coat. Add the salt and mushrooms; sauté 4 minutes or until the mushrooms begin to release liquid, stirring occasionally. Stir in the carrots and ginger; cook 1 minute. Add the broth mixture; cook 30 seconds or until the sauce begins to thicken. Remove from the heat; stir in the tofu and onions. Serve over the rice; sprinkle with the peanuts.

CALORIES 389; FAT 14.3g (sat 2.1g, mono 5.5g, poly 6.2g); PROTEIN 17g; CARB 52g; FIBER 2g; SUGARS 3g (est. added sugars 0g); CHOL 0mg; IRON 4mg; SODIUM 619mg; CALCIUM 92mg

1,300-CALORIE PLAN: Serve with ⅔ cup Miso Mixed Vegetable Salad, page 203 (65 calories).
1,400-CALORIE PLAN/1,500-CALORIE PLAN: Serve with ⅔ cup Miso Mixed Vegetable Salad, (65 calories) and increase the rice to a 1-cup serving (for an additional 51 calories).

Butternut-Eggplant Vegetable Bowl DF V

Hands-on: 27 minutes | Total: 27 minutes | Serves 4 (serving size: 2½ cups)

The key to making this delicious meal quickly is to have your vegetables cut about the same size. Aim for bite-sized pieces, about ¾-inch.

2 cups cubed butternut squash
¼ cup water
2½ cups unsalted vegetable stock
1 cup medium bulgur wheat
1 teaspoon freshly ground black pepper
¾ teaspoon kosher salt
3 tablespoons extra-virgin olive oil
2 cups cubed eggplant
1 cup chopped yellow squash
4 cups chopped lacinato kale
1 tablespoon chopped fresh thyme
2 tablespoons apple cider vinegar
2 teaspoons honey

1. Combine the butternut squash and ¼ cup water in a microwave-safe bowl; cover with plastic wrap. Microwave at HIGH until almost tender, about 5 minutes.
2. Bring the stock to a boil in a medium saucepan over high. Add the bulgur and ¼ teaspoon each of the pepper and salt. Cover and reduce the heat to medium-low. Simmer until tender, about 12 minutes. Remove from the heat, and let stand 5 minutes.
3. Heat a large nonstick skillet over medium-high heat. Add 1 tablespoon of the oil to the pan; swirl to coat. Add the eggplant and yellow squash; cook, stirring occasionally, until almost tender, about 6 minutes. Add the butternut squash and kale; cook, stirring occasionally, until the kale begins to wilt, about 2 minutes. Sprinkle with the remaining ¾ teaspoon pepper and ½ teaspoon salt.
4. Whisk together the thyme, vinegar, honey, and remaining 2 tablespoons oil in a small bowl. Divide the bulgur among 4 bowls. Top each with 1¾ cups vegetable mixture, and drizzle each with about 1 tablespoon dressing.

CALORIES 322; FAT 11.7g (sat 1.7g, mono 8.2g, poly 1.5g); PROTEIN 10g; CARB 51g; FIBER 11g; SUGARS 8g (est. added sugars 3g); CHOL 0mg; IRON 3mg; SODIUM 551mg; CALCIUM 150mg

serve with:

- 1 (1-ounce) slice French bread (82 calories)

1,300-CALORIE PLAN: Increase the serving of French bread to 1½ ounces (123 calories).
1,400-CALORIE PLAN/1,500-CALORIE PLAN: Increase the serving of French bread to 1½ ounces and drizzle with 1 teaspoon olive oil (163 calories).

Kale

This leafy green has a somewhat bitter flavor that shines when raw, baked, sautéed, or stewed. It's available fall through the spring. When buying, look for bunches that are dark green and free of yellow or brown blemishes. Place cut kale in a plastic produce bag in your refrigerator for up to a week.

Lasagna Bowl GF V

Hands-on: 35 minutes | Total: 35 minutes | Serves 4 (serving size: 1½ cups)

If you can't find cremini mushrooms, use white button. The trick to making zucchini "noodles?" Purchase zucchini that's narrower than your vegetable peeler's blade.

1 medium zucchini
¾ teaspoon kosher salt
2 tablespoons olive oil
1 cup chopped yellow onion
1 tablespoon finely chopped garlic
16 ounces sliced cremini mushrooms
1 tablespoon unsalted tomato paste
1 (28-ounce) can unsalted diced fire-roasted tomatoes, undrained
1 teaspoon freshly ground black pepper
5 ounces fresh baby spinach
4 ounces part-skim ricotta cheese (about ½ cup)
3 ounces preshredded reduced-fat mozzarella cheese (about ¾ cup)
¼ cup loosely packed basil leaves

1. Using a vegetable peeler, peel the zucchini into long, even strips. Toss together the zucchini strips and ¼ teaspoon of the salt in a colander. Let stand until ready to use.

2. Heat a Dutch oven over medium-high heat. Add the oil to the pan; swirl to coat. Add the onion and garlic; cook, stirring often, until tender, about 3 minutes. Add the mushrooms; cook, stirring often, until browned, about 5 minutes. Add the tomato paste, and cook 1 minute. Stir in the tomatoes, pepper, and remaining ½ teaspoon salt; bring to a simmer, stirring often. Reduce the heat to medium-low, and simmer, stirring occasionally, until slightly reduced, about 6 minutes. Gently stir in the spinach. Cover and cook until the spinach is wilted, about 3 minutes. Remove from the heat. Gently stir in the zucchini strips. Stir together the ricotta and mozzarella. Dot the zucchini mixture with the cheese mixture. Sprinkle with the basil.

CALORIES 282; FAT 13g (sat 4.7g, mono 6.6g, poly 1g); PROTEIN 16g; CARB 28g; FIBER 6; SUGARS 13g (est. added sugars 0g); CHOL 23mg; IRON 3mg; SODIUM 628mg; CALCIUM 329mg

serve with:

- 1 (1½-ounce) slice gluten-free or non-gluten-free Italian bread (116 calories), rubbed with crushed garlic and toasted

1,300-CALORIE PLAN: Drizzle the Italian bread with 1 teaspoon olive oil before toasting (40 calories).

1,400-CALORIE PLAN/1,500-CALORIE PLAN: Drizzle the Italian bread with 1 teaspoon olive oil and top with 1½ tablespoons Parmesan cheese before toasting (72 calories). Opt for vegetarian Parmesan cheese if you want to keep this meal vegetarian.

Roasted Vegetable Plate with Herbed Dressing GF

Hands-on: 20 minutes | Total: 20 minutes
Serves 4 (serving size: 1 cup salad, ½ cup vegetables, about 2 teaspoons almonds, and about ½ tablespoon Parmesan cheese)

Don't be scared of a hot oven—roasting the veggies at 500°F gets the job done quickly and gives the vegetables a nice golden color.

1 (10-ounce) package cauliflower florets
8 ounces Brussels sprouts, trimmed and halved
1 cup chopped peeled sweet potato (about 1 small sweet potato)
2 large shallots, quartered lengthwise
1 teaspoon grated lemon rind
½ teaspoon freshly ground black pepper
¼ cup olive oil
1 ounce Parmesan cheese, grated (about ¼ cup)
⅝ teaspoon kosher salt
2 tablespoons chopped fresh tarragon
2 tablespoons white wine vinegar
1 (5-ounce) container baby arugula
3 tablespoons chopped toasted almonds

1. Place a rimmed baking sheet in the oven, and preheat the oven to 500°F. (Do not remove the pan while the oven preheats.)
2. Toss together the cauliflower, Brussels sprouts, sweet potato, shallots, rind, pepper, 2 tablespoons of the oil, half of the Parmesan cheese, and ⅜ teaspoon of the salt. Spread the mixture on the preheated baking sheet; bake at 500°F until golden brown, about 15 minutes.
3. Whisk together the tarragon, vinegar, remaining 2 tablespoons oil, and remaining ¼ teaspoon salt in a large bowl. Add the arugula; toss to coat.
4. Divide the arugula mixture among 4 plates. Top with the roasted vegetable mixture. Sprinkle with the toasted almonds and the remaining Parmesan cheese.

CALORIES 290; FAT 19.5g (sat 3.4g, mono 12.5g, poly 2.4g); PROTEIN 10g; CARB 24g; FIBER 6g; SUGARS 5g (est. added sugars 0g); CHOL 6mg; IRON 2mg; SODIUM 463mg; CALCIUM 215mg

serve with:

- 1 (5-ounce) glass white wine (116 calories)

1,300-CALORIE PLAN: Add 1 small whole-grain dinner roll (60 calories).
1,400-CALORIE PLAN/1,500-CALORIE PLAN: Add 1 small whole-grain dinner roll smeared with 1 teaspoon butter (94 calories).

373
TOTAL CALORIES

Tomato, Basil, and Corn Pizza (V)

Hands-on: 15 minutes | Total: 25 minutes | Serves 6 (serving size: 1 slice)

This pizza is fresh, fast, and impressive. If you don't have a rectangular pizza stone, use a heavy baking sheet instead. You can often find fresh mozzarella in the grocery store where the more expensive cheeses are, but it is not expensive.

1 pound refrigerated fresh pizza dough
1 tablespoon plain yellow cornmeal
½ cup lower-sodium marinara sauce (such as Dell'Amore)
1 large tomato, thinly sliced
⅔ cup fresh corn kernels (from 2 ears)
3½ ounces fresh mozzarella cheese, torn
2 large garlic cloves, thinly sliced
½ teaspoon kosher salt
½ teaspoon freshly ground black pepper
¼ cup loosely packed basil leaves, torn
¼ teaspoon crushed red pepper
1 teaspoon olive oil
1 tablespoon balsamic glaze

1. Place a rectangular pizza stone in the oven, and preheat the oven to 500°F. (Do not remove the pizza stone while the oven preheats.)
2. Place the dough in a microwave-safe bowl. Cover with plastic wrap, and microwave at HIGH until the dough is slightly warmed, about 30 seconds. Place the dough on a lightly floured surface, and roll out into a 15 x 12-inch rectangle. Sprinkle the cornmeal on a large piece of parchment paper; place the dough rectangle on the cornmeal. Let stand 5 minutes.
3. Place the parchment and dough on a flat baking sheet. Bake in the preheated oven 3 minutes. Remove the pizza crust from the oven, and spread the marinara sauce on the crust. Top evenly with the tomato slices, corn, mozzarella, and garlic. Sprinkle with the salt and black pepper. Gently slide the pizza onto the preheated pizza stone. Bake at 500°F until well browned and the crust is crispy, about 12 minutes. Sprinkle with the basil and red pepper; drizzle with the oil and balsamic glaze. Cut into 6 slices.

CALORIES 285; FAT 7.3g (sat 3.1g, mono 1.9g, poly 1.1g); PROTEIN 10g; CARB 43g; FIBER 6g; SUGARS 5g (est. added sugars 2g); CHOL 12mg; IRON 1mg; SODIUM 552mg; CALCIUM 12mg

serve with:

- 1½ cups chopped romaine lettuce, 2 tablespoons reduced-fat Caesar dressing, and 2 tablespoons grated vegetarian Parmesan cheese (88 calories)

1,300-CALORIE PLAN: Add ¼ cup plain croutons to your salad (31 calories).
1,400-CALORIE PLAN/1,500-CALORIE PLAN: Serve with 1 (5-ounce) glass wine (116 calories).

Pizza Dough

Refrigerated fresh pizza dough is a wonderful convenience product available in the bakery section of large supermarkets. When time is of the essence, you can use the quick microwave rising method we've used in the recipe.

Roasted Asparagus, Mushroom, and Onion Pizza (V)

Hands-on: 51 minutes | Total: 1 hour, 31 minutes
Serves 8 (serving size: 2 slices)

You can easily cut this recipe in half if you're only serving 4. Use any hearty vegetables you like.

1½ pounds refrigerated fresh pizza dough
2 pounds cremini mushrooms, quartered
2 small red onions, each cut into 12 wedges
Cooking spray
1 pound asparagus spears, trimmed and cut into thirds
2 tablespoons cornmeal
⅔ cup lower-sodium marinara sauce (such as Dell'Amore)
5 ounces fresh mozzarella cheese, torn into small pieces (about 1¼ cups)
3 ounces fontina cheese, shredded (about ¾ cup)
1½ tablespoons extra-virgin olive oil
1½ tablespoons balsamic vinegar
¾ teaspoon crushed red pepper
¼ cup basil leaves
¼ teaspoon kosher salt

1. Cut dough in half. Let stand at room temperature, covered, 30 minutes.
2. Place 2 heavy baking sheets in the oven. Preheat the oven to 500°F. (Do not remove the pans while the oven preheats.)
3. Combine the mushrooms and onions on a jelly-roll pan; coat with cooking spray. Bake at 500°F for 15 minutes. Add the asparagus to the pan; bake at 500°F for 15 minutes. Remove from the oven; cool.
4. Roll each piece of dough to a 15 x 9-inch rectangle on a lightly floured work surface. Carefully remove baking sheets from the oven; sprinkle with cornmeal. Arrange dough on baking sheets; coat with cooking spray. Bake at 500°F for 8 minutes. Spread ⅓ cup sauce over each crust, leaving a ½-inch border. Top with vegetable mixture and cheeses. Bake at 500°F for 10 to 11 minutes. Combine the oil, vinegar, and pepper in a bowl; drizzle over the pizzas. Sprinkle with the basil and salt. Cut each pizza into 8 slices.

CALORIES 397; FAT 12.6g (sat 5g, mono 5.2g, poly 1.2g); PROTEIN 18g; CARB 53g; FIBER 9g; SUGARS 7g (est. added sugars 3g); CHOL 27mg; IRON 3mg; SODIUM 571mg; CALCIUM 100mg

1,300-CALORIE PLAN: Serve with ⅔ cup Kale Salad with Creamy Peppercorn Dressing, page 203 (33 calories) and 1 small plum (30 calories).
1,400-CALORIE PLAN/1,500-CALORIE PLAN: Serve with ⅔ cup Kale Salad, page 203 (33 calories) and 2 small plums (60 calories).

Pepperoni Pizza GF

Hands-on: 17 minutes | Total: 1 hour, 20 minutes
Serves 6 (serving size: 1 slice)

You won't miss the gluten in this crust! Topped with cheesy goodness and turkey pepperoni, this pizza is bound to be a hit with the whole family.

½ cup warm water (100° to 110°F)
2 teaspoons granulated sugar
1 package dry yeast (about 2¼ teaspoons)
3.65 ounces white rice flour (about ¾ cup)
1.4 ounces sweet white sorghum flour (about ⅓ cup)
1.4 ounces tapioca flour (about ⅓ cup)
1.7 ounces potato starch (about ⅓ cup)
0.9 ounce flaxseed meal (about ¼ cup)
1 teaspoon xanthan gum
¼ teaspoon salt
2 tablespoons olive oil
2 large egg whites
1 large egg
¾ cup lower-sodium marinara sauce (such as Dell'Amore)
4 ounces part-skim mozzarella cheese, shredded (about 1 cup)
2 ounces sliced turkey pepperoni*
2 tablespoons grated fresh Parmesan cheese

1. Combine ½ cup warm water, sugar, and yeast in a small bowl, stirring with a whisk. Let stand 5 minutes or until the yeast mixture is bubbly.
2. Weigh or lightly spoon the flours, potato starch, and flaxseed meal into dry measuring cups; level with a knife. Combine the flours, potato starch, flaxseed meal, xanthan gum, and salt in a large bowl; beat with a mixer at medium speed until blended. Add the yeast mixture, 1 tablespoon of the oil, egg whites, and egg; beat at low speed 1 minute or until combined. Increase the speed to medium; beat 2 minutes.
3. Coat a baking sheet with 1 teaspoon oil. Scrape the dough onto the pan. Lightly coat your hands with oil. Press the dough into a 14-inch circle, coating hands with oil as needed to prevent the dough from sticking. Coat the top of the dough with any remaining oil. Cover with plastic wrap, and let rise in a warm place (85°F), free from drafts, for 30 minutes.
4. Preheat the oven to 400°F.
5. Remove the plastic wrap, and bake the crust at 400°F for 17 minutes or until the bottom lightly browns. Cool completely. Increase the oven temperature to 425°F.
6. Spread the marinara over the crust, leaving a ½-inch border; top with the mozzarella cheese, pepperoni, and Parmesan cheese. Bake at 425°F for 16 minutes or until the crust is golden and the cheese melts. Cut into 6 slices.

Pizza Toppings

Pizzas are open to endless flavor combinations. Here are a few ideas for substitutions and additions:

- Thinly sliced steak, hot or mild Italian chicken sausage, grilled or sautéed shrimp
- Crumbled feta or goat cheese
- Chopped broccoli
- Roasted halved or sliced Brussels sprouts
- Roasted bell peppers
- Sliced beets

*Make sure the turkey pepperoni is certified gluten free.

CALORIES 346; FAT 13.8g (sat 4.5g, mono 5.2g, poly 1.3g); PROTEIN 17g; CARB 40g; FIBER 4g; SUGARS 4g (est. added sugars 2g); CHOL 59mg; IRON 1mg; SODIUM 599mg; CALCIUM 236mg

serve with:

- 2 cups baby spinach tossed with 2 tablespoons gluten-free reduced-fat salad dressing (54 calories)

1,300-CALORIE PLAN: Add ¼ cup fresh raspberries or sliced strawberries and 1 tablespoon pine nuts to your salad (72 calories).
1,400-CALORIE PLAN/1,500-CALORIE PLAN: Add ¼ cup fresh raspberries or sliced strawberries, 1 tablespoon crumbled feta cheese, and 1 tablespoon pine nuts to your salad (97 calories).

Flank Steak

Flank steak is a lean cut of beef that has a lot of tough fibers running through it. It's usually thinly sliced and cut against the grain to maximize its tenderness. In this classic Cuban dish, it's slowly simmered in an aromatic sauce, which transforms it into tender, succulent shreds.

Slow-Cooker Ropa Vieja DF GF

Hands-on: 15 minutes | Total: 8 hours, 30 minutes
Serves 6 (serving size: ½ cup rice and 1 cup steak mixture)

Cooking spray
1 tablespoon olive oil
1 (1½-pound) flank steak, trimmed
¾ teaspoon kosher salt
½ teaspoon freshly ground black pepper
1 cup thinly sliced white onion
1 cup thinly sliced red bell pepper
1 cup thinly sliced green bell pepper
4 garlic cloves, minced
⅓ cup golden raisins
1 cup unsalted beef stock
3 tablespoons unsalted tomato paste
1 teaspoon ground cumin
½ teaspoon dried oregano
1 (14.5-ounce) can unsalted fire-roasted diced tomatoes
⅓ cup pimiento-stuffed olives, halved
3 tablespoons chopped fresh cilantro
3 cups hot cooked rice

1. Coat a 6-quart slow cooker with cooking spray.
2. Heat a large nonstick skillet over medium-high heat. Add 2 teaspoons of the oil to the pan; swirl to coat. Cut the steak into quarters. Sprinkle the steak with ¼ teaspoon each of the salt and black pepper; add the steak to the pan. Cook 4 minutes on each side or until browned. Transfer the steak to the slow cooker. Add the onion, bell peppers, garlic, and remaining 1 teaspoon oil to pan; cook 3 minutes or until slightly softened, stirring occasionally. Stir in the raisins; transfer the onion mixture to slow cooker.
3. Combine the stock, tomato paste, cumin, oregano, tomatoes, the remaining ½ teaspoon salt, and the remaining ¼ teaspoon black pepper in a medium bowl. Pour the tomato mixture over the steak and vegetables in the slow cooker. Cover and cook on LOW for 8 hours and 15 minutes or until the steak is very tender.
4. Remove the steak from the cooker; shred using 2 forks. Stir the steak, olives, and cilantro into the sauce. Serve the steak mixture over the rice.

CALORIES 381; FAT 10.8g (sat 2.9g, mono 4.7g, poly 1.4g); PROTEIN 29g; CARB 41g; FIBER 5g; SUGARS 11g (est. added sugars 1g); CHOL 70mg; IRON 3mg; SODIUM 482mg; CALCIUM 63mg

1,300-CALORIE PLAN: Serve with either 1 (¾-ounce) slice whole-grain gluten-free bread (58 calories) or 1 small whole-grain roll (60 calories).
1,400-CALORIE PLAN/1,500-CALORIE PLAN: Increase the rice to a ¾-cup serving (an additional 51 calories) and serve with either 1 (¾-ounce) slice whole-grain gluten-free bread (58 calories) or 1 small whole-grain roll (60 calories).

Posole DF GF

Hands-on: 35 minutes | Total: 1 hour, 55 minutes
Serves 8 (serving size: 1 cup stew, 2 tablespoons radish, 1 tablespoon cilantro, 1 tablespoon onion, and ⅛ of the tortilla strips)

Posole is a traditional Mexican soup, which boasts exuberant flavors of hominy, chiles, pork shoulder, and corn tortillas. Top it with cilantro and thinly sliced radishes to make it a year-round favorite.

2 stemmed seeded dried ancho chiles
3 cups boiling water
2½ cups unsalted chicken stock (such as Swanson)
2 tablespoons olive oil
2 pounds boneless pork shoulder (Boston butt), trimmed and cut into 1-inch pieces
1 teaspoon kosher salt
2 cups chopped white onion
6 garlic cloves, minced
1½ teaspoons dried oregano
¾ teaspoon ground coriander
¾ teaspoon ground cumin
1 (14.5-ounce) can unsalted fire-roasted diced tomatoes
2 (15-ounce) cans white hominy, rinsed and drained
Cooking spray
3 (6-inch) corn tortillas, halved and cut into ¼-inch strips*
1 cup thinly sliced radishes
½ cup cilantro leaves

1. Heat a small skillet over medium heat. Add the chiles to the pan; cook 1 minute or until toasted, turning occasionally. Place the chiles in a medium bowl; add 3 cups boiling water. Let stand 15 minutes. Drain the chiles; discard the liquid. Place the chiles in a blender. Add the stock; blend until smooth. Set aside.

2. Heat a large Dutch oven over medium heat. Add 1 tablespoon of the oil to the pan; swirl to coat. Sprinkle the pork with ½ teaspoon of the salt. Add half of the pork to the pan; cook 6 minutes or until browned, turning occasionally. Place the browned pork on a plate. Repeat the procedure with the remaining pork.

3. Add 1 teaspoon of the oil to the pan. Add 1½ cups of the onion and the garlic; cook 3 minutes, stirring occasionally. Add the oregano, coriander, and cumin; cook 30 seconds, stirring constantly. Add the reserved chile mixture, tomatoes, pork and accumulated juices, and remaining ½ teaspoon salt; bring to a simmer. Reduce the heat, and cook, partially covered, 1 hour. Stir in the hominy; simmer, partially covered, 20 minutes or until the pork is tender.

4. Preheat the oven to 425°F.

5. Coat a baking sheet with cooking spray. Toss the tortilla strips with the remaining 2 teaspoons oil. Spread the strips on the prepared baking

sheet in a single layer; bake at 425°F for 7 minutes or until the strips are browned and crisp.

6. Ladle the stew into 8 bowls. Top each serving with the radish, cilantro, the remaining onion, and the tortilla strips.

* Make sure the corn tortillas are certified gluten free.

CALORIES 305; FAT 12.6g (sat 3.4g, mono 6.3g, poly 1.7g); PROTEIN 26g; CARB 20g; FIBER 4g; SUGARS 6g (est. added sugars 0g); CHOL 76mg; IRON 3mg; SODIUM 520mg; CALCIUM 55mg

serve with:

- 1 (1-ounce) piece cornbread (80 calories)

1,300-CALORIE PLAN: Top the Posole with ¼ cup cubed avocado (60 calories).

1,400-CALORIE PLAN/1,500-CALORIE PLAN: Top the Posole with ¼ cup cubed avocado and increase the serving of cornbread to 1 (1½-ounce) piece smeared with 1 teaspoon butter (133 calories).

Fast Chicken Chili DF GF

Hands-on: 13 minutes | Total: 18 minutes
Serves 4 (serving size: 1½ cups chili, 1 tablespoon cilantro leaves, and 2 lime wedges)

This quickie chili comes together in a flash, making it ideal for busy weeknights. Green chiles, cumin, cilantro, and lime add a touch of Mexican flavor.

1 tablespoon canola oil
1 pound skinless, boneless chicken breast, cut into bite-sized pieces
¼ teaspoon salt
½ cup vertically sliced onion
2 teaspoons minced fresh garlic
2 teaspoons ground cumin
1 teaspoon ground coriander
½ teaspoon dried oregano
¼ teaspoon ground red pepper
3 cups no-salt-added canned cannellini beans, rinsed and drained
1 cup water
2 (4-ounce) cans chopped green chiles, undrained
1 (14-ounce) can fat-free, lower-sodium chicken broth
¼ cup cilantro leaves
1 lime, cut into 8 wedges

1. Heat a Dutch oven over medium-high heat. Add the oil to the pan; swirl to coat. Sprinkle the chicken with ⅛ teaspoon of the salt. Add the chicken to the pan; sauté 4 minutes. Add the onion and next 5 ingredients (through red pepper); sauté 3 minutes. Add 2 cups beans, 1 cup water, 1 can of the chiles, broth, and remaining ⅛ teaspoon salt; bring to a boil.
2. Mash the remaining 1 cup beans and remaining 1 can chiles in a bowl. Add to the soup; simmer 5 minutes. Serve with the cilantro and lime.

CALORIES 284; FAT 6.5g (sat 0.8g, mono 2.7g, poly 1.5g); PROTEIN 33g; CARB 23g; FIBER 8g; SUGARS 2g (est. added sugars 0g); CHOL 66mg; IRON 5mg; SODIUM 636mg; CALCIUM 101mg

serve with:

- ¾ ounce gluten-free corn chips, about 24 chips (120 calories)

1,300-CALORIE PLAN: Increase the serving of corn chips to 1 ounce, about 32 chips (an additional 40 calories).
1,400-CALORIE PLAN/1,500-CALORIE PLAN: Increase the serving of corn chips to 1 ounce, about 32 chips (an additional 40 calories) and add ½ cup grapes (52 calories).

Virginia Woman Focuses on the Positive, Loses 30 Pounds

"THE WORST THING IN THE WORLD is to come home after you've had a horrible day at work and then you have to figure out what you're going to make."

Those are the words of Stephanie Bellanger, a federal contract specialist from Richmond, VA. But gone now are the days she has to experience them, as she and her family have made the switch to the Cooking Light Diet. Her post-work thoughts are now focused more on the positive.

"It's the best thing in the world to be on the way home and know, 'Oh gosh, I'm going to have those beef kabobs, and they're amazing!'" [Laughs]

> "It's the best thing in the world to be on the way home and know, 'Oh gosh, I'm going to have those beef kabobs, and they're amazing!"

Before dinner planning became a cakewalk, though, Stephanie had to find the Cooking Light Diet. And, like many, Stephanie's discovery of the CLDiet was born of a desire to make positive changes due to health concerns.

"After I had my son (who's 3), I was diagnosed with postpartum cardiomyopathy. And I kind of just allowed myself to live with that diagnosis like, 'Well, I guess that's it, and this is how things are going to be now.' And besides the pregnancy weight, I'd gained even more after that. Then my sister's fiancé was diagnosed with diabetes, and almost immediately his health went down terribly and he ended up having to have his foot amputated. And then we had a family friend in his 50s die of a massive heart attack. So I was going for my yearly checkup with all these things in the back of my mind. And the cardiologist said, 'You have prediabetes. You have sleep apnea. You're too young to have these types of conditions, and you really need to get this under control.' I asked what was causing all this, and she said it was my weight.

So Stephanie decided to make a change, but was determined to "do something that I knew I was going to stick with." She wasn't about to start anything she'd struggle with. And that's when she discovered the Cooking Light Diet.

Stephanie is now down 30 pounds*, and she's more motivated than ever to keep going with the CLDiet. In her own words: "This is something that we—my family—can do for the rest of our lives."

**Members following The Cooking Light Diet lose more than half a pound per week, on average.*

Cincinnati Chili

399 TOTAL CALORIES

Hands-on: 40 minutes | Total: 2 hours, 40 minutes
Serves 6 (serving size: about 1¼ cups chili, 2 tablespoons pasta, 2 tablespoons cheese, and 2 tablespoons onion)

2 cups water
14 ounces lean ground sirloin (90% lean)
6 ounces lean ground chuck (80% lean)
1½ cups finely chopped sweet onion
2 teaspoons cider vinegar
1½ teaspoons Worcestershire sauce
1½ tablespoons smoked sweet paprika
1½ teaspoons ground cumin
1½ teaspoons ground cinnamon
1½ teaspoons ground allspice
1¼ teaspoons kosher salt
½ teaspoon ground red pepper
½ ounce bittersweet chocolate, finely chopped
3 garlic cloves, crushed
1 (15-ounce) can unsalted tomato sauce (such as Muir Glen)
1 (15-ounce) can unsalted kidney beans, rinsed and drained
1 cup cooked bucatini pasta or spaghetti (about 2 ounces uncooked)
¼ cup water
½ teaspoon canola oil
3 ounces reduced-fat cheddar cheese, finely shredded (about ¾ cup)
¾ cup finely chopped white onion

1. Bring 2 cups water to a boil in a large Dutch oven. Reduce heat to a simmer. Add beef, stirring to crumble. Stir in sweet onion, 1 teaspoon of the vinegar, Worcestershire sauce, and next 9 ingredients. Return to a simmer. Partially cover, and cook 2 hours, stirring occasionally. Stir in kidney beans; cook 5 minutes. Remove from heat; stir in remaining 1 teaspoon vinegar.
2. Combine the cooked pasta, ¼ cup water, and oil in a large nonstick skillet; heat over medium-high heat. Cook until the water evaporates and the pasta is lightly browned, stirring occasionally, about 12 minutes. Coarsely chop the pasta. Serve the chili with the pasta, cheese, and white onion.

CALORIES 352; FAT 15.2g (sat 6.2g, mono 5.8g, poly 0.8g); PROTEIN 27g; CARB 27g; FIBER 7g; SUGARS 7g (est. added sugars 1g); CHOL 66mg; IRON 4mg; SODIUM 581mg; CALCIUM 133mg

serve with:

- ¼ cup low-sodium oyster crackers (47 calories)

1,300-CALORIE PLAN: Replace the oyster crackers with 1 (1-ounce) piece cornbread (80 calories).

1,400-CALORIE PLAN/1,500-CALORIE PLAN: Replace the oyster crackers with 1 (1-ounce) piece cornbread smeared with 1 teaspoon butter (114 calories).

Chili Toppers

Chili toppers let everyone at the table get creative. Below is a mix of choices to help you keep your bowl in check:

- 1 tablespoon reduced-fat sour cream (24 calories)
- 1 tablespoon plain 2% Greek yogurt (9 calories)
- 1 tablespoon chopped onions (4 calories)
- 1 tablespoon sliced black olives (10 calories)
- 1 tablespoon shredded cheddar cheese (28 calories)
- 2 tablespoons cubed avocado (30 calories)
- ¼ cup diced tomato (8 calories)

Classic Slow-Cooker Beef Stew

Hands-on: 45 minutes | Total: 8 hours
Serves 8 (serving size: about 1¼ cups)

A nutty dark beer adds richness and depth to the stew. Be careful not to choose a beer that's super-hoppy; it will taste too bitter.

2 pounds trimmed boneless chuck roast, cut into 2-inch cubes
1½ teaspoons kosher salt
1 teaspoon freshly ground black pepper
2 tablespoons canola oil
3 medium-sized yellow onions, halved lengthwise and cut crosswise into ½-inch-thick slices
6 garlic cloves, thinly sliced
1 (12-ounce) bottle nut brown ale
1¼ cups unsalted beef stock
1½ pounds baby Dutch potatoes, halved
1 pound carrots, peeled and cut diagonally into 2-inch pieces
4 thyme sprigs
2 bay leaves
2 tablespoons all-purpose flour
1 tablespoon Dijon mustard
1 tablespoon red wine vinegar
¼ cup flat-leaf parsley leaves

1. Heat a large skillet over medium-high heat. Sprinkle the beef with ¼ teaspoon each of the salt and pepper. Add 1½ teaspoons of the oil to the pan; swirl to coat. Add half of the beef to the pan; cook 6 minutes, turning until well browned on all sides. Remove the beef from the pan. Repeat the procedure with 1½ teaspoons of the oil and the remaining beef; remove the beef and any juices from the pan.

2. Add the remaining 1 tablespoon oil to the pan; swirl to coat. Add the onions and garlic; sauté 4 minutes. Add the beer, scraping pan to loosen browned bits. Bring to a boil; cook 2 minutes. Stir in 1 cup of the stock, the remaining 1¼ teaspoons salt, and remaining ¾ teaspoon pepper. Bring to a simmer. Carefully pour the mixture into a 6-quart slow cooker. Add the beef, potatoes, carrots, thyme, and bay leaves. Cover and cook on LOW for 7 hours.

3. Combine remaining ¼ cup stock and flour, stirring with a whisk. Stir flour mixture into stew; cook 15 minutes or until thickened. Stir in mustard and vinegar. Discard thyme sprigs and bay leaves. Sprinkle with the parsley.

CALORIES 386; FAT 18g (sat 5.9g, mono 8.3g, poly 1.6g); PROTEIN 25g; CARB 28g; FIBER 4g; SUGARS 5g (est. added sugars 1g); CHOL 86mg; IRON 3mg; SODIUM 509mg; CALCIUM 48mg

1,300-CALORIE PLAN: Serve with 1 small whole-grain roll (60 calories).
1,400-CALORIE PLAN/1,500-CALORIE PLAN: Serve with 1 small whole-grain roll (60 calories) and 2 teaspoons preserves or 1 teaspoon butter (33 calories).

Five-Bean Chili DF GF V

383 TOTAL CALORIES

Hands-on: 30 minutes | Total: 1 hour, 15 minutes
Serves 8 (serving size: about 1½ cups chili and 2 tablespoons cheese)

This make-ahead chili is loaded with beans that give the dish a rich character. Waiting to serve this chili the next day lets the flavors meld. If the beans soak up a lot of liquid overnight, you can add more vegetable broth or even water to thin it out.

1 tablespoon canola oil
2 cups prechopped onion
1 cup chopped carrot
2 tablespoons unsalted tomato paste
2 tablespoons minced fresh garlic
1½ teaspoons dried oregano
1½ teaspoons chili powder
1 teaspoon kosher salt
½ teaspoon Spanish smoked paprika
4 cups stemmed and torn kale
3 cups organic vegetable broth
2 red bell peppers, chopped
1 jalapeño pepper, seeded and chopped
1 (14.5-ounce) can unsalted diced tomatoes, undrained
1 (15-ounce) can unsalted black beans, rinsed and drained
1 (15-ounce) can unsalted kidney beans, rinsed and drained
1 (15.5-ounce) can unsalted chickpeas (garbanzo beans), rinsed and drained
1 (15.8-ounce) can unsalted Great Northern beans, rinsed and drained
1 (16-ounce) can unsalted pinto beans, rinsed and drained
4 ounces shredded cheddar cheese (about 1 cup)

Heat oil in a large Dutch oven over medium heat. Add the onion and carrot; sauté 10 minutes or until tender. Stir in the tomato paste and the next 5 ingredients; cook 2 minutes, stirring constantly. Add the kale and the next 9 ingredients (through pinto beans). Cover and simmer 45 minutes. Ladle the chili into 8 bowls; top each serving with cheese.

CALORIES 276; FAT 7.3g (sat 3.2g, mono 1.4g, poly 0.9g); PROTEIN 14g; CARB 40g; FIBER 12g; SUGARS 7g (est. added sugars 0g); CHOL 13mg; IRON 3mg; SODIUM 602mg; CALCIUM 253mg

serve with:

- 1 (1-ounce) piece cornbread (107 calories)

1,300-CALORIE PLAN: Add 1½ cups spinach tossed with 1½ tablespoons light vinaigrette (53 calories).
1,400-CALORIE PLAN/1,500-CALORIE PLAN: Add 1½ cups spinach tossed with 1½ tablespoons light vinaigrette (100 calories) and sprinkled with 1 tablespoon chopped toasted pecans.

SNACKS, DESSERTS & EXTRAS

Cranberry-Pistachio Bars DF V

As a cross between a cookie and a brownie, this treat is just the thing to satisfy a chocolate craving.

Hands-on: 9 minutes | Total: 30 minutes | Serves 20 (serving size: 1 bar)

Cooking spray
1 cup uncooked old-fashioned rolled oats
¾ cup uncooked quinoa
¾ cup sweetened dried cranberries, coarsely chopped
½ cup salted, dry-roasted pistachios, chopped
⅓ cup unsweetened dried flaked coconut
2 tablespoons flaxseed meal
1 ounce bittersweet chocolate, finely chopped
½ cup unsalted creamy almond butter
6 tablespoons honey
1 tablespoon canola oil
¼ teaspoon salt

1. Preheat the oven to 350°F. Coat an 8-inch square glass or ceramic baking dish with cooking spray.
2. Spread the oats and quinoa on a baking sheet. Bake at 350°F for 8 minutes or until lightly browned; cool. Place oat mixture in a large bowl; stir in the cranberries, pistachios, coconut, flaxseed meal, and chocolate.
3. Combine the almond butter, honey, oil, and salt in a small saucepan over medium heat; bring to a boil. Cook 1 minute, stirring constantly. Pour the almond butter mixture over the oat mixture; toss well to coat. Press the mixture into the prepared baking dish. Bake at 350°F for 13 minutes or until lightly browned. Cool completely in dish. Cut into 20 bars.

CALORIES 158; FAT 8.1g (sat 1.7g, mono 3.7g, poly 1.8g); PROTEIN 4g; CARB 19g; FIBER 3g; SUGARS 9g (est. added sugars 6g); CHOL 0g; IRON 1mg; SODIUM 58mg; CALCIUM 32mg

158 TOTAL CALORIES

Portion Size Pointer

Portion size matters, especially when you're snacking on some nutrient-rich, yet calorically dense snacks, such as nuts and avocados. **Research has shown snackers eat more if a larger portion is offered to them. So to keep between-meal snacking in check, measure out your snacks before you're so hungry you're ready to devour them.**

Peanut Butter–Oatmeal Raisin Bars DF V

Substitute golden raisins for the cranberries and chopped salted, dry-roasted peanuts for the pistachios. Omit the coconut and chocolate. Add ½ teaspoon ground cinnamon to the oat mixture in step 2. Substitute creamy peanut butter for the almond butter.

SERVES 18 (serving size: 1 bar): CALORIES 158; FAT 7g (sat 1.2g, mono 3.3g, poly 2g); PROTEIN 4g; CARB 21g; FIBER 2g; SUGARS 10g (est. added sugars 6g); CHOL 0mg; IRON 1mg; SODIUM 78mg; CALCIUM 15mg

Oatmeal-Raisin Bars DF V

Hands-on: 10 minutes | Total: 2 hours, 15 minutes
Serves 10 (serving size: 1 bar)

These bars can easily be made gluten free by using oats that are certified gluten free.

1 cup golden raisins
1 cup boiling water
Cooking spray
1 cup quick-cooking oats
1 cup walnuts
½ teaspoon vanilla extract
¼ teaspoon fine sea salt
¼ teaspoon ground cinnamon

1. Combine the raisins and 1 cup boiling water in a bowl; cover and let stand 5 minutes or until soft. Drain and pat dry with paper towels.
2. Line a 9 x 5-inch loaf pan with plastic wrap. Coat the plastic wrap with cooking spray. Place the oats in a food processor; process 30 seconds or until finely ground. Add the raisins, walnuts, and remaining ingredients; process 1 minute or until the mixture is finely chopped and pulls away from the sides of the processor bowl.
3. Transfer the fruit mixture to the prepared pan. Coat a piece of plastic wrap with cooking spray. Place the plastic wrap, coated side down, on the surface of the fruit mixture, and press into an even layer using your fingers. Leave the plastic wrap pressed directly onto fruit mixture to cover; chill 2 hours.
4. Cut the fruit mixture into 10 bars. Wrap each bar individually with plastic wrap.

Note: Store in the refrigerator for up to 2 weeks.

CALORIES 151; FAT 7.4g (sat 0.7g, mono 1.1g, poly 4.7g); PROTEIN 3g; CARB 20g; FIBER 2g; SUGARS 9g (est. added sugars 0g); CHOL 0mg; IRON 1mg; SODIUM 40mg; CALCIUM 25mg

Cherry Pie Bars DF V

Combine 1 cup boiling water, ⅓ cup whole pitted dates, and 1 (5-ounce) package dried tart cherries in a bowl; cover and let stand 10 minutes or until soft. Drain and pat dry with paper towels. Place the cherry mixture, 1 cup raw unblanched almonds, ½ teaspoon vanilla extract, and ¼ teaspoon fine sea salt in a food processor; process 1 minute or until the mixture is finely chopped and pulls away from the sides of the processor bowl. Transfer the fruit mixture to the prepared pan and prepare as directed.

SERVES 10 (serving size: 1 bar): CALORIES 146; FAT 7.1g (sat 0.5g, mono 4.4g, poly 1.7g); PROTEIN 4g; CARB 19g; FIBER 6g; SUGARS 10g (est. added sugars 0g); CHOL 0mg; IRON 1mg; SODIUM 60mg; CALCIUM 20mg

Easy Energy Bars

These make-ahead, freezable bars—made from wholesome grains, healthy nuts, and fruit—help satisfy cravings.

1. Sunflower, Strawberry, and Butterscotch Bars (V)

Hands-on: 10 minutes | Total: 40 minutes

Preheat the oven to 350°F. Coat an 11 x 7-inch glass or ceramic baking dish with cooking spray. Combine ⅓ cup sunflower seed butter, ⅓ cup corn syrup, 1 tablespoon olive oil, 1 teaspoon vanilla extract, and ½ teaspoon salt in a microwave-safe bowl. Microwave at HIGH 1 minute or until bubbly. Combine 1¼ cups puffed barley cereal, 1 cup old-fashioned rolled oats, ⅔ cup chopped dried strawberries, ⅓ cup coarsely chopped pecans, and 3 tablespoons butterscotch morsels in a medium bowl. Pour the sunflower seed butter mixture over the barley mixture; toss well to coat. Press into the prepared dish. Sprinkle with 2 tablespoons golden flaxseeds, pressing to adhere. Bake at 350°F for 10 minutes. Cool completely in the dish. Cut into 14 bars.

SERVES 14 (serving size: 1 bar): CALORIES 153; FAT 8.2g (sat 1.5g, mono 4.4g, poly 1.8g); PROTEIN 3g; CARB 19g; FIBER 2g; SUGARS 8g (est. added sugars 3g); CHOL 0mg; IRON 1mg; SODIUM 112mg; CALCIUM 13mg

2. Peanut Butter–Chocolate Bars (DF)

Hands-on: 15 minutes | Total: 45 minutes

Preheat the oven to 350°F. Coat an 11 x 7-inch glass or ceramic baking dish with cooking spray. Combine ⅓ cup creamy peanut butter, ⅓ cup light agave nectar, 1 tablespoon olive oil, 1 teaspoon vanilla extract, and ½ teaspoon salt in a microwave-safe bowl. Microwave at HIGH 1 minute or until bubbly. Combine 1¼ cups puffed barley cereal, 1 cup old-fashioned rolled oats, ⅔ cup dried mixed berries, ⅓ cup dry-roasted salted peanuts, and ⅓ cup mini marshmallows in a medium bowl. Pour the peanut butter mixture over the barley mixture; toss well to coat. Press into the prepared baking dish. Bake at 350°F for 10 minutes or until set. Place 2 ounces chopped bittersweet chocolate in a small microwave-safe bowl; microwave at HIGH 30 seconds or until melted, stirring until smooth. Drizzle over the bars. Cool completely in the dish. Cut into 14 bars.

SERVES 14 (serving size: 1 bar): CALORIES 166; FAT 7.5g (sat 1.8g, mono 3.6g, poly 1.7g); PROTEIN 4g; CARB 22g; FIBER 2g; SUGARS 14g (est. added sugars 2g); CHOL 0mg; IRON 1mg; SODIUM 115mg; CALCIUM 13mg

3. Pumpkinseed, Date, and Tahini Bars DF V

Hands-on: 15 minutes | Total: 45 minutes

Preheat the oven to 350°F. Coat an 11 x 7-inch glass or ceramic baking dish with cooking spray. Combine ⅓ cup tahini, ⅓ cup brown rice syrup, 1 tablespoon olive oil, 1 teaspoon vanilla extract, and ½ teaspoon salt in a microwave-safe bowl. Microwave at HIGH 1 minute or until bubbly. Combine 1¼ cups puffed barley cereal, 1 cup old-fashioned rolled oats, ⅔ cup prechopped dates, and ⅓ cup toasted pumpkinseed kernels in a medium bowl. Pour the tahini mixture over the barley mixture; toss well to coat. Press into the prepared baking dish. Sprinkle with 3 tablespoons toasted uncooked quinoa, pressing to adhere. Bake at 350°F for 10 minutes or until set. Cool completely in the dish. Cut into 14 bars.

SERVES 14 (serving size: 1 bar): CALORIES 149; FAT 6.2g (sat 0.9g, mono 2.5g, poly 2.3g); PROTEIN 4g; CARB 21g; FIBER 2g; SUGARS 11g (est. added sugars 7g); CHOL 0mg; IRON 1mg; SODIUM 103mg; CALCIUM 16mg

4. Coconut, Almond, and Goji Bars DF V

Hands-on: 15 minutes | Total: 45 minutes

Preheat the oven to 350°F. Coat an 11 x 7-inch glass or ceramic baking dish with cooking spray. Combine ⅓ cup almond butter, ⅓ cup honey, 1 tablespoon olive oil, 1 teaspoon vanilla extract, and ½ teaspoon salt in a microwave-safe bowl. Microwave at HIGH 1 minute or until bubbly. Combine 1¼ cups puffed barley cereal, 1 cup old-fashioned rolled oats, ⅔ cup dried goji berries, ⅓ cup coarsely chopped toasted almonds, and ⅓ cup flaked, unsweetened coconut in a medium bowl. Pour the almond butter mixture over the barley mixture; toss well to coat. Press into the prepared baking dish. Sprinkle with 1 tablespoon sesame seeds, pressing to adhere. Bake at 350°F for 10 minutes or until set. Cool completely in the baking dish. Cut into 14 bars.

SERVES 14 (serving size: 1 bar): CALORIES 146; FAT 7.7g (sat 1.7g, mono 3.7g, poly 1.5g); PROTEIN 4g; CARB 17g; FIBER 2g; SUGARS 7g (est. added sugars 7g); CHOL 0mg; IRON 1mg; SODIUM 115mg; CALCIUM 38mg

5. Pistachio-Apple Bars with Chia Seeds DF V

Hands-on: 15 minutes | Total: 45 minutes

Preheat the oven to 350°F. Coat an 11 x 7-inch glass or ceramic baking dish with cooking spray. Combine ⅓ cup cashew butter, ⅓ cup honey, 1 tablespoon olive oil, 1 teaspoon vanilla extract, and ½ teaspoon salt in a microwave-safe bowl. Microwave at HIGH 1 minute or until bubbly. Combine 1¼ cups puffed barley cereal, 1 cup old-fashioned rolled oats, ¼ cup finely chopped dried apple, ¼ cup chopped sweetened dried cranberries, and ⅓ cup chopped dry-roasted pistachios in a medium bowl. Pour the cashew butter mixture over the barley mixture; toss well to coat. Press into the prepared baking dish. Sprinkle with 1 teaspoon black chia seeds, pressing to adhere. Bake at 350°F for 10 minutes or until set. Cool completely in the dish. Cut into 14 bars.

SERVES 14 (serving size: 1 bar): CALORIES 125; FAT 5.9g (sat 1g, mono 3.3g, poly 1.2g); PROTEIN 3g; CARB 17g; FIBER 2g; SUGARS 10g (est. added sugars 7g); CHOL 0mg; IRON 1mg; SODIUM 122mg; CALCIUM 8mg

Crispy Rice Bars

These bars are a perennial favorite. They're a sweet snack-time idea. Start here: Coat a 13 x 9–inch pan with cooking spray. Melt 2 tablespoons butter and 10 ounces marshmallows over medium-low heat. Add one of the flavor combinations below and 6 cups rice cereal. Press the mixture into the prepared pan.

1. Double Chocolate Bars DF

Stir ¼ cup unsweetened cocoa into the melted marshmallows; cook 3 minutes. Add the cereal; toss well to combine. Press the cereal mixture into the prepared pan. Place 4 ounces chopped bittersweet chocolate in a microwave-safe dish. Microwave at HIGH 45 seconds or until melted, stirring every 15 seconds; drizzle over the cereal mixture. Chill 10 minutes before cutting into 20 bars.

SERVES 20 (serving size: 1 bar): CALORIES 116; FAT 3.9g (sat 2g, mono 0.4g, poly 0.1g); PROTEIN 1g; CARB 22g; FIBER 1g; SUGARS 11g (est. added sugars 10g); CHOL 3mg; IRON 3mg; SODIUM 66mg; CALCIUM 3mg

2. Maple-Bacon Bars DF

Stir 3 tablespoons maple syrup and 4 cooked, drained, chopped applewood smoked bacon slices into the melted marshmallows. Add the cereal, and toss well to combine. Press the mixture into the prepared pan.

SERVES 20 (serving size: 1 bar): CALORIES 105; FAT 2.2g (sat 1.1g, mono 0.3g, poly 0.1g); PROTEIN 2g; CARB 20g; FIBER 0g; SUGARS 11g (est. added sugars 10g); CHOL 5mg; IRON 3mg; SODIUM 110mg; CALCIUM 4mg

3. Cherry-Chip Bars

Stir 1 cup finely chopped dried cherries and ¼ teaspoon vanilla extract into the melted marshmallow mixture. Add the cereal, and toss well to combine. Press the cereal mixture into the prepared pan. Sprinkle the mixture evenly with ⅓ cup semisweet chocolate minichips.

SERVES 20 (serving size: 1 bar): CALORIES 105; FAT 2.1g (sat 1.3g, mono 0.6g, poly 0.1g); PROTEIN 1g; CARB 26g; FIBER 0g; SUGARS 15g (est. added sugars 9g); CHOL 3mg; IRON 3mg; SODIUM 67mg; CALCIUM 2mg

4. Espresso-Toffee Bars

Stir 1 tablespoon espresso powder into the melted butter before adding the marshmallows. Add 1 cup toffee bits and the cereal; toss well to combine. Press the cereal mixture into the prepared pan.

SERVES 20 (serving size: 1 bar): CALORIES 154; FAT 5.5g (sat 2.8g, mono 0.4g, poly 0.3g); PROTEIN 1g; CARB 27g; FIBER 0g; SUGARS 16g (est. added sugars 15g); CHOL 7mg; IRON 0mg; SODIUM 83mg; CALCIUM 4mg

5. Chocolate-Butterscotch Bars

Press the cereal mixture into the prepared pan. Place 1 cup chocolate chips in a microwave-safe bowl. Microwave at HIGH 1 minute, stirring every 20 seconds. Spread over the cereal mixture. Place ½ cup butterscotch chips and 2 teaspoons fat-free milk in a microwave-safe bowl. Microwave at HIGH 30 seconds; stir once. Dollop the butterscotch mixture over the chocolate; swirl with a knife. Chill.

SERVES 20 (serving size: 1 bar): CALORIES 149; FAT 5g (sat 3.3g, mono 1.3g, poly 0.2g); PROTEIN 1g; CARB 27g; FIBER 1g; SUGARS 16g (est. added sugars 14g); CHOL 3mg; IRON 3mg; SODIUM 71mg; CALCIUM 6mg

6. Browned Butter–Pecan Bars

Before adding the marshmallows, cook the melted butter 3 minutes or until browned. Add ¼ teaspoon kosher salt and ¼ teaspoon vanilla extract to the melted marshmallows; stir well. Add the cereal; toss well to combine. Press the cereal mixture into the prepared pan; sprinkle evenly with ½ cup chopped toasted pecans.

SERVES 20 (serving size: 1 bar): CALORIES 105; FAT 3.3g (sat 0.9g, mono 1.4g, poly 0.7g); PROTEIN 1g; CARB 19g; FIBER 0g; SUGARS 9g (est. added sugars 8g); CHOL 3mg; IRON 3mg; SODIUM 90mg; CALCIUM 3mg

7. S'mores Chewy Bars

Char the marshmallows under the broiler for 2 minutes before melting. Stir ½ cup graham cracker crumbs and ½ cup semisweet chocolate minichips into the melted marshmallows before adding the cereal; toss well to combine. Press the cereal mixture into the prepared pan.

SERVES 20 (serving size: 1 bar): CALORIES 120; FAT 3g (sat 1.6g, mono 0.9g, poly 0.3g); PROTEIN 1g; CARB 24g; FIBER 1g; SUGARS 12g (est. added sugars 11g); CHOL 3mg; IRON 0mg; SODIUM 33mg; CALCIUM 5mg

8. Lemon–White Chocolate Bars

Stir 1 tablespoon grated lemon rind into the melted marshmallows before adding the cereal. Press the cereal mixture into the prepared pan. Place 4 ounces chopped premium white chocolate in a microwave-safe bowl. Microwave at HIGH 1½ minutes or until melted, stirring every 20 seconds; drizzle over the cereal mixture. Refrigerate for 15 minutes before cutting into 20 bars.

Serves 20 (serving size: 1 bar): CALORIES 116; FAT 3.1g (sat 1.9g, mono 0.9g, poly 0.1g); PROTEIN 1g; CARB 22g; FIBER 0g; SUGARS 12g (est. added sugars 11g); CHOL 4mg; IRON 0mg; SODIUM 71mg; CALCIUM 13mg

North Carolina Woman Overcomes Genetic Weight-Loss Struggle

RALEIGH RESIDENT KENNAN HESTER IS NO STRANGER TO WEIGHT STRUGGLES. Her mother was overweight most of her life prior to lap band surgery, as was her sister. Those battles waged by family members were motivation enough for Kennan to stay active throughout high school, but it became more of a challenge in college. She turned to diet services and products, but nothing really fit.

"With other diets I've tried, it was really easy to get derailed and completely gain everything back that I had already lost," Kennan said. "I tried Weight Watchers, I tried some juice diets, I tried cutting out alcohol. I tried Lean Cuisine right after college. Weight Watchers kind of worked a little bit, but it just wasn't sustainable."

Eager to try something new with wedding season right around the corner, Kennan and her husband, Joey, discovered the Cooking Light Diet. They joined, and their start was promising.

"In the first two weeks, we both started losing weight," Kennan said. "I've now maintained 14 pounds* of weight loss in fifteen weeks. My whole family has asked me what I'm doing, and how they can do it, too! And I've had coworkers start noticing, and I feel awesome. I'm loving it."

Navigating wedding season with the CLDiet was smooth sailing. "With the Cooking Light Diet, we had seven weddings this year, and I was able to attend all those weddings and still lose 20 pounds*," Kennan said.

In addition to the obvious benefits of weight-loss success, Kennan has loved that the Cooking Light Diet still lets her indulge.

"[I love] the fact that it occasionally tells me to sub a snack for wine," Kennan laughed. "[But] The Cooking Light Diet is crucial to where I am today. It completely changed the way that I can lose weight, and how I can be healthy. I am still eating amazing food, and still enjoying those other indulgences whenever I want."

**Members following The Cooking Light Diet lose more than half a pound per week, on average.*

> "The Cooking Light Diet is crucial to where I am today. It completely changed the way that I can lose weight, and how I can be healthy."

Easy and Convenient 150-Calorie Snack Ideas

Homemade Guacamole and Chips 

Place 2 tablespoons chopped onion, 2 tablespoons chopped fresh cilantro, ⅛ teaspoon salt, and 1 medium chopped avocado in a food processor; pulse 8 times or until combined. Serve with 13 baked tortilla chips per serving.

SERVES 4 (serving size: about 3 tablespoons guacamole and 13 chips): CALORIES 147; FAT 7g (sat 0.6g, mono 3.8g, poly 0.6g); PROTEIN 2g; CARB 19g; FIBER 5g; SUGARS 0g (est. added sugars 0g); CHOL 0mg; IRON 1mg; SODIUM 156mg; CALCIUM 29mg

Turkey and Cheese Roll 

Top 2 ounces of lean lower-sodium deli roasted turkey breast with 2 ultra-thin slices of provolone cheese (0.8 ounces cheese total) and roll up.

SERVES 1: CALORIES 142; FAT 7.6g (sat 4.4g, mono 1.7g, poly 0.2g); PROTEIN 15g; CARB 4g; FIBER 0g; SUGARS 1g (est. added sugars 0g); CHOL 36mg; IRON 0mg; SODIUM 692mg; CALCIUM 171mg

Greek Yogurt and Strawberry Snack 

Stir ¼ cup sliced strawberries into ½ cup plain fat-free Greek yogurt. Stir in 1 teaspoon of honey.

SERVES 1: CALORIES 105; FAT 0.1g (sat 0g, mono 0g, poly 0.1g); PROTEIN 10g; CARB 16g; FIBER 1g; SUGARS 12g (est. added sugars 6g); CHOL 0mg; IRON 0mg; SODIUM 43mg; CALCIUM 82mg

Crunch-Crunch-Crunch Mix DF V

Combine ½ cup dried cherries, 2 cups whole-grain Rice Chex, ½ cup roasted unsalted pistachios, and 3 cups Kashi Go Lean Crunch Cereal.

SERVES 1: CALORIES 116; FAT 3.1g (sat 0.4g, mono 1.7g, poly 1g); PROTEIN 4g; CARB 19g; FIBER 3g; SUGARS 10g (est. added sugars 3g); CHOL 0mg; IRON 2mg; SODIUM 67mg; CALCIUM 37mg

Raspberry-Ricotta Waffle 

Toast 1 frozen whole-wheat waffle (such as Van's). Dollop with 1 tablespoon part-skim ricotta cheese and 2 teaspoons raspberry preserves.

SERVES 1: CALORIES 134; FAT 4.2g (sat 0.8g, mono 1.7g, poly 1g); PROTEIN 3; CARB 24g; FIBER 3g; SUGARS 10g (est. added sugars 9g); CHOL 0mg; IRON 1mg; SODIUM 67mg; CALCIUM 37mg

Salty-Sweet Mix

Combine 1½ cups Post Honey Nut Shredded Wheat, 1 cup dried mangoes, 3 cups Triscuit Whole-Wheat Thin Crisps, and ½ cup roasted almonds; toss well.

SERVES 12 (serving size: ½ cup): CALORIES 126; FAT 4.6g (sat 0.5g, mono 2.1g, poly 0.8g); PROTEIN 3; CARB 20g; FIBER 2g; SUGARS 9g (est. added sugars 2g); CHOL 0mg; IRON 1mg; SODIUM 57mg; CALCIUM 36mg

Chocolate-Granola Apple Wedges 

Place 2 ounces finely chopped semisweet chocolate in a medium-sized microwave-safe bowl. Microwave at HIGH 1 minute, stirring every 15 seconds, or until the chocolate melts. Place ⅓ cup low-fat granola without raisins in a shallow dish. Dip 1 large Braeburn apple, cut into 16 wedges, skin side up, in the chocolate; allow excess chocolate to drip back into bowl. Dredge the wedges in the granola. Place the wedges, chocolate side up, on a large plate. Refrigerate 5 minutes or until set. Note: If you can't find Braeburn apples, Gala or Fuji varieties also stand up to dipping and add a touch more sweetness.

SERVES 4 (serving size: 4 apple wedges): CALORIES 132; FAT 4.8g (sat 2.6g, mono 1.4g, poly 0.1g); PROTEIN 2g; CARB 24g; FIBER 3g; SUGARS 14g (est. added sugars 8g); CHOL 10mg; IRON 1mg; SODIUM 22mg; CALCIUM 13mg

Gluten-Free Peanut Butter–Chocolate Chip Cookies GF V

Hands-on: 10 minutes | Total: 20 minutes
Serves 20 (serving size: 1 cookie)

You probably have everything on hand to make these chewy, chocolaty peanut butter cookies. To fit the cookies on a single sheet pan, divide the cookies into five rows of four. Pressing the cookies flat helps them bake quickly and get lovely crisp edges; otherwise they'll be too round and undercooked.

¼ teaspoon salt
1 large egg white
1 cup chunky peanut butter
⅓ cup granulated sugar
¼ cup brown sugar
¼ cup semisweet chocolate minichips

1. Preheat the oven to 375°F. Line a baking sheet with parchment paper.
2. Place the salt and egg white in a medium bowl; stir with a whisk until the white is frothy. Add the peanut butter, granulated sugar, brown sugar, and chocolate chips, stirring to combine.
3. Divide the dough into 20 equal portions (about 1 tablespoon each); arrange the dough 2 inches apart on the prepared baking sheet. Gently press the top of each cookie with a fork; press the top of each cookie again to form a crisscross pattern, and flatten to a 2-inch diameter. Bake at 375°F for 10 minutes or until lightly browned. Cool on a wire rack.

CALORIES 131; FAT 5.6g (sat 1.4g, mono 2.6g, poly 1.4g); PROTEIN 3g; CARB 13g; FIBER 1g; SUGARS 9g (est. added sugars 7g); CHOL 0mg; IRON 0mg; SODIUM 121mg; CALCIUM 3mg

Fudgy Skillet Cookie (V)

Hands-on: 10 minutes | Total: 29 minutes
Serves 16 (serving size: 1 wedge)

148 TOTAL CALORIES

As a cross between a cookie and a brownie, this treat is just the thing to satisfy a chocolate craving. Sprinkle with additional chocolate chips, if you like, while the cookie is still warm for melty chocolate goodness.

2 ounces semisweet chocolate
3 tablespoons canola oil
2 tablespoons unsalted butter
½ cup brown sugar
¼ cup granulated sugar
1 large egg
3.4 ounces all-purpose flour (about ¾ cup)
½ cup unsweetened cocoa
½ teaspoon baking soda
½ teaspoon salt
2½ ounces milk chocolate, chopped

1. Preheat the oven to 350°F.

2. Place the semisweet chocolate, canola oil, and butter in a microwave-safe bowl. Microwave at HIGH 45 seconds, stirring occasionally. Stir in the brown sugar, granulated sugar, and egg. Weigh or lightly spoon flour into dry measuring cups; level with a knife. Stir in the flour, cocoa, baking soda, and salt. Stir in the chopped milk chocolate. Scrape into a 10-inch cast-iron skillet. Bake at 350°F for 19 minutes. Cut into 16 wedges.

CALORIES 148; FAT 7.4g (sat 3.1g, mono 2.6g, poly 1g); PROTEIN 2g; CARB 21g; FIBER 1g; SUGARS 14g (est. added sugars 13g); CHOL 16mg; IRON 1mg; SODIUM 123mg; CALCIUM 21mg

Candy Craving

Sometimes a small taste of your favorite candy is what you're craving. You can have the sweet treat—and stay within your calorie limit. Each of these treats has about 150 calories.

- 2 snack-sized York Peppermint Patties
- 6 Werther's Original Creamy Caramel-Filled Candies
- 7 regular-sized pretzels
- 9 M&M Almond candies
- 44 plain M&M candies
- 1½ tablespoons Nutella Hazelnut Spread
- 5 pieces Dove dark chocolate
- 6 Hershey's Kisses
- 2 fun-size Milky Way bars
- 4 miniature Milky Way Midnight bars

Maple-Pecan Bars GF V

Hands-on: 20 minutes | Total: 55 minutes | Serves 20 (serving size: 1 bar)

Reminiscent of pecan pie, these bars deserve a spot at your holiday dessert buffet. Use pure maple syrup to form the gooey brown sugar and pecan mixture needed to make these heavenly bars.

CRUST

2.6 ounces white rice flour (about ½ cup)
2.3 ounces cornstarch (about ½ cup)
2.1 ounces sweet white sorghum flour (about ½ cup)
½ cup packed brown sugar
6 tablespoons butter
1 teaspoon xanthan gum
2 teaspoons vanilla extract
¼ teaspoon salt

FILLING

½ cup pure maple syrup
⅓ cup packed brown sugar
¼ cup 1% low-fat milk
1 tablespoon butter
½ cup whole pecans
½ teaspoon vanilla extract

1. Preheat the oven to 375°F.
2. Line a 9-inch square metal baking pan with parchment paper.
3. Make the crust: Weigh or lightly spoon the white rice flour, cornstarch, and sorghum flour into dry measuring cups; level with a knife. Place the white rice flour, cornstarch, sorghum flour, ½ cup brown sugar, and the next 4 ingredients (through salt) in a food processor; pulse until mixture resembles fine meal. Press the flour mixture into the bottom of the prepared pan. Bake at 375°F for 15 minutes or until the edges of the crust are slightly browned.
4. While the crust bakes, make the filling: Combine the syrup and the next 3 ingredients (through 1 tablespoon butter) in a medium saucepan; bring to a boil over medium heat. Cook 2 minutes, stirring constantly with a whisk until the sugar dissolves. Remove from the heat; add the pecans and ½ teaspoon vanilla, stirring with a whisk. Pour the mixture into the hot crust. Bake at 375°F for 10 minutes or until the filling is bubbly. Cool completely in the pan. Cut into 20 bars.

CALORIES 149; FAT 6.2g (sat 2.8g, mono 2.2g, poly 0.8g); PROTEIN 1g; CARB 23g; FIBER 1g; SUGARS 14g (est. added sugars 14g); CHOL 11mg; IRON 0mg; SODIUM 7mg; CALCIUM 23mg

Lemon Squares

Hands-on: 17 minutes | Total: 3 hours, 10 minutes
Serves 16 (serving size: 1 square)

A tender shortbread cookie crust meets a delectably bold, tart lemon filling in these luscious treats.

Cooking spray
3.4 ounces all-purpose flour (about ¾ cup)
¼ cup powdered sugar
3 tablespoons pine nuts, toasted and coarsely chopped
⅛ teaspoon salt
2 tablespoons chilled unsalted butter, cut into small pieces
2 tablespoons canola oil
¾ cup granulated sugar
2 tablespoons all-purpose flour
1 teaspoon grated lemon rind
½ cup fresh lemon juice
2 large eggs
1 large egg white
2 tablespoons powdered sugar

1. Preheat the oven to 350°F. Coat an 8-inch square glass or ceramic baking dish with cooking spray.
2. Weigh or lightly spoon the flour into dry measuring cups; level with a knife. Place the flour, ¼ cup powdered sugar, pine nuts, and salt in a food processor; pulse 2 times to combine. Add the butter and canola oil. Pulse 3 to 5 times or until the mixture resembles coarse meal. Place the mixture into the bottom of the prepared baking dish. Press into the bottom of the pan. Bake at 350°F for 20 minutes or until lightly browned. Reduce the oven temperature to 325°F.
3. Combine the granulated sugar and the next 5 ingredients (through egg white) in a medium bowl, stirring with a whisk until smooth. Pour the mixture over the crust. Bake at 325°F for 20 minutes or until set. Remove from the oven, and cool completely in the pan on a wire rack. Cover and chill for at least 2 hours. Sprinkle the squares with 2 tablespoons powdered sugar. Cut into 16 squares.

CALORIES 124; FAT 5g (sat 1.3g, mono 2g, poly 1.2g); PROTEIN 2g; CARB 19g; FIBER 0g; SUGARS 12g (est. added sugars 12g); CHOL 30mg; IRON 1mg; SODIUM 31mg; CALCIUM 6mg

124 TOTAL CALORIES

Quick, Convenient Sweet Snacks

GRANOLA BARS
Watch for sugar and look for one with fiber

- Nature Valley Dark Chocolate & Nut Chewy Trail Mix Bar
  1 bar: 140 calories, 14g sugar, 1g fiber
- Kasha TLC Trail Mix Chewy Granola Bar
  1 bar: 140 calories, 6g sugar, 4g fiber
- Nature Valley Oats 'n Honey Crunchy Granola Bar
  2 bars: 190 calories, 12g sugar, 2g fiber

ICE CREAM
Watch for saturated fat

- Edy's/Dreyer's Chocolate Rich & Creamy Grand Ice Cream
  ½ cup: 140 calories, 4g sat fat
- Breyers Original Chocolate
  ½ cup: 140 calories, 4.5g sat fat

148
TOTAL CALORIES

Butterscotch Bars (V)

Hands-on: 12 minutes | Total: 57 minutes | Serves 36 (serving size: 1 bar)

A small square of these rich bars can satisfy a sweet craving. The flour and oats mixture is somewhat dry after combining, but it serves as both a solid base for the soft butterscotch chip layer and a crumbly, streusel-like topping.

Cooking spray
1 cup packed brown sugar
5 tablespoons butter, melted
1 teaspoon vanilla extract
1 large egg, lightly beaten
9 ounces all-purpose flour (about 2 cups)
2½ cups quick-cooking oats
½ teaspoon salt
½ teaspoon baking soda
¾ cup fat-free sweetened condensed milk
1¼ cups butterscotch morsels (about 8 ounces)
⅛ teaspoon salt
½ cup finely chopped toasted walnuts

1. Preheat the oven to 350°F. Coat a 13 x 9-inch metal baking pan with cooking spray.
2. Combine the sugar and butter in a large bowl. Stir in the vanilla and egg. Weigh or lightly spoon the flour into dry measuring cups; level with a knife. Combine the flour, oats, ½ teaspoon salt, and baking soda in a bowl. Add the oat mixture to the sugar mixture; stir with a fork until combined (mixture will be crumbly). Place 3 cups oat mixture into the bottom of the prepared pan. Press into the bottom of the pan.
3. Place the sweetened condensed milk, butterscotch morsels, and ⅛ teaspoon salt in a medium-sized microwave-safe bowl; microwave at HIGH 1 minute or until butterscotch morsels melt, stirring every 20 seconds. Stir in the walnuts. Scrape the mixture into the pan, spreading evenly over the crust. Sprinkle with the remaining oat mixture, gently pressing into the butterscotch mixture. Bake at 350°F for 30 minutes or until the topping is golden brown. Place the pan on a cooling rack; run a knife around the outside edge. Cool completely. Cut into 36 bars.

CALORIES 148; FAT 5.1g (sat 2.7g, mono 0.9g, poly 1.1g); PROTEIN 3g; CARB 23g; FIBER 1g; SUGARS 14g (est. added sugars 14g); CHOL 11mg; IRON 1mg; SODIUM 87mg; CALCIUM 31mg

Chocolate–Pecan Pie Truffles ⓥ

Hands-on: 20 minutes | Total: 2 hours, 20 minutes
Serves 24 (serving size: 2 truffles)

These rich truffles are quick and easy to make and are perfectly portioned bites.

16 ounces pecan pie (about ½ pie), chilled and cut into 3-inch pieces
¼ cup unsweetened cocoa
1½ tablespoons bourbon
7½ ounces chopped dry-roasted, salted almonds

1. Place the pie in a food processor; pulse 30 seconds or until the mixture resembles chunky peanut butter. Add the cocoa, bourbon, and 4 ounces of the almonds; pulse 3 to 4 times or until combined. Remove the mixture to a bowl; cover and chill 1 hour.
2. Line a baking sheet with parchment paper. Drop the pecan pie mixture by 2 teaspoonfuls onto the prepared baking sheet to form 48 balls. Place in the freezer for 1 hour or until the truffles are firm.
3. While the truffles chill, very finely chop the remaining almonds; place in a shallow dish. Remove the truffles from freezer; gently shape each mound into a ball. Roll the truffles in the nuts to coat. Keep the truffles chilled in an airtight container. Let stand 2 or 3 minutes at room temperature before serving.

CALORIES 126; FAT 8.2g (sat 1.4g, mono 4.1g, poly 1.7g); PROTEIN 3g; CARB 11g; FIBER 1g; SUGARS 4g (est. added sugars 3g); CHOL 10mg; IRON 1mg; SODIUM 77mg; CALCIUM 33mg

126
TOTAL CALORIES

Quick, Convenient Salty Snacks

CRACKERS

Watch for sodium and go for the fiber

- Kellogg's Special K Multi-Grain Crackers
  24 crackers: 120 calories, 3g fat, 250mg sodium, 3g fiber
- Back To Nature Harvest Whole Wheat Crackers
  6 crackers: 120 calories, 4.5g fat, 180mg sodium, 3g fiber
- Ak-Mak 100% Whole Wheat Stone Ground Sesame Crackers
  5 crackers: 115 calories, 2g fat, 220mg sodium, 4g fiber

CHIPS

Watch for sodium

- Stacy's Simply Naked Chips
  10 chips: 130 calories, 270mg sodium
- Kangaroo Sea Salt
  9 chips: 110 calories, 180mg sodium

Chocolate Pavlovas with Mixed Berries

Hands-on: 20 minutes | Total: 5 hours, 20 minutes
Serves 8 (serving size: 1 meringue, about 3 tablespoons whipped topping, and about ¼ cup berry mixture)

These pavlovas with their mild chocolate flavor are crisp and tender, but become chewy when the fruit syrup soaks in. A heavy-duty stand mixer works best for whipping the meringue, but you can use any mixer you have on hand.

4 large egg whites, at room temperature
¼ teaspoon cream of tartar
¾ cup plus 1 tablespoon granulated sugar
½ teaspoon vanilla extract
2 tablespoons unsweetened cocoa
1 cup sliced strawberries
¾ cup fresh raspberries
½ cup fresh blueberries
1½ cups frozen reduced-fat whipped topping, thawed

1. Preheat the oven to 250°F. Cover a large baking sheet with parchment paper. Draw 8 (4-inch) circles on the paper. Turn the parchment paper over; secure the paper to the baking sheet with masking tape.
2. Beat the egg whites and cream of tartar with a heavy-duty stand mixer at medium speed until foamy, about 1 minute. Increase speed to high; beat until soft peaks form, about 1 minute. Reduce speed to medium, and add ¾ cup of the sugar, 1 tablespoon at a time, beating well after each addition.
3. Increase the mixer speed to high; beat the mixture just until stiff peaks form and sugar dissolves (do not overbeat). Beat in the vanilla. Sift the cocoa over the meringue mixture; gently fold into the mixture using a rubber spatula until blended, being careful not to deflate the meringue. Divide the mixture among the 8 drawn circles on the prepared pan. Shape the meringues into nests with 1-inch sides using the back of a spoon.
4. Bake at 250°F for 2 hours or until dry, turning the pan halfway around (on same rack) after 1 hour. Turn the oven off; let the meringues stand in the oven, with the door closed, 3 hours or overnight. Carefully remove the meringues from the paper. Store in an airtight container for up to 2 days.
5. Combine the strawberries, raspberries, and blueberries in a bowl; sprinkle with the remaining 1 tablespoon sugar. Let the berry mixture stand, stirring occasionally, until syrupy, about 30 minutes. Top each meringue with whipped topping and berry mixture. Serve immediately.

CALORIES 141; FAT 2.2g (sat 1.7g, mono 0.2g, poly 0.1g); PROTEIN 3g; CARB 29g; FIBER 2g; SUGARS 26g (est. added sugars 20g); CHOL 0mg; IRON 0mg; SODIUM 39mg; CALCIUM 20mg

Strawberry Cheesecake Pops

Hands-on: 15 minutes | Total: 4 hours, 15 minutes
Serves 6 (serving size: 1 ice pop)

These pops are a frosty twist on cheesecake. They're rich, creamy, fruity, and all kinds of good.

1 (5-ounce) can evaporated low-fat milk
¼ cup sugar
3 ounces ⅓-less-fat cream cheese, softened
¼ cup plain fat-free Greek yogurt
1 teaspoon vanilla extract
3 tablespoons light-colored corn syrup
1 teaspoon fresh lemon juice
10 ounces strawberries, hulled
¼ cup graham cracker crumbs

1. Combine the milk and sugar in a saucepan over medium heat; cook 3 minutes. Place the cream cheese in a medium bowl; gradually add the milk mixture, whisking until smooth. Stir in the yogurt and vanilla. Cool completely.
2. Place the corn syrup, juice, and berries in a blender; process until smooth. Divide half of the cream cheese mixture among 6 (4-ounce) ice-pop molds. Top with the strawberry mixture, followed by the remaining cream cheese mixture. Stir slightly with a skewer. Freeze 4 hours or until solid.
3. Unmold ice pops; dip tips in graham cracker crumbs.

CALORIES 154; FAT 4.1g (sat 1.9g, mono 1g, poly 0.3g); PROTEIN 4g; CARB 26g; FIBER 1g; SUGARS 18g (est. added sugars 12g); CHOL 14mg; IRON 0mg; SODIUM 101mg; CALCIUM 91mg

Chocolate Cookie Ice Cream Sandwiches

Hands-on: 18 minutes | Total: 2 hours, 35 minutes
Serves 18 (serving size: 1 sandwich)

If you've ever bitten into an ice cream sandwich only to feel cheated out of cookie, you won't be disappointed in these little rounds. They have the ideal ratio of cookie to ice cream.

Cooking spray
4.5 ounces all-purpose flour (about 1 cup)
¼ teaspoon baking soda
⅛ teaspoon salt
½ cup packed dark brown sugar
¼ cup butter, softened
½ cup granulated sugar
⅓ cup unsweetened cocoa
2 large egg whites
2¼ cups cookies-and-cream light ice cream, softened

1. Preheat the oven to 350°F. Coat 2 baking sheets with cooking spray.
2. Weigh or lightly spoon the flour into a dry measuring cup; level with a knife. Combine the flour, baking soda, and salt in a medium bowl, stirring with a whisk.
3. Place the brown sugar and butter in a medium bowl. Beat with a mixer at medium speed until creamy; gradually add the granulated sugar, beating well. Add the cocoa and egg whites, beating well. Gradually add the flour mixture, beating until well blended. Drop by rounded teaspoonfuls 1½ inches apart onto the prepared baking sheets.
4. Bake at 350°F for 10 minutes or just until the edges are set. Cool on pans for 2 minutes; remove from the pans. Cool completely on wire racks.
5. Spread about 2 tablespoons ice cream onto the flat side of 18 cookies; top each with another cookie, pressing gently to form a sandwich. Freeze until firm, about 2 hours.

CALORIES 124; FAT 3.3g (sat 2g, mono 0.8g, poly 0.2g); PROTEIN 2g; CARB 22g; FIBER 1g; SUGARS 14g (est. added sugars 12g); CHOL 8mg; IRON 1mg; SODIUM 70mg; CALCIUM 21mg

Cucumber Pimm's Cup

Cucumber Pimm's Cup DF GF V

152 TOTAL CALORIES

Hands-on: 11 minutes | Total: 8 hours, 11 minutes | Serves 6

A traditional Pimm's Cup may include slices of lemon and orange, mint, and sometimes rosemary or thyme, along with cucumber spears. We steeped the lemonade overnight with cucumber slices to bring out their flavor.

2 cups prepared lemonade
1 large cucumber, cut into ½-inch-thick slices
1 cup Pimm's No. 1, chilled
1 cup ginger ale, chilled
6 cucumber spears (optional)
Mint leaves (optional)

1. Combine the prepared lemonade and cucumber slices in a large pitcher. Refrigerate 8 hours or overnight.
2. Add the Pimm's and ginger ale to the pitcher. Pour 1 cup of the mixture into each of 6 ice-filled glasses. Garnish with cucumber spears and mint leaves, if desired.

CALORIES 152; FAT 0.2g (sat 0g, mono 0g, poly 0g); PROTEIN 1g; CARB 16g; FIBER 1g; SUGARS 14g (est. added sugars 13g); CHOL 0g; IRON 0mg; SODIUM 10mg; CALCIUM 15mg

Bottled Manhattans DF LC V

128 TOTAL CALORIES

Hands-on: 11 minutes | Total: 8 hours, 11 minutes
Serves 12 (serving size: about 2 ounces)

Garnish this classic cocktail with an orange twist and a maraschino cherry.

2 cups rye whiskey
1 cup sweet (Italian) vermouth
2 teaspoons Angostura bitters
12 orange twists
12 maraschino cherries

1. Combine the first 3 ingredients in a large bowl; stir gently.
2. Funnel the mixture into a clean 750-milliliter bottle, leaving an inch of headroom at the top of the bottle; seal with a cork or cap. Store in the refrigerator or in a cool, dark place for long aging.
3. To make 1 cocktail, pour 2 ounces of the whiskey mixture into a pint glass filled with ice. Stir rapidly for 20 to 30 seconds. Strain into a chilled cocktail glass or tumbler filled with ice. Garnish with an orange twist and a maraschino cherry.

CALORIES 128; FAT 0g (sat 0g, mono 0g, poly 0g); PROTEIN 0g; CARB 5g; FIBER 0g; SUGARS 2g (est. added sugars 1g); CHOL 0mg; IRON 0mg; SODIUM 2mg; CALCIUM 4mg

Know Your Alcohol

The benefits of alcohol are real. Any alcohol, *consumed within the recommended guidelines,* which translates to 5 ounces of wine, 12 ounces of beer, or 1½ ounces of distilled spirits, confers cardiovascular benefit. Just remember your weight also plays a role in health, and alcohol has calories, too. Bottom line: Choose wisely, and know where the calories hide.

How Many Calories are in that Drink?

ULTRA LIGHT BEER
64 calories
(2.5% alcohol)

Low cal but low alcohol. If you're looking to take the edge off, it might take a few of these.

WINE SPRITZER
72 calories
(3 ounces club soda, 3 ounces wine)

A smart, delicate sip for moderate drinking.

CHAMPAGNE
85 calories
(4 ounces)

Bubbles make for a lighter and brighter sip. Flutes are smaller than wineglasses, so you'll be less likely to overpour.

SCOTCH ON THE ROCKS
96 calories
(1.5 ounces)

Clean, simple, stiff. No mixer here—which is where a lot of calories hide.

LIGHT BEER
110 calories
(4% alcohol)

Although there's no governmental standard for "light" beer, calories must be listed to make the claim. Most have 100 to 120.

GIN & TONIC
120 calories
(2 ounces tonic, 1.5 ounces gin)

Tonic is no different from a soda—a teaspoon of sugar in about 2 ounces. Same as bourbon and cola.

WINE
125 calories
(5 ounces)

Equal calories for red, white, and rosé.

AMERICAN LAGER
150 calories
(12 ounces, 5% alcohol)

Calories come from alcohol (7 per gram) and carbs (4 per gram). More alcohol = more calories.

VODKA MARTINI
210 calories
(3 ounces vodka, ½ ounce vermouth)

Martini glasses may hold 5 to 6 ounces. Making it dirty adds 450mg sodium per ½ ounce olive juice.

WHITE RUSSIAN
222 calories
(2 ounces vodka, 1 ounce coffee liqueur, 1 ounce half-and-half)

The liqueur has 12g of sugar per ounce—the amount in about a tablespoon.

SANGRÍA
260 calories
(8 ounces)

When wine meets brandy, juice, fruit, and sugar, calories add up.

MARGARITA
273 calories
(the frozen 8-ounce happy hour pour)

More than 50% of these lime-coated calories come from sugar.

HIGH-GRAVITY BEER
291 calories (16 ounces)

Higher alcohol (8% to 10%) means more calories. Be aware that pints are 16 ounces, not 12, like the typical can or bottle.

PIÑA COLADA
425 calories (12 ounces frozen)

Rich cream of coconut adds 8g sat fat, while rum and sugar-fllled juice spike calories.

WHAT'S THE HEALTHIEST: *Beer, Wine, or Liquor?*

GIVEN THE HIGHLY PRAISED BENEFITS OF RESVERATROL, a compound found in grape skins, wine seems the obvious choice. Studies suggest it can help fight cancer, preserve memory, ease depression, and more. But the research is still evolving, says Joseph Wu, PhD, a professor of biochemistry and molecular biology at New York Medical College.

When it comes to reducing cardiovascular risk, though—which is of special concern, as heart disease is the number-one killer of both men and women—the type of alcohol doesn't matter. "About 97% of the studies suggest it's the ethanol content in alcohol that's most beneficial," says Eric Rimm, ScD, director of the program in cardiovascular epidemiology at the Harvard T.H. Chan School of Public Health.

"You can study people who drink beer in Germany, spirits in Finland, and wine in France, and they all end up with about a 30% reduction in heart disease," says Rimm.

Why Should Women Drink Less Than Men?

YOU MIGHT THINK the one-drink-per-day limit for women versus two for men is because women tend to be smaller, and you'd be partly right. A more surprising factor is that women are deficient in an enzyme (called alcohol dehydrogenase) that breaks down alcohol in the stomach and liver.

"For genetic reasons, women have considerably less of this enzyme than men. If a man and woman weighed the same and drank the same amount of alcohol, the woman would have higher blood levels of alcohol than the man for a longer period of time," explains preventive medicine specialist David Katz, MD, MPH, founding director of the Yale-Griffin Prevention Research Center.

"Whether alcohol and its metabolic breakdown products have toxic effects depends on how high blood levels go and how long they stay elevated." One drink can vary widely in both calorie and alcohol range, so make smart choices and sip slowly.

Miso Bloody Mary DF V

Hands-on: 6 minutes | Total: 6 minutes

Combine 2 tablespoons fresh lime juice, 4 teaspoons white miso paste, 1 teaspoon prepared horseradish, and 1 teaspoon celery seeds in a pitcher; muddle with back of a wooden spoon. Stir in 1½ cups low-sodium tomato juice, ¾ cup vodka, 2 tablespoons fresh lime juice, 2 teaspoons hot sauce, 1 teaspoon Worcestershire sauce, and ½ teaspoon freshly ground black pepper. Pour ⅔ cup into each of 4 ice-filled glasses. Garnish with celery stalks and lime wedges.

SERVES 4 (serving size: about ⅔ cup): CALORIES 134; FAT 0.2g (sat 0g, mono 0g, poly 0g); PROTEIN 1g; CARB 18g; FIBER 2g; SUGARS 4g (est. added sugars 0g); CHOL 0mg; IRON 0mg; SODIUM 253mg; CALCIUM 22mg

Cucumber-Mint Tequila Tonic DF GF V

Hands-on: 10 minutes | Total: 1 hour, 10 minutes

Place 2 cups chopped English cucumber, ½ cup mint leaves, ⅓ cup agave nectar, ¼ cup cilantro leaves, 2 tablespoons fresh lime juice, and a dash of salt in a food processor; pulse until smooth. Scrape mixture into a bowl; stir in ½ cup tequila blanco. Chill. Strain. Stir in ¾ cup chilled tonic water. Serve over ice. Garnish with cucumber slices and fresh mint leaves.

SERVES 1: CALORIES 114; FAT 0g (sat 0g, mono 0g, poly 0g); PROTEIN 1g; CARB 19g; FIBER 1g; SUGARS 17g (est. added sugars 12g); CHOL 0mg; IRON 0mg; SODIUM 45mg; CALCIUM 17mg

Piña Coladas GF V

Hands-on: 18 minutes | Total: 4 hours, 18 minutes

Combine 2 cups flaked sweetened coconut and 1 (12-ounce) can evaporated fat-free milk in a medium saucepan over medium heat; cook until tiny bubbles form around the edge (do not boil), about 7 minutes. Remove from the heat. Cover and chill at least 4 hours or up to overnight. Arrange 2 cups cubed fresh pineapple in a single layer on a baking sheet; freeze at least 1 hour or until firm. Strain coconut mixture through a sieve over a medium bowl, pressing coconut with the back of a spoon to remove as much milk as possible. Discard solids. Place the frozen pineapple, 2½ cups ice cubes, ¾ cup gold rum (such as Bacardi Gold), ¼ cup pineapple juice, and 2 tablespoons light agave nectar in a blender; process the mixture until smooth. Add the milk mixture, and process until smooth. Pour about ⅔ cup into each of 8 glasses. Serve each with a fresh pineapple slice.

SERVES 8 (serving size: about ⅔ cup): CALORIES 158; FAT 2.1g (sat 2.2g, mono 0g, poly 0g); PROTEIN 0g; CARB 22g; FIBER 2g; SUGARS 18g (est. added sugars 2g); CHOL 0mg; IRON 0mg; SODIUM 20mg; CALCIUM 14mg

Maple-Bourbon Sour DF V

Hands-on: 5 minutes | Total: 5 minutes

Combine 6 tablespoons bourbon, 2 tablespoons maple syrup, and 2 tablespoons fresh lemon juice, stirring well. Pour mixture into a cocktail shaker filled with ½ cup ice. Cover and shake. Strain the mixture. Divide between 2 glasses. Serve over ice and garnish with lemon slices, if desired.

SERVES 2 (serving size: about ⅓ cup): CALORIES 152; FAT 0g (sat 0g, mono 0g, poly 0g); PROTEIN 0g; CARB 14g; FIBER 0g; SUGARS 12g (est. added sugars 12g); CHOL 0mg; IRON 0mg; SODIUM 3mg; CALCIUM 21mg

BULKING UP YOUR MEALS

Bulking Up Your Meals

WHO NEEDS TO BULK UP THEIR MEALS?

Some of you may need a higher calorie level because you are very active individuals, males (who generally need more calories than females), or have reached your desired weight and want to follow a maintenance plan to maintain your weight loss. Once you determine your calorie level at CookingLightDiet.com (see page 10 for more details), you can use these suggestions to follow a daily menu plan of 1,600 to 2,000 calories.

Breakfast

For those following a 1,600- to 2,000-calorie meal plan, your breakfast should generally contain about 400 calories. You can use the breakfast recipes in Chapter 2 (page 22) as a starting point. If you follow the suggestions for the 1,200- to 1,400-calorie menu plans, you'll need to add some of the 100-calorie ideas below. If you follow the menu suggestions for the 1,500-calorie plan, choose from the list below to add 50 additional calories.

CALORIE LEVEL	BREAKFAST
1,600	400
1,700	400
1,800	400
1,900	400
2,000	400

10 WAYS TO ADD ABOUT 50 CALORIES

- ½ small (6-inch) banana (45 calories)
- 1½ teaspoons peanut butter (48 calories)
- ¼ cup low-fat granola, such as Kellogg's (56 calories)
- ½ cup 1% low-fat milk or milk substitute (51 calories)
- 1 tablespoon maple syrup (52 calories)
- 2 slices center-cut bacon (50 calories)
- ½ cup orange juice (55 calories)
- ½ grapefruit (46 calories)
- 1 (45-calorie) slice toasted multigrain bread
- 2 teaspoons jam (50 calories)

10 WAYS TO ADD ABOUT 100 CALORIES

- Scrambled eggs made with 1 large egg and 1 egg white (90 calories)
- 1 part-skim mozzarella cheese stick (80 calories)
- 1 ounce cooked turkey sausage link (90 calories)
- 1 cup 1% low-fat milk or milk substitute (102 calories)
- ½ cup plain fat-free Greek yogurt with ¼ cup fresh blueberries (88 calories)
- 1 (45-calorie) slice toasted multigrain bread with 2 teaspoons jam (95 calories)
- 1 slice toasted raisin bread (86 calories)
- 2 gluten-free rice cakes and 2 teaspoons cream cheese (105 calories)
- 1 flax, oat bean, and whole-wheat pita bread, such as Joseph's, with 1 teaspoon almond butter (92 calories)
- 1 small (6-inch) banana (90 calories)

Working Mom Makes Diet Work for Her, Not Other Way Around

AMY PERRONE OF FABIUS, NY, has four kids and directs her local YMCA's preschool. Needless to say, there was little time left in the day to focus on her struggle with fluctuating weight.

"My weight is something I've struggled with pretty much my whole life," Amy said. "And having to think, 'Okay, now what am I going to have for dinner? What am I going to have for lunch?' It's hard. I just need someone telling me, 'Here's what you get. This is your menu.'"

That's where the Cooking Light Diet came in, and it was a game-changer.

"Having [a menu] on paper and having someone say to me, 'This is what you get today?' Done and done," Amy said. "The only thing that's not getting done for me is actually preparing it, and that's not something I mind. Being told, 'Here's your menu for the week and here's your grocery list'...it doesn't get any simpler than that."

Cooking Light Diet's ease of use and heavy lifting with menu planning allowed Amy to refocus on the weight-loss struggle. This renewed focus has led to Amy being 35 pounds* down so far. And that doesn't include exercise, which is something Amy is still trying to figure out.

"It's not that I don't want to go work out," Amy said. "I mean, I work at a YMCA. I just put my kids first a lot of the time. But I'm happy with the fact that by sticking to this, I'm losing the weight, and I'm hoping to make time for the exercise to become secondary. It's just the best ever. You have everything. You print out the menus, and then you get a grocery list [if using the online program]. It's a no-brainer! I don't have to worry about forgetting anything. It's wonderful."

So wonderful, in fact, that Amy plans to keep going once she hits her desired weight-loss goal.

"The important thing is to look at this as more of a lifestyle change as opposed to just, 'Okay, I'm going to be on a diet for six months and then go back to my old way of eating,'" Amy said. "This is absolutely something I will continue to follow."

**Members following The Cooking Light Diet lose more than half a pound per week, on average.*

> "The important thing is to look at this as more of a lifestyle change...this is absolutely something I will continue to follow."

Chilled Tomato Soup with Avocado Relish, page 94

Wheat Berry Salad with Goat Cheese, page 116

Lunch

For those following 1,600- to 2,000-calorie menu plans, your lunch should range in calories from 450 to 500. Start with the recipes in Chapter 3 (page 72) and follow the suggestions for the 1,500-calorie lunch plan (which has 400 calories) and include some additional items to round out the meal.

- 1,600- and 1,700-calorie plans: add 50 calories to the menu
- 1,800- and 1,900-calorie plans: add 100 calories to the menu
- 2,000-calorie plans: add 150 calories to the menu

CALORIE LEVEL	LUNCH
1,600	450
1,700	450
1,800	500
1,900	500
2,000	550

10 WAYS TO ADD ABOUT 50 CALORIES

- ¼ cup chopped cooked chicken breast (58 calories)
- 1 serving of a 50-calorie side dish (page 202)
- 10 dry-roasted peanuts (53 calories)
- 2 tablespoons guacamole with 6 (4-inch) pieces celery (54 calories)
- ¼ cup low-fat cottage cheese (41 calories)
- 1 (2-inch) kiwifruit (42 calories)
- ½ cup fresh mango slices (50 calories)
- 1 fresh peach (38 calories)
- ¾ cup fresh pineapple chunks (56 calories)
- 1 small pack raisins (42 calories)

10 WAYS TO ADD ABOUT 100 CALORIES

- 1 serving of a 100-calorie side dish or 2 servings of a 50-calorie side dish (page 202)
- 1 medium pear (103 calories)
- 1 medium apple (95 calories)
- 2 graham cracker sheets (110 calories)
- 13 dry-roasted almonds (99 calories)
- 30 pistachios (98 calories)
- 1 mini light Swiss cheese wedge, such as The Laughing Cow, with 9 almonds (104 calories)
- Pita wedges made from ½ (6-inch) pita bread, split and toasted, with 1 tablespoon hummus (110 calories)
- ½ cup of plain fat-free Greek yogurt with ½ cup sliced strawberries (94 calories)
- 1 tablespoon peanut butter with 4 celery sticks (99 calories)

10 WAYS TO ADD ABOUT 150 CALORIES

- 2 hard-cooked eggs (155 calories)
- 10 thin wheat crackers and ⅓ cup 1% or fat-free cottage cheese (144 calories)
- 1 whole-wheat graham cracker topped with 2 teaspoons chocolate-hazelnut spread and ¼ cup sliced strawberries (135 calories)
- 2 (45-calorie) slices bread topped with 2 ounces thinly sliced lean deli turkey, 2 leaves leaf lettuce, and 1 teaspoon stone-ground mustard (157 calories)
- 9 multigrain pita chips, such as Stacy's (140 calories)
- 1 cup vegetable soup and 2 multigrain crackers (154 calories)
- 1 ounce goat cheese and 1 cup sliced cucumber (91 calories)
- 1 cup plain fat-free Greek yogurt swirled with 1½ teaspoons honey (152 calories)
- 18 baked light tortilla chips (147 calories)
- 1 small apple with 1 ounce cheddar cheese (163 calories)

Dinner

For the 1,600- to 2,000-calorie menu plans, use the dinner recipes in Chapter 4 (page 144). Follow the 1,500-calorie dinner plan (which is 500 calories) and include the appropriate number of additional calories.

- 1,600-calorie plan: No changes. Follow the 1,500-calorie dinner menu.
- 1,700-calorie plan: add 50 calories to the menu
- 1,800- and 1,900-calorie plans: add 100 calories to the menu
- 2,000-calorie plans: add 150 calories to the menu

CALORIE LEVEL	DINNER
1,600	500
1,700	550
1,800	600
1,900	600
2,000	650

10 WAYS TO ADD ABOUT 50 CALORIES

- 1 serving of a 50-calorie side dish (page 202)
- 1½ cups fresh baby salad greens tossed with 1½ tablespoons reduced-fat dressing (48 calories)
- ½ cup baked new potato wedges, such as Simply Potatoes (50 calories)
- 1 cup steamed or roasted green beans with 2 teaspoons sliced almonds (57 calories)
- 1 cup steamed or roasted broccoli with 2 teaspoons grated Parmesan cheese (34 calories)
- 1 cup butternut squash puree (57 calories)
- 4 whole-grain saltine crackers (48 calories)
- 1 (¾-ounce) slice French bread (54 calories)
- 1 medium tangerine (47 calories)
- 2 small plums (60 calories)

10 WAYS TO ADD ABOUT 100 CALORIES

- 1 serving of a 100-calorie side dish or 2 servings of a 50-calorie side dish (page 202)
- 1 hamburger or hot dog bun (114 calories)
- 1 (2½-inch) dinner roll (96 calories)
- 1 (¾-ounce) slice French bread with 1 teaspoon butter (88 calories)
- ½ cup cooked long-grain white rice (103 calories)
- ½ cup couscous (88 calories)
- ½ cup mashed potatoes, such as Simply Potatoes (100 calories)
- 1 cup baked new potato wedges, such as Simply Potatoes (100 calories)
- An additional 2 ounces lean beef (114 calories)
- An additional 2 ounces rotisserie chicken, skin removed (117 calories)

10 WAYS TO ADD ABOUT 150 CALORIES

- 1½ cups fresh baby salad greens tossed with 2 tablespoons reduced-fat dressing and 2 tablespoons sliced almonds (125 calories)
- ¾ cup edamame (142 calories)
- 1 ounce baked sweet potato fries, such as Alexia (142 calories)
- 1 small baked potato (145 calories)
- 1 (¾-ounce) slice French bread with 2 teaspoons olive oil (134 calories)
- 1 cup cooked wild rice (166 calories)
- ¾ cup cooked brown rice (164 calories)
- ¾ cup cooked quinoa (166 calories)
- 6 ounces white wine (144 calories)
- 6 ounces red wine (150 calories)

Chicken Parmesan with Zucchini Noodles, page 180

Arizona Woman and Family Lose Over 130 Pounds

SCOTTSDALE, AZ, RESIDENT JOYCE VAN HUIS knew it was time for a change after an unsettling doctor's visit.

"I went to the doctor one day, and I'd just turned 60 years old," Joyce said. "And I decided, you know, I've been on a diet my entire life, in one form or the other, and I'm not doing this anymore. So after indulging for maybe 6 months I went to the doctor, and he said, 'I'm sorry. You've got Type 2 diabetes.' And I thought, 'Ok, yet another diet I have to get on.' So I thought I'd give the Cooking Light Diet a try, because it was inexpensive to subscribe, and I knew how good the food was. So it just went from there."

"Who would've thought that the old tried-and-true, counting calories, is the best plan?"

And went it did. Joyce and her husband Bob started shedding pounds, and after they each got past the 20-pound mark, Joyce's sister-in-law and mother-in-law noticed and decided to join. So far, the four have a combined weight loss of over 130 pounds* with the Cooking Light Diet!

"I mean, I've been on the liquid diet, the no-carb diet, the you-name-it, I've been on it," Joyce said. "And this is just so simple...delicious food that requires minimum attention. And when you love food like I do, that's what you want. You don't want to deprive or starve yourself."

In addition to the amazing weight-loss success Joyce has shared with her family, she also received great news from her doctor regarding her diabetes and glucose levels.

"Before I got on the CLDiet, my A1C levels were high," Joyce said. "And when I went for my three-month follow-up—the doctor had put me on medication—they'd dropped to a level that's considered prediabetic. And I'm very diligent about following the Cooking Light Diet and not cheating, because you know what? It's common sense. The more weight you lose, the better your numbers get."

Joyce says the Cooking Light Diet has made a huge difference in her life, and she loves its simplicity the most.

"I was saying to my sister-in-law, 'Who would've thought that the old tried-and-true, counting calories, is the best plan?'"

**Members following The Cooking Light Diet lose more than half a pound per week, on average.*

Snacks

For the 1,600- to 2,000-calorie menu plans, you can use the snack recipes in Chapter 5 (page 234). All the snacks in that chapter are around 150 calories, so you can increase the serving size, if you'd like, or add another snack to meet your calorie needs.

CALORIE LEVEL	SNACK
1,600	250
1,700	300
1,800	300
1,900	300
2,000	400

10 WAYS TO ADD ABOUT 50 CALORIES FOR A SNACK

- ¾ cup strawberries and blueberries (48 calories)
- ¾ cup fresh pineapple chunks (56 calories)
- 1 medium peach (38 calories)
- 1 small pack raisins (42 calories)
- 1 (2-inch) kiwifruit (42 calories)
- 1 mini light cheese round, such as Babybel (50 calories)
- 1½ cups air-popped popcorn (46 calories)
- 1 rye crispbread, such as Wasa, topped with 1 tablespoon part-skim ricotta cheese (59 calories)
- 5 large green olives (50 calories)
- 1 mini Milky Way bar (40 calories)

10 WAYS TO ADD ABOUT 100 CALORIES FOR A SNACK

- 1 small banana (100 calories)
- 1 (100-calorie) pack of cocoa-dusted roasted almonds or 13 dry-roasted almonds (100 calories)
- ½ cup 2% plain Greek yogurt drizzled with 1 teaspoon honey (96 calories)
- 3 cups air-popped popcorn with 1 teaspoon cinnamon sugar (107 calories)
- 1 (1-ounce) bag freeze-dried strawberries, such as Simply Balanced (110 calories)
- 1 part-skim mozzarella cheese stick (80 calories)
- 4 whole-grain crackers and 1 mini light cheese round, such as Babybel (104 calories)
- 4 Hershey's Kisses (102 calories)
- 2 dark chocolate squares, such as Ghirardelli (105 calories)
- 1 fun-size Snickers (74 calories)

NUTRITIONAL INFORMATION

How to Use It and Why

At *Cooking Light*, our team of food editors, experienced cooks, and registered dietitians builds recipes with whole foods and whole grains, and bigger portions of plants and seafood than meat. We emphasize oil-based fats more than saturated, and we promote a balanced diet low in processed foods and added sugars (those added during processing or preparation).

Not only do we focus on quality ingredients, but we also adhere to a rigorous set of nutrition guidelines that govern calories, saturated fat, sodium, and sugar based on various recipe categories. The numbers in each category are derived from the most recent set of USDA Dietary Guidelines for Americans, as shown in the following chart. As you look through our numbers, remember that the nutrition stats included with each recipe are for a single serving. When we build recipes, we look at each dish in context of the role it plays in an average day: A one-dish meal that fills a plate with protein, starch, and vegetables will weigh more heavily in calories, saturated fat, and sodium than a recipe for roasted chicken thighs. Similarly, a bowl of ice cream may contain more than half of your daily added sugar recommendation, but balances out when the numbers are folded into a day's worth of healthy food prepared at home.

When reading the chart, remember that recommendations vary by gender and age; other factors, including lifestyle, weight, and your own health—for example, if you're pregnant or breast-feeding or if you have genetic factors such as risk for hypertension—all need consideration. Go to choosemyplate.gov for your own individualized plan.

In Our Nutritional Analysis, We Use These Abbreviations

sat saturated fat
mono monounsaturated fat
poly polyunsaturated fat
carb carbohydrates
chol cholesterol
g gram
mg milligram
est. estimated (added sugars)

Daily Nutrition Guide

	Women ages 25 to 50	Women over 50	Men ages 25 to 50	Men over 50
Calories	2,000	2,000*	2,700	2,500
Protein	50 g	50 g	63 g	60 g
Fat	65 g*	65 g*	88 g*	83 g*
Saturated Fat	20 g*	20 g*	27 g*	25 g*
Carbohydrates	304 g	304 g	410 g	375 g
Fiber	25g to 35 g	25 g to 35 g	25 g to 35 g	25 g to 35 g
Added Sugars	38 g	38 g	38 g	38 g
Cholesterol	300 mg*	300 mg*	300 mg*	300 mg*
Iron	18 mg	8 mg	8 mg	8 mg
Sodium	2,300 mg*	1,500 mg*	2,300 mg*	1,500 mg*
Calcium	1,000 mg	1,200 mg	1,000 mg	1,000 mg

*Or less, for optimum health

Nutritional values used in our calculations either come from The Food Processor, Version 10.4 (ESHA Research), or are provided by food manufacturers.

METRIC EQUIVALENTS

Cooking/Oven Temperatures

	Fahrenheit	Celsius	Gas Mark
Freeze Water	32° F	0° C	
Room Temp.	68° F	20° C	
Boil Water	212° F	100° C	
Bake	325° F	160° C	3
	350° F	180° C	4
	375° F	190° C	5
	400° F	200° C	6
	425° F	220° C	7
	450° F	230° C	8
Broil			Grill

Liquid Ingredients by Volume

¼ tsp	=					1 ml				
½ tsp	=					2 ml				
1 tsp	=					5 ml				
3 tsp	=	1 Tbsp	=	½ fl oz	=	15 ml				
2 Tbsp	=	⅛ cup	=	1 fl oz	=	30 ml				
4 Tbsp	=	¼ cup	=	2 fl oz	=	60 ml				
5⅓ Tbsp	=	⅓ cup	=	3 fl oz	=	80 ml				
8 Tbsp	=	½ cup	=	4 fl oz	=	120 ml				
10⅔ Tbsp	=	⅔ cup	=	5 fl oz	=	160 ml				
12 Tbsp	=	¾ cup	=	6 fl oz	=	180 ml				
16 Tbsp	=	1 cup	=	8 fl oz	=	240 ml				
1 pt	=	2 cups	=	16 fl oz	=	480 ml				
1 qt	=	4 cups	=	32 fl oz	=	960 ml				
				33 fl oz	=	1000 ml	=	1 l		

Dry Ingredients by Weight

(To convert ounces to grams, multiply the number of ounces by 30.)

1 oz	=	1⁄16 lb	=	30 g
4 oz	=	¼ lb	=	120 g
8 oz	=	½ lb	=	240 g
12 oz	=	¾ lb	=	360 g
16 oz	=	1 lb	=	480 g

Length

(To convert inches to centimeters, multiply inches by 2.5.)

1 in	=					2.5 cm		
12 in	=	1 ft			=	30 cm		
36 in	=	3 ft	=	1 yd	=	90 cm		
40 in	=					100 cm	=	1 m

Equivalents for Different Types of Ingredients

Standard Cup	Fine Powder (ex. flour)	Grain (ex. rice)	Granular (ex. sugar)	Liquid Solids (ex. butter)	Liquid (ex. milk)
1	140 g	150 g	190 g	200 g	240 ml
¾	105 g	113 g	143 g	150 g	180 ml
⅔	93 g	100 g	125 g	133 g	160 ml
½	70 g	75 g	95 g	100 g	120 ml
⅓	47 g	50 g	63 g	67 g	80 ml
¼	35 g	38 g	48 g	50 g	60 ml
⅛	18 g	19 g	24 g	25 g	30 ml

INDEX

D

E

F

G

N

O

P

Q

R

S

T

V

W